Hear this, ye old men,

and give ear, all ye inhabitants of the land.

Hath this been in your days,

or even in the days of your fathers?

Tell ye your children of it,

and let your children tell their children,

and their children another generation.

BOOK OF JOEL
CHAPTER ONE, VERSES 2 AND 3

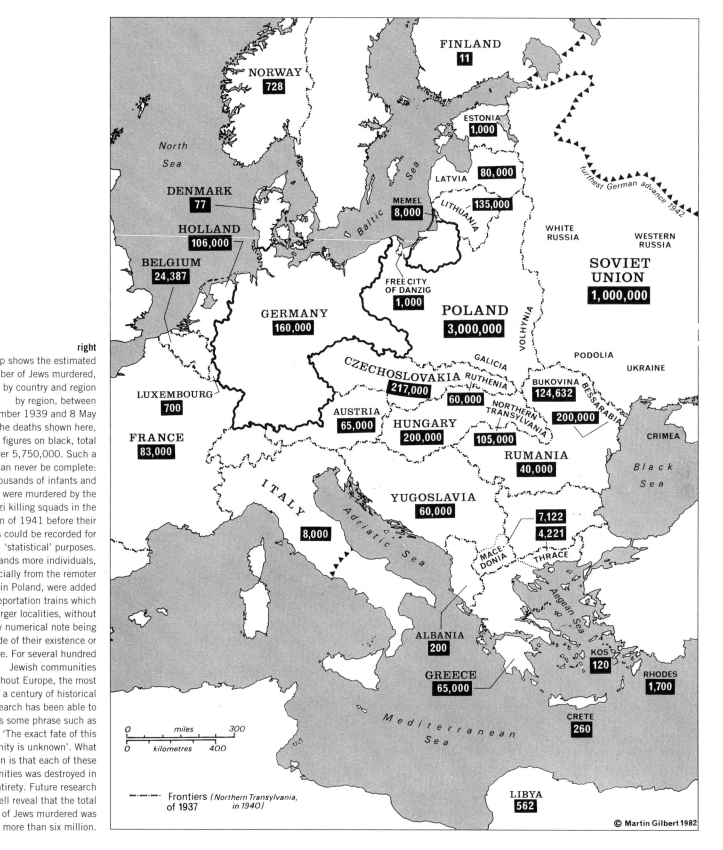

right

This map shows the estimated number of Jews murdered, country by country and region by region, between 1 September 1939 and 8 May 1945. The deaths shown here, in white figures on black, total just over 5,750,000. Such a total can never be complete: thousands of infants and babies were murdered by the Nazi killing squads in the autumn of 1941 before their births could be recorded for 'statistical' purposes. Thousands more individuals, especially from the remoter villages in Poland, were added to the deportation trains which left larger localities, without any numerical note being made of their existence or their fate. For several hundred Jewish communities throughout Europe, the most that half a century of historical research has been able to record is some phrase such as 'The exact fate of this community is unknown'. What is known is that each of these communities was destroyed in its entirety. Future research may well reveal that the total number of Jews murdered was more than six million.

FINLAND **11**

NORWAY **728**

North Sea

ESTONIA **1,000**

Baltic Sea

LATVIA **80,000**

DENMARK **77**

MEMEL **8,000**

LITHUANIA **135,000**

WHITE RUSSIA

WESTERN RUSSIA

furthest German advance 1942

HOLLAND **106,000**

BELGIUM **24,387**

FREE CITY OF DANZIG **1,000**

GERMANY **160,000**

POLAND **3,000,000**

VOLHYNIA

PODOLIA

UKRAINE

SOVIET UNION **1,000,000**

LUXEMBOURG **700**

CZECHOSLOVAKIA **217,000**

GALICIA

RUTHENIA

BUKOVINA **124,632**

BESSARABIA

FRANCE **83,000**

AUSTRIA **65,000**

60,000

HUNGARY **200,000**

NORTHERN TRANSYLVANIA **200,000**

CRIMEA

105,000

RUMANIA **40,000**

Black Sea

ITALY

Adriatic Sea

YUGOSLAVIA **60,000**

8,000

7,122

4,221

MACE-DONIA

THRACE

Aegean Sea

ALBANIA **200**

KOS **120**

RHODES **1,700**

GREECE **65,000**

CRETE **260**

Mediterranean Sea

| 0 | miles | 300 |

| 0 | kilometres | 400 |

LIBYA **562**

© Martin Gilbert 1982

—·—·— Frontiers *(Northern Transylvania,* of 1937 *in 1940)*

NEVER AGAIN

A HISTORY OF THE HOLOCAUST

MARTIN GILBERT

UNIVERSE

CONTENTS

Bread and soup distribution in the Theresienstadt ghetto. A drawing done in the ghetto by a twelve-year-old girl, Helga Weissová. She survived the war, and lives today in the Czech Republic.

Two young boys in the Lodz Ghetto, photographed by Mendel Grossman, who survived the ghetto but died on a death march in Germany shortly before the end of the war. He was thirty-two years old. Most of the children in the Lodz ghetto did not survive the war.

(preceding page)
page 1
A group of Jews from Berehovo, Ruthenia, shortly after reaching Auschwitz, and before being sent to the gas chambers, photographed by an SS Sergeant (*see page 139*).

INTRODUCTION

top
Anne Frank was a German Jewish girl who, with her family, found refuge in Holland before the war. Her diary was written between June 1942 and August 1944 while she was in hiding in Amsterdam. After being deported with her family to Auschwitz, she was transferred to Belsen. She died there at the beginning of March 1945, less than six weeks before the camp was liberated. Her diary was first published, as *The Diary of a Young Girl*, in 1947.

above
Justyna Davidson Draenger used scraps of paper smuggled into her prison cell in 1943 to write about Jewish resistance in Cracow. She escaped from prison, but was killed fighting the Germans in the forests east of Cracow. *Justyna's Narrative* was first published in Polish in 1946, in English in 1996.

Shortly before he was murdered in 1941, in Riga, the Jewish historian Simon Dubnov called out the words: 'Write and record!' Thousands of Jews, unaware of Dubnov's call, tried to keep some record of what was happening to them during the Holocaust – in diaries, letters and scribbled notes. Some of these notes have survived, and been published.

Artists and photographers recorded the fate of their fellow-Jews in paintings, sketches and photographs. Historians, authors and poets tried to convey in writing and verse their fate, and that of those around them.

The most intense period of the Holocaust lasted for less than four years, starting with the German invasion of the Soviet Union in June 1941. It was only brought to an end in May 1945 by the defeat of the German armies on the battlefield. When it ended, six million Jews had been murdered.

Polish-born Rafael Scharf, many of whose family and friends were murdered in the Holocaust, has written: 'It calls for a painful mental effort to envisage this apocalyptic world, for which there is no analogy in history. There have been wars, foreign occupations, oppression, persecution and murder on a massive scale; such horrors continue to abound, but it is totally without precedent that a whole people, without exception, should be separated from its surroundings and condemned to death....'

'Who will write our story?': this was the anguished question of Justyna Davidson Draenger, who was active in Jewish resistance in Cracow.

ACKNOWLEDGEMENTS

Every historian of the Holocaust owes a debt of gratitude to the work of those who have assembled the basic documentation, without which no account, however short, can be compiled. More than twenty thousand Jewish communities – large and small – were destroyed in Europe between 1940 and 1945. The task of listing their names and giving the number of Jews living in the communities before the war was undertaken after the war by Yad Vashem, the Holocaust memorial in Jerusalem, and published in 1965 as *Blackbook of Localities Whose Jewish Population was Exterminated by the Nazis*.

Serge Klarsfeld's pioneering work, published in 1978, listing the name of every deportee from France to Auschwitz, has much influenced my work on the Holocaust. Since 1978 he and the Beate Klarsfeld Foundation have published documentary collections on the Belgian Jewish deportations, the fate of Roumanian Jewry, and the destruction of the Jews of Grodno.

My work on the Holocaust was also stimulated by Reuben Ainsztein, whose pioneering book *Jewish Resistance in Nazi-occupied Eastern Europe*, published 1974, remains a basic source; and by Szymon Datner, who helped me in Warsaw in the early 1980s towards a fuller understanding of the scale of what had happened.

While I was doing research at Yad Vashem in the 1980s, the personal encouragement of Israel Gutman and Shmuel Krakowski meant a great deal to me. I have also been influenced by John Garrard, who found and made available on the internet the names of those who were murdered in the ghetto of Brest-Litovsk.

The Holocaust exhibition at the Imperial War Museum opened in the year 2000. I am grateful to all those at the museum for their contribution to my work. Special thanks are due to the Director-General, Robert Crawford, and to Suzanne Bardgett, Kathy Jones, Alison Murchie, Dr Steve Paulsson and James Taylor.

Among survivors of the Holocaust whose friendship has meant a great deal to me, who have given me good guidance – often over many years – and have allowed me to quote in this book from their recollections, are Harry Balsam, Judge Moshe Bejski, Benjamin Bender, Sala Bernholz, Victor Breitburg, Leo Bretholz, Howard Chandler, Rose Dajch, Michael Etkind, John Fox, Ben Giladi, Moniek Goldberg, Abraham Goldstein, Pinchas Gutter, Roman Halter, Arek Hersh, Solly Irving, Lorraine Justman-Wissnicki, Jack Kagan, Bronka Klibanska, Freddie Knoller, Lilli Kopecky, Luba Krugman-Gurdus, Pinkus Kurnedz, Leo Laufer, Dov Levin, Michael Novice, Ray Mandel, Michel Mielnicki, Vladka Meed, Moishe Nurtman, Salek Orenstein, Mania Salinger, Agnes Sassoon, Harry Spiro, Martin Spitzer, George Topas, Leon Weliczker Wells, Krulik Wilder, Rella Wizenberg, Alexander Zvielli and Aron Zylberszac.

Ben Helfgott gave his usual perceptive guidance. Jack Brauns helped me with material and recollections of the Kovno ghetto. Rudolf Vrba encouraged me to examine the economic aspect of Nazi policy towards the Jews, and gave me permission to quote from his account of 'Canada' in Auschwitz. Elie Wiesel answered my queries and gave me permission to quote from his recent writings.

Helen Epstein, Gisele Naichouler Feldman, Abraham Foxman, Robert Krell, Ann Shore and Stella Tzur gave me permission to quote from their reflections as hidden children. Nicole David, also a hidden child, provided me with important historical material about children in hiding, both in Belgium and elsewhere.

Among those who left Germany before the war, I was helped by, and have quoted the recollections of, Tom Bermann, Johnny Blunt, Gisela Feldman (the voyage of the *St Louis*), Leslie Frankel, Professor Otto Hutter, Rabbi Harry Jacobi, Lisa Mendel Loshin (the voyage of the *St Louis*), Eric Lucas and Eddie Nussbaum. Ruth Mandel and Naomi Gryn let me quote from their writings as members of the 'second generation' – the children of Holocaust survivors.

Benjamin Ferencz let me quote from his account of entering Mauthausen as a war crimes investigator; Joseph Finklestone from his 1945 article describing the arrival of young survivors in Britain.

Hugo Gryn, my rabbi and my friend, always shared aspects of his past with me: his childhood in Berehovo (then part of Czechoslovakia), his experiences of Auschwitz, slave labour camps, death marches, liberation and the journey to England after the war. In this book I have drawn on his memories and wisdom, and on his recollections, which have been published by his daughter Naomi Gryn.

I am indebted for material about particular episodes and individuals to Leslie Blau (the Jews of Bonyhad); Eve Line Blum (the Paris deportation of 15 May 1944); David Borde, *New York Times* (Elie Wiesel's visit to Kosovo in 1999); Peter Coombs (the liberation of Belsen); Robert Engel (the fate of two passengers on the *St Louis*); Sam Goldsmith (the liberation of Dachau); Marilyn Herman (the death marches); Michael D. Hull (Dr Aristides de Sousa Mendes); Robert Kirschner, Programme Director, Skirball Cultural Centre, Los Angeles, and Arnold Schwartzman (Hitler's signature on the Nuremberg Laws); Harry Jacobi (Gertrud Wijsmuller's rescue work); Tony McNulty MP (the proposed Holocaust memorial day in Britain); Benjamin Meirtchak (the fate of Jewish soldiers in the Polish army and underground); Robin O'Neil (the activities of Julius Madritsch); Lawrence M. Rothbaum (the Jews of Albania); Elaine Shnieder (Greek Jews); Gerhard Shoenberner (Holocaust memorials); Sigmund Sobolewski and Rabbi Roy D. Tanenbaum (the Jewish *Sonderkommando* revolt in Auschwitz-Birkenau); John Wilkins, editor of *The Tablet* (the Vatican and the Jews of Rome).

Enid Wurtman helped me with enquiries in Israel. Freddie Knoller – whom I have already thanked above – and Eric D. Sugerman, of the Israel-Judaica Stamp Club, gave me access to their philatelic collections. I also received material from Ondine Brent and Martha Hauptman (Office of Professor Elie Wiesel).

In an attempt to portray the geographic range of the Holocaust, I am grateful to Tim Aspden, who transformed my rough ideas and sketches into maps that offer a visual geographic perspective. Barbara Dixon of HarperCollins was always ready with help and guidance. Paul Calver and Mabel Chan worked on the design aspects. Mark Stevens incorporated my texts and materials into graphic pages. Michelle Pickering gave the book her expert editorial scrutiny. Erica Hunninger gave the benefit of her publishing and editorial expertise.

Kay Thomson helped with the considerable correspondence, and with advice on the content and arrangement of each topic. My son Joshua contributed his time and judgment for the presentation of the material.

Martin Gilbert
Merton College, Oxford
18 February 2000

top
Zofia Kubar, a university student in Poland before the war, was in the Warsaw ghetto for two and a half years. She escaped while on a forced labour detail outside the ghetto, and survived the rest of the war pretending to be Christian, helped by Christians. After the war she emigrated to the United States. Her memoirs, *Double Identity*, were published in 1989.

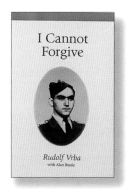

above
Rudolf Vrba was born in Slovakia. In the summer of 1942 he was deported to Auschwitz. After almost two years there he escaped, and, with a fellow-Slovak Jew, Alfred Wetzler, brought out the news of the truth about Auschwitz. His memoirs, *I Cannot Forgive*, were first published in 1963.

European Jewry

right
Jewish youngsters photographed in
western Russia in the early 1920s.
Their homes and their lives were
to be devastated following
the German invasion of the
Soviet Union in June 1941.

The story told in these pages is of a people – the Jews – who had lived in Europe for many hundreds of years. Some Jewish communities in early twentieth-century Europe dated back more than a thousand years. Jews had been living in the central and southern areas of the European continent since Roman times, and in the Aegean and Mediterranean area since Greek times more than two and a half thousand years before the outbreak of the Second World War.

The Holocaust witnessed the savage destruction of six million Jewish lives – of men, women, children and babies – as well as the destruction of Jewish life itself – of long-established patterns of religious worship, ethics, culture, languages and livelihoods.

Chapter One looks at some of the Jewish experiences and contributions to life in Europe up to the moment in 1933 when Hitler and the Nazi Party came to power in Germany. Until then, Jewish life in Germany, and elsewhere in Europe, had not been free from external struggle and conflict, but it had seen a growth and a flourishing, a pattern of vigorous participation and the hope of even more fulfilling times to come. It had seen a variety of Jewish experience that stimulated literature and art, music and science, commerce and self-confidence – vibrant manifestations of Jewishness in more than a dozen countries, as well as confident assimilation in the national life of all the countries of Europe, both before and after the First World War.

The prevalence of anti-Semitism, the two-thousand-year-old Christian hostility to Jews, was challenged by Pope Pius XI when he told a group of Christian pilgrims on 20 September 1938: 'Abraham is our patriarch and forefather. Anti-Semitism is incompatible with that lofty thought. It is a movement with which we Christians can have nothing to do. Spiritually we are all Semites.'

JEWISH LIFE IN EUROPE

Some of the oldest Jewish communities in Europe were in Greece: they had been in existence for more than two thousand years, since the flourishing of Ancient Greece, at a time when there was still a Jewish Temple in Jerusalem. In the late nineteenth century, and during the inter-war years, the Jews of Salonika played a central part in the life of the port, as dockworkers and stevedores as well as merchants.

Jews had lived in Italy for more than two thousand years. They had been an integral part of the life of the Roman Empire, at a time when the Temple was destroyed by Rome and the city of Jerusalem reduced to rubble. Jews had spread with the Romans to every corner of the Roman world, benefiting from the law and order, relative tolerance and social peace of Roman rule.

Jews were to be found living in scattered communities throughout the Roman provinces that later became France, Hungary and Roumania. Indeed, large Jewish communities existed in every European country many hundreds of years before the founding of the national States of which they were later to be a part.

The Jews of Germany had already been living continuously in different parts of Germany for more than 1,500 years when the German Empire was established in 1870.

The contribution of Jewish life to the new Germany was appreciated. Bismarck, the architect of German unity, had been present at the opening of the Oranienburger Strasse synagogue in Berlin in 1866. It was a triumphal moment for him, as Prussian troops were even then on their way back to Berlin, having defeated the Austrian army and paved the way for a united Germany. Berlin Jews welcomed this unification, and were as patriotic as any Germans in their national fervour. Their service in the Prussian army in the war against France in 1812 had led to an edict that gave

left
Three postcards published in Salonika at the end of the nineteenth century: a Jewish lady, a ninety-year-old Jew (on another version of this postcard he is described as being a hundred years old) and three Jewish fruit sellers. In 1943 almost all Salonika's Jews were deported to Auschwitz, where more than 43,000 were murdered.

them equality within the Prussian domains.

Jews fought as national patriots in all the armies of the First World War. They were to be found in the opposing trenches on both the western and eastern fronts. Jewish soldiers died on the battlefield fighting in the ranks of the Entente armies (Britain, France, Italy and Russia) and as part of the forces of the Central Powers (Germany, Austria-Hungary and Turkey). In each of these armies, Jews won the highest awards for bravery. In the German army, 12,000 Jewish soldiers were killed in action on the battlefields.

Jewish life, with its own inner religious and cultural experiences and links, was also intertwined with the life of the nations among whom the Jews lived. The Biblical prophet Jeremiah had expressed this aspect of the Jewish experience when he declared, after tens of thousands of Jews had been carried off as captives from Jerusalem to Babylon: 'Seek the peace of the city whither I have caused you to be carried away captives, and pray unto the Lord for it; for in the peace thereof shall you have peace.'

No Jewish community had a continuous, entirely peaceful existence in the two thousand years from the ascendancy of the Roman Empire to the creation of the modern nation States in the nineteenth and early twentieth centuries. Again and again, local rulers, the Church or a population incited by hatred and prejudice, turned against the Jews and drove them out. Central European cities such as Prague saw several expulsions, but the Jews always returned, re-founding – often three or four times – their broken communities, rebuilding their homes and re-creating their shattered livelihoods.

By the opening years of the twentieth century, many Jewish homes and livelihoods were as secure as they had ever been, yet there were still large areas of poverty, particularly in eastern Poland and western Russia, nor had anti-Jewish prejudice disappeared, even in the most modern and cultured States of Europe.

Jewish life in Europe had survived two millennia since Roman times. Despite continual upsurges in persecution and expulsion, it had flourished, but, even in the age of parliamentary democracies, liberalism and enlightenment, it was far from secure.

above

A Jewish physician, Issahar Beer Teller, who practised in Prague (top). He died in Prague in 1688. The detail above is from his tombstone in the Old Jewish Cemetery in Prague. The bear (*Beer*) is holding a pair of medical pincers.

left

The Oranienburger Strasse synagogue (the New Synagogue) in Berlin: opened in 1866, the scene of a violin recital by Albert Einstein in 1930, ransacked during the Kristallnacht of 1938 but saved from burning by the courage of a non-Jewish German police lieutenant, Wilhelm Krützfeld, severely damaged during a British bombing raid on Berlin in 1943, reinaugurated (as a museum) to all its former external glory in 1995. This photograph was taken in 1996.

LANGUAGES AND CULTURE

As the Roman Empire spread north of the Alps, the Jews also moved north. Many of those who settled in Germany, particularly along the river Rhine, were later expelled eastward. They settled in what became Poland and Lithuania, bringing with them their own medieval German language, known as Yiddish.

After the expulsion of the Jews from Spain in 1492, Spanish Jews settled throughout the south of Europe, North Africa and Holland, where they continued to speak a version of the Spanish language of the time of their expulsion: it was known as Ladino.

However remote were the places in which Jews settled, as the result of expulsion or migration, they also maintained the Hebrew language – the language of their religion, of the Old Testament and their prayer book. Biblical Hebrew provided a link between all Jewish communities. With the advent of printing in the fifteenth century, Jewish prayer books were printed in Hebrew throughout Europe. The first Rome prayer book was printed in 1486, the first Cracow prayer book in 1592, the first Berlin prayer book in 1798. Many of the towns in which such printing took place were to see mass deportation during the Holocaust.

The cultural impact of Hebrew throughout the Jewish world was stimulated from the earliest years of the twentieth century by the growth of Jewish nationalism – the Zionist movement – which called on Jews to see Palestine as their national home, and to use the Hebrew language – modernized for the new century – as the language of daily life.

above
The *Gazeta de Amsterdam*, the first Jewish newspaper to be published in Amsterdam, on 19 August 1675. It is written in Ladino (Judaeo-Spanish),the language of the descendants of Jews expelled from Spain (Sepharad in Hebrew) in 1492. Its front page carried reports from Venice and Paris.

right
A Jewish family celebration. This photograph was found after the war in the southern Polish town of Radomsko, almost all of whose 12,000 Jews were deported to the death camp at Treblinka and murdered in the Holocaust. The Jews of Radomsko were Yiddish-speaking Ashkenazi Jews, the descendants of Jews who had come from Germany (Ashkenaz in Hebrew) in the Middle Ages. During the late nineteenth and early twentieth centuries, in common with all Polish Jewry, they had seen much emigration to France, Britain, the United States and, increasingly, to Palestine.

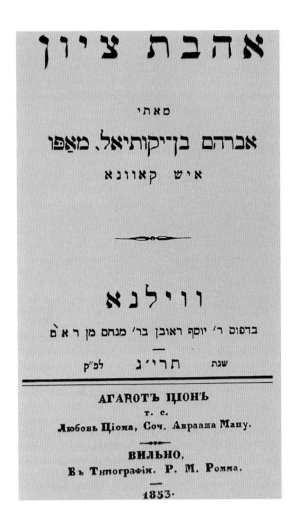

above

A West German stamp, issued in 1979, to commemorate the two-hundredth anniversary of the birth of Moses Mendelssohn, German Jewish philosopher and leading advocate of religious toleration. Mendelssohn's grave was among those desecrated in Berlin when the tombstones in the Jewish cemetery in Grosse Hamburger Strasse were taken away in 1941 for trench supports on the battlefield.

far left

Dinstagische Kurant (The Sunday Courant), a weekly newspaper published in Amsterdam in Yiddish. This issue is dated 27 August 1687.

near left

The title page, in modern Hebrew, of the novel *Ahavat Ziyyon* (The Love of Zion), by Abraham Mapu, the creator of the modern Hebrew novel. It was published in Vilna in 1853. Below the Hebrew lettering, the title, author's name and place of publication are printed in Russian. Mapu also published a textbook for the teaching of elementary modern Hebrew in schools.

left

The masthead and headlines of *Chwila* (The Moment), a Jewish newspaper published in Lvov, in Polish. This issue, of 18 May 1939, headed 'White Paper', brings news of a strike among the Jews of Palestine against the British government's official White Paper, which imposed restrictions on Jewish immigration into Palestine.

By 1933, hundreds of thousands of Jews, particularly in Poland and Lithuania, but also in Germany and throughout central Europe, spoke modern Hebrew as well as Yiddish, Polish or Lithuanian. Modern Hebrew was taught at Jewish high schools, and had a growing literature.

Jewish culture was manifested in many forms, and in all the languages spoken by Jews as the twentieth century dawned. Jewish printing presses produced books, novels, histories, and even Jewish cookbooks, in many languages, including modern Hebrew. Jewish newspapers appeared in every European language.

RELIGION

During two thousand years of dispersal and persecution after the Roman destruction of the Temple in Jerusalem in AD 70, the twin traditions of communal and family worship gave the Jews a powerful sense of continuity with the Biblical narrative and its ethical commandments, serving as an emotional shield during hard times, and as a powerful source of unity despite wide geographic dispersal.

Observance of the Holy Days – including the Day of Atonement when Jews everywhere fast and seek forgiveness for their sins, and the Rejoicing of the Law, when the Scrolls containing the Five Books of Moses (the Torah) are carried around the synagogue in joyous triumph – gave each community a sense of solidarity.

Just as each Jewish family maintained the traditions of weekly observance, so rabbis and teachers maintained the study of the Divine Will, perpetuating the all-pervading sense of Jewishness and the observance of the Jewish spiritual heritage.

Between the years 1000 and 1642, a series of rabbinical councils laid down laws for Jewish communal life. Some of the towns in which these councils were held saw the deportation and destruction of their Jewish communities hundreds of years later. One such council was held in the Rhineland city of Worms in 1196. During the Holocaust, the 300 Jews then living in Worms were deported 800 miles eastward to their deaths. A rabbinical council was also held in Corfu in 1642. During the Holocaust, 1,800 Jews were deported from Corfu to their deaths 900 miles away.

Among the most powerful Jewish religious movements was Hassidism. Founded in the 1730s, and manifesting itself in the vibrant rejoicing at religious worship, Hassidism flourished throughout Eastern Europe for two hundred years. The main centres of Hassidism were to be destroyed, and hundreds of thousands of its adherents murdered, in the brief period of the Holocaust.

The weekly Sabbath ritual in each home, with the lighting of the candles and the blessings on wine and bread, thanking God for his goodness, strengthened – in good times and bad – the belief in the common

destiny of the Jewish people, as a people chosen by God to carry out his commandments.

Hugo Gryn, born in Berehovo, Czechoslovakia, in 1930, later recalled:

'Home life and religious life were inseparable.... Prayer books, elegant editions of Bibles as well as well-thumbed ones dotted the shelves in our home. One of my earliest literary activities was to cut open the pages of the religious books to which we had endless subscriptions.

Set prayers were recited three times a day. Although my father considered himself an emancipated man, he would never fail to put on his *tefillin* – the leather phylacteries – while reciting the morning prayers before breakfast. Gabi and I usually joined him, each with our own prayer books. During the winter months we joined him in reciting the evening service before supper as well.

As far as I know, virtually every Jewish home in Berehovo observed a high level of *kashrut*: only ritually slaughtered meat and poultry were eaten – and great care was taken to remove every possible trace of blood. Meat and dairy dishes were strictly separated and it would never have occurred to anyone that any of the Biblically forbidden foods were even tempting!

Before baking bread or *challot* – the special

plaited loaves for Shabbat – my mother would take a small ball of dough and throw it into an open fire in memory of the Temple of Jerusalem. I cannot recall actually learning, but only knowing the blessings before eating and after meals, or before tasting fruits or cakes. I came to recite the special blessings instinctively on seeing lightning, hearing thunder and looking at a rainbow.... In one of my more pious phases I actually kept a list to make sure that in the course of any given day I recited the recommended one hundred benedictions.

There was a blessing on waking up and to this day I cannot drop off to sleep before invoking the archangel Michael on my right, Gabriel on the left, Uriel ahead of me and Raphael behind, and the Shechinah, or the presence of God, always above my head....'

opposite
The inside of the synagogue in Lancut, Poland, photographed in 1996, shortly after it had been restored. Jews were first recorded living in Lancut in 1563. The baroque-style synagogue was built in the 1730s, to replace the wooden synagogue that had been destroyed by fire. After the outbreak of war in September 1939, many of the town's 2,700 Jews managed to escape to the Soviet Union. Those who could not escape were murdered in a nearby camp and forest in 1942 and 1943.

above left
Jewish boys at a Yeshiva (religious academy) in the town of Nowogrodek, eastern Poland, pose for a photograph with their two teachers. This photograph was taken a few years before the outbreak of the Second World War.

left
Jewish boys at their religious studies, Trnava, Czechoslovakia. This photograph was taken by Roman Vishniac, who travelled throughout Eastern Europe between 1933 and 1938, photographing Jewish communities.

SELF-HELP

During the nineteenth century, as industrialization spread, and cities grew in size, there was a dramatic increase in the Jewish population in Europe, as in the general population. With the increase in numbers came new challenges but also new pressures. By the late nineteenth century there were more than a million Jewish poor in Russia and Eastern Europe.

In the Eastern Galician region of the Austro-Hungarian Empire there was intense Jewish poverty. In the White Russian (Belorussian) and Pripet marsh regions of western Russia many Jews lived in the poorest of *shetls* – small towns and villages in which they eked a precarious living, from the soil and from such trade as was possible with Jew and non-Jew alike.

Prosperous Jewish communities existed, and there were wealthy Jews who flourished in the expansion of nineteenth-century commerce and industry. Jews were among the leading railway builders, sugar manufacturers and even tea distributors of the Russian Empire. Jews were also at the forefront of the modernization of the newly united Germany, which since 1870 was Europe's most rapidly expanding industrial nation.

The Jewish sense of responsibility for fellow Jews in distress led to the growth of many charitable societies. The emphasis was on self-help: teaching a trade and providing an education to make it possible to meet the challenges of daily life.

The Alliance Israelite Universelle, founded in Paris in 1860, set up free Jewish schools in the poorest regions, including the Balkans. The Society to Promote Trades and Agriculture (ORT) was set up in Russia in 1880; after the Russian revolution, it moved, in 1921, to Berlin.

Also founded in Russia, in 1912, the Society to Promote Health Among Jews (OSE) established hospitals, kindergartens and children's homes. It too moved its headquarters to Berlin after the Russian revolution, and, like ORT, was then forced to move again, after Hitler came to power in Germany in 1933. Both set up their new headquarters in Paris.

above

Samuel Poliakov, a Russian Jewish financier and railway builder, who in 1880 was one of the founders of ORT, The Society to Promote Trades and Agriculture among the Jews of Russia. Poliakov died in 1888, at the age of fifty-two. This drawing was by Hillel Turok.

right

Jewish citizens in the Polish town of Chelm – famous in Jewish folklore for its archetypal fools – pose for a photograph during the rebuilding of a Home for Elderly Jews. This was a project embarked upon by the town's Jewish community before the Second World War. In 1939 there were 15,000 Jews in Chelm, half the town's population. During the Holocaust those who had been unable to escape eastward to the Soviet Union (the border of which was then only sixteen miles away) were deported to the nearby Sobibor death camp – only twenty miles to the north – and murdered there. Only fifteen Jewish workers at the town's prison survived the war in Chelm itself.

די עירות פֿון געזעל' מלבוש ערומים אין חעלים

Individual Jewish families also made substantial contributions to the well-being of their fellow Jews. The Rothschild family, originally from Frankfurt, financed schools, orphanages and poorhouses throughout Europe, and in Vienna set up a Home for Poor Musicians.

With the upheavals of the First World War, the American Jewish Joint Distribution Committee, known colloquially as the 'Joint', and still, like ORT, in existence at the start of the twenty-first century, made strenuous efforts to alleviate the plight of Jewish refugees in Eastern Europe who fled from the war zones. After the First World War the Joint took a lead in helping the dispossessed, and the widows and orphans of the war.

More than a million Jews emigrated from continental Europe – in particular from Russia – before 1914. Many of them settled in Britain and the United States. As soon as they were able to do so, they sent back what money they could to their family members still in Europe, or to the communities from which they had come. This was especially true of Jews who had come from the poorer regions of Russian Poland.

Baltic Sea
GERMANY
LITHUANIA
Kovno
Vilna
Minsk
Warsaw
WHITE RUSSIA
(BELORUSSIA)
POLAND
Pripet
Marshes
Chelm
RUSSIA
Kiev
AUSTRIA-
HUNGARY
EASTERN
GALICIA
Berdichev
Kharkov
UKRAINE
ROUMANIA
Odessa
0 kilometres 300
0 miles 150
© Martin Gilbert 2000
Black Sea

⋯ Northern and eastern border of the Jewish Pale of Settlement, within which most Russian Jews had to live.

▨ Areas of the Pale in which 20 per cent of all Jews were in receipt of poor relief from the Jewish community.

above
Members of the Chelm charitable society, The Clothing of the Naked. The society – of a sort that was found in many Jewish communities – was active in collecting donations from those who could afford to make even a small contribution. The money was used to purchase material from which clothes and shoes were made for those in need. The craftsmen employed by the society gave their services free. Each Passover (in the spring) and Sukkot festival (in the autumn), two to three hundred sets of clothing were distributed; in this photograph the shoes and clothing are being displayed. The Yiddish heading (in Hebrew lettering) gives the full name of the society.

POGROMS

The word pogrom comes from the Russian word for a violent mass attack against a section of the community. For the Jews of Russia, sudden violent attacks were a dreaded feature of their daily life. The most terrible of all such assaults took place almost three hundred years before the Holocaust, over an eight-year period between 1648 and 1656. These attacks were organized by a Cossack leader, Bogdan Chmielnicki, who, having defeated the Polish landed gentry and its army, joined forces with the local Ukrainian peasantry to attack the Jews.

More than 100,000 Jews were killed during the Chmielnicki massacres, and many more tortured or wounded. Jewish folk-memory of that time of torment persisted into the twentieth century. Jewish schoolchildren in Poland in the inter-war years from 1919 to 1939 were taught about the Chmielnicki massacres as a time of catastrophe for the Jews: a catastrophe that would surely not be seen again. Yet during the Holocaust, every town in which these frightening massacres took place was to have its Jewish community totally destroyed.

In the nineteenth century, violence returned to torment the Jews of Russia. It came in the form of pogroms that were often condoned by the Tsarist government, eager to find a scapegoat for its own economic failures – just as Hitler would seek to turn the German people against the Jews by falsely accusing them of controlling the wealth of Germany.

In the late nineteenth century four million Jews were living in Tsarist Russia, most of them in a specially designated area known as the Pale of Settlement, to which they had been restricted. The first organized pogrom broke out in Odessa in 1871. Jews were attacked in the streets and beaten up, Jewish shops were looted and Jewish homes destroyed. Waves of pogroms broke out in 1881 and 1882, and again between 1902 and 1905.

The period of the pogroms was a testing time for Jews throughout Russia. Self-defence groups were formed, and sometimes succeeded in driving the attackers away. But right-wing extremists, local hooligans and peasant economic discontent against the government found fierce outlets in the form of violence against Jews.

As the pogroms spread, as many as a million Jews emigrated to the United States. Many Jews from the Lithuanian region of Russia sought a new life in South Africa. Hundreds of thousands of others went to Britain and Western Europe, several thousand to Palestine.

During the Holocaust, among the Jews to be deported from Paris to Auschwitz in 1942 were those who had been born in Russia, who had emigrated in order to escape the pogroms, and found a new life and livelihood in France. Some of those who were deported to their deaths from Paris had been born in cities like Odessa where the pogroms had been at their most severe.

The Jewish deaths in the pogroms shocked Christian Europe. Three hundred Jews were killed in Odessa, eighty in Bialystok, forty-nine in Kishinev, several dozen in cities such as Brest-Litovsk, Minsk and Kiev. In the Holocaust, which began thirty-five years after the last of the Tsarist pogroms, tens of thousands of Jews were to be murdered from each of these same towns: 50,000 in Kishinev alone.

above
Map showing some of the towns in the Jewish Pale of Settlement in pre-1914 Tsarist Russia, in which Jews were attacked and Jewish property destroyed between 1871 and 1906. The map also shows, as a brown shaded area, the main region affected by the Chmielnicki massacres in the mid-seventeenth century.

opposite
A painting by Józef Mitler, entitled *After a Pogrom*. This stylized painting was used as an illustration in 1982 – a hundred years after the main wave of pogroms – by the editors of *Polish Jewry: History and Culture*, from the Jewish art collections then in Poland.

ANTI-SEMITISM

below
Historic hatreds: a woodcut from Schedel's *Chronicle of the World*, printed in Nuremberg in 1493 (one of the earliest printed books), showing the burning of Jews. It was in Nuremberg, in 1923, that Julius Streicher founded his anti-Semitic magazine, *Der Sturmer* (The Attacker). In 1938, in an article entitled 'War against the world enemy', he called for the total destruction of the Jewish people.

The Jews were a group against whom, century after century, violence was done in every land in which they lived. The expulsion of whole Jewish communities, and the murder of Jews, were features of Christian Europe throughout the Middle Ages and beyond.

In 1919, within a year of the end of the First World War, prejudice against Jews erupted in southern Russia, in which at least 85,000 Jews were murdered. Once again, as in the pogroms before the First World War, there were brave efforts at Jewish self-defence, but the attackers were armed with weapons, and with a vicious hatred.

A member of the post-war democratic government in Germany, Walther Rathenau, who had been one of the leaders of Germany's First World War preparedness, was murdered by anti-Semites in 1922. Their crude street slogan had been: 'Knock off Walther Rathenau, the dirty God-damned Jewish sow.'

In 1925, a thirty-six-year-old German political agitator, Adolf Hitler, who had applauded Rathenau's

murder, was in prison after his attempt to seize power in Munich. While in prison he wrote a book, *Mein Kampf* (My Struggle). In it he asked: 'Was there any shady undertaking, any form of foulness, especially in cultural life, in which at least one Jew did not participate? On putting the probing knife carefully to that kind of abscess, one immediately discovered, like a maggot in a putrescent body, a little Jew who was often blinded by the sudden light.'

Between the wars, laws that discriminated against Jews were passed in Poland, Latvia, Lithuania, Roumania and Greece. Many European countries put an upper limit on the percentage of Jews who could go to university. Nor did the fact that 40,000 Jews had been killed fighting in the ranks of the Austro-Hungarian army during the First World War prevent such anti-Jewish legislation being passed in both Austria and Hungary.

In Austria, extremist politicians called for a 'resolute

struggle' against what they described as the 'Jewish peril', and warned of the 'destructive' influence of Austria's Jews. Hitler, who had been born in Austria, had imbibed much anti-Jewish hatred in Vienna before the First World War.

In many European countries between the wars Jews were accepted as equal and respected citizens, and made substantial contributions to public well-being, as indeed they also did, or tried to do, in countries where anti-Jewish feeling had been intensified by agitators such as Hitler. France's most reforming inter-war Prime Minister, Léon Blum, was a Jew. This was used against him by extremist French politicians, especially those who, after 1933, saw merit in Hitler's anti-Jewish legislation.

Even in countries where there was widespread popular dislike of Jews, there could also be a close and constructive working together of Jews and non-Jews. In

Poland, Jews were among the country's most respected writers, poets, doctors and scientists.

There was anti-Semitism throughout Europe between the wars, but it needed a particularly dynamic and evil force to turn it into mass murder.

EUROPE'S INTER-WAR JEWISH POPULATION

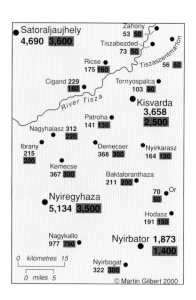

above

Towns in central Hungary, giving (in black) the number of Jews living there in 1930, and (in red) the number of those killed at Auschwitz in 1944.

As a result of the First World War, Jews became citizens of new and much altered countries. Europe after 1919 included several new nations that had been created after the defeat of the German, Austro-Hungarian and Russian Empires. Among the largest of these new nations were Poland and Czechoslovakia. The Baltic provinces of Russia became independent as Lithuania, Latvia and Estonia. Serbs joined with Croats and Slovenes to become Yugoslavia. Hungary and Austria were established as separate States. The territory of Germany was reduced – some going to France, some to Poland. The territory of Roumania was enlarged.

Every European country had a Jewish population. In Poland, one-tenth of the total population was Jewish. The Jews of the new Poland were given specifically Jewish representation in the parliament. In the new democratic Germany there were many Jewish members of parliament. In Czechoslovakia, Jews were welcomed as participants in the building up of the new institutions of statehood.

Many Jews were city dwellers, active in trade and commerce, in the life of the universities, and as teachers and doctors. Other Jews lived in small towns and villages, as shopkeepers and traders, and as farmers.

Jews lived in an estimated 30,000 localities throughout Europe. There was hardly a town without its Jewish community.

European Jewry after the First World War looked forward to toleration and progress. Following the establishment of the League of Nations in 1920, all countries were encouraged to introduce legislation that would protect all minorities. Better times ahead was the aspiration of all the peoples of Europe, as nations began to build up their institutions and create social policies that it was hoped would eliminate not only poverty, but also injustice and prejudice. Such aspirations were, however, under continual strain. Two severe economic crises, in the early and late 1920s, caused inflation, high prices, the collapse of many small businesses (including many Jewish small businesses) and the search for someone to blame emerged again.

A minority was an easy target for popular prejudice and anger. The Jews, even when they themselves were the victims of economic hardship in common with all citizens, were often singled out by demagogic politicians for particular abuse. In Germany, Adolf Hitler did this with particular venom, as he struggled

The Jews of Europe

The pre-Second World War Jewish populations of countries in Europe from which Jews were to be murdered during the Holocaust. Some of these figures were calculated precisely as a result of a census, others are approximations made at the time. They add up to almost eight million.

Poland	3,225,000
Soviet Union	1,300,000
Roumania	796,000
Germany	554,000
Hungary	473,000
Czechoslovakia	356,830
France	300,000
Austria	181,778
Lithuania	153,743
Holland	139,687
Latvia	93,479
Belgium	90,000
Greece	77,000
Yugoslavia	70,000
Italy	48,000
Denmark	5,577
Estonia	4,566
Norway	1,728
Albania	400
Total	**7,870,788**

Less than half a million European Jews lived in countries that the Germans did not control, or from which the Germans were unable to deport them.

left
A group of Hassidic Jews in a town in inter-war Ruthenia, when it was part of Czechoslovakia. The wall posters are in Czech. The road sign (top right) is in three languages – Czech, Hungarian and Ukrainian.

to build up a small, extremist political party into a national movement. Anti-Jewish feeling was also to be found, and flourished, in Poland and Roumania; there, as elsewhere in Europe where Hitler was in due course to extend his conquest or control, anti-Jewish sentiment was widespread, often strong enough to fan into violence, and stimulating considerable Jewish emigration, particularly to France and Palestine.

POLISH JEWRY BETWEEN THE WARS

Nadzia and I remembered our childhood in Hotz, the times we spent by the lake where in the summer we swam and in the winter we ice-skated. We reminisced about the walks through the hills covered in pine trees and about the places where in June we picked wild strawberries, and in August and September collected baskets full of mushrooms. Hotz was a lovely place for us; it was our world, as we didn't know any other.

We had food every day, but we had no running water in the house. The water was brought daily in buckets from a well and two metal containers were filled – one for washing up and the other for drinking and cooking. We had no proper toilet in the house; the wooden structure with a pit below was a sort of 'thunder-box', and it was situated at some distance from the house.

Roman Halter (twelve years old when war broke out), one of only four survivors of the Jewish community of eight hundred in Chodecz – known in Yiddish as Hotz – reminiscing with another survivor, Nadzia Pinczewska, fifty years after the war

More than three million Jews lived in Poland before the Second World War. In the Polish capital, Warsaw, the 352,659 Jews recorded in the census of 1931 constituted almost thirty per cent of the city's population. Jews had lived in Warsaw since the end of the fourteenth century.

The variety of Jewish life in Warsaw before the Second World War was reflected in the education system: there were six Hebrew language elementary schools, four Yiddish secular schools, a Yiddish-Hebrew school, an Orthodox religious school, two bi-lingual (Polish-Hebrew) elementary schools, and many private secondary schools of every Jewish religious and secular persuasion. Many Jewish children also went to Polish-language State schools.

Among other Jewish institutions were several hospitals, the orphanage run by Janusz Korczak, newspapers, publishing houses, theatres and restaurants.

The second largest number of Jews in Poland was in the industrial city of Lodz, whose 202,497 Jews made up a third of the population. Cracow, where Jews had lived since the fourteenth century, had a Jewish population of 56,515, just over a quarter of the city's inhabitants. Vilna, a centre of Jewish learning for five hundred years, had 55,000 Jews, well over a quarter of the population.

In the towns of eastern Poland, Jews were an even larger percentage of the population. In Pinsk the 20,220 Jews constituted two-thirds of the population.

The **top map** shows all Polish towns with more than 25,000 Jewish inhabitants in 1939, as well as other towns mentioned on these and the following two pages.

Despite the large number of Polish Jews living in cities and towns, hundreds of thousands more lived in villages and hamlets. The **bottom map** shows a rural area along the river San. The largest town in the region, Sanok, had a Jewish population of 4,000, more than forty per cent of the total population. The numbers shown on the map are the number of Jews living in 1931 in each of the towns and villages marked.

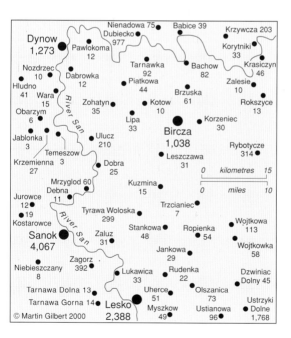

Recalling the pre-war years

Everybody was hungry for education. I think that European Jews were the most knowledgeable people on earth, because they wanted to know about the world around them.

Those early years of my life were good times for me. I knew everybody by their first name and everybody knew me. We had a good feeling toward one another. It was our domain. There was time for everything. Life was good.

John Fox, from Tuszyn, aged eleven at the outbreak of war

above left
A Jewish mother (Regina) and her children. The two boys on the left are wearing their prayer shawls (*talitot*). The photograph, found after the war, had been taken in the town of Naleczow between 1934 and 1937. Henryk Mazurek of Lublin later recalled: 'Her name was Taube, or Tauber, or maybe Tauberg. I remembered the name from stories told by my mother. Regina was her very good friend from a home-tailoring course or a lace-making course. She had seven children.'

left
A group of Jewish friends from Lodz, on holiday at the Polish resort town of Sopot in the early 1930s. The woman on the far right is Ala Salomonczyk, from Lodz. A graduate of a fine-art school, at the beginning of the Second World War Ala Salomonczyk managed to reach her husband, Dr Liebeskind, in Lvov. She was one of 250,000 Polish Jews who escaped into the Soviet Union in September and October 1939. She died there in unknown circumstances.

A PRE-WAR JEWISH COMMUNITY IN POLAND

Nowogrodek was a small town in eastern Poland. Of its 12,000 inhabitants, half were Jews. The first records of Jews in the town date back to 1484. The name of the first Jew in the town is known, Ilya Moisevitch, a tax collector for one of the Polish kings.

Every Monday and Thursday the White Russian farmers from the villages around Nowogrodek would come with their wares to the market. Jewish traders sold shoes, clothing, pottery, paint, saddles and scythes. Jewish butchers catered for non-Jewish customers.

The Jewish institutions in the town, typical of Jewish communities in eastern Poland, included a hospital – with twenty-five beds – together with a dispensary and an ambulance. The Jewish orphanage included many children whose fathers had been killed in the First World War. Sixty orphans were living there in 1930. Schooling was provided by The Society to Promote Trades and Agriculture (ORT), where the orphans learned a trade: the girls to become tailors and the boys carpenters. Most of the other Jewish children in the town went to a Hebrew-language school, where the curriculum was

that of the Jewish schools in Palestine. Orthodox Jewish children went to a special religious school, where boys and girls studied separately.

The Jewish sports organization Maccabi fostered football, cycling and general sports, and had its own club. Some of the footballers emigrated to Palestine in the 1930s. Jewish children from poor families were taken on holiday by a nationwide organization, TOZ, their place of relaxation was a village in a pine forest fifteen miles away.

A loan society, typical of each small Jewish community, enabled poor Jews to borrow money free of interest. The Jewish communal library had more than 7,000 books. The town fire brigade, a volunteer organization, was mostly Jewish, and had its own band.

There were two central synagogues, and synagogues for each trade (such as tailors, butchers, shopkeepers). A school of religious learning for boys (a Yeshiva) attracted boys from throughout the region. The Jewish Old Age Home had thirty residents. Jewish political Parties, mostly Socialist and Zionist, flourished and held vigorous debates.

above
Jewish children, mostly from poor families, on holiday at a village in the pine forest fifteen miles from Nowogrodek. Of the forty children shown here, only two survived the war. One of them, Shoshana Israelit, was hidden by a local White Russian farmer. She lives today in Israel. The other, Maurice Schuster, who escaped to Russia with his family, lives today in New York. The two survivors are both circled on the photograph.

left
Samovar break at the Jewish orphanage in Nowogrodek, mid-1930s. The samovar – tea urn – is on the right.

Nazi Germany

right
Hitler surrounded by admiring German youth.

above
A German stamp of the Nazi era.

There were three Germanys in the first thirty-three years of the twentieth century. The first was Imperial Germany, ruled by the Kaiser. Although, in 1900, Germany had only been united as a single country for thirty years, it was confident of its military abilities.

From 1914 to 1918 Imperial Germany fought against France, Britain and Russia. Elated by initial successes on the battlefield, it was cast down by the final defeat.

In 1919 a second Germany arose, the Weimar Republic. It was based on an elected parliament (the Reichstag) and democratic institutions, committed to maintain the rule of law. Jews were among those active in rebuilding the nation; one of them, Hugo Preuss, Minister of the Interior in the first post-war government, prepared the draft of the Weimar constitution.

Starting in 1930, Adolf Hitler's National Socialist German Workers Party, known by the first two syllables of *Nazional* (National) – as the Nazi Party – began to assert its political power. In September 1930 it won 107 seats in the Reichstag and, with more than six million votes, became the second largest Party in Germany. In July 1932 its seats increased to 230. Hitler was then in a position, within the parliamentary framework, to form a government.

In the election held in November 1932 the number of Nazi Party seats fell to 196. Had even two of Hitler's three main political opponents – Socialists, Communists and the Catholic Centre Party – united, they could have outvoted him. But they lacked sufficient sense of danger. In addition, Hitler's popular appeal remained strong.

On 30 January 1933 Hitler was asked by President Hindenburg to form a government. He did so. From that moment, he changed the laws and quickly acquired dictatorial power.

THE NAZI PROGRAMME AND THE JEWS

As early as 1920, Hitler made clear his personal attitude towards the Jews. The Nazi Party of which he had just become the leader published its twenty-five point official programme on 25 February 1920. The Party had only sixty members then, but it had all the determination of fanaticism.

'None but members of the Nation', read Point Four of the programme, 'may be citizens of the State. None but those of German blood, whatever their creed, may be members of the Nation. No Jew, therefore, may be a member of the Nation.'

Fifteen years later, this crude separation of one integral part of the German people was carried into law – the Nuremberg Laws of 1935.

Another demand first put forward in 1920 was that all Jews who had come to Germany after 1914 should be forced to leave. It did not matter to the Nazis that these immigrants were taking a productive and constructive part in German life, seeking to be, and becoming, good citizens. In 1938 this demand was carried out, in the mass expulsion, overnight, of 18,000 German Jews, most of them pre-1914 immigrants from

below
Hitler making a speech in 1923, at the time of the Nazi Party's first programme.

the Polish provinces of the Russian Empire.

On 13 August 1920 Hitler spoke to his supporters for two hours, in a beer cellar in Munich, his political base. His theme was 'Why we are against the Jews'. During his speech he promised that the Nazi Party alone would 'free you from the power of the Jew!' and he announced a new slogan, for Germany and for the world: 'Anti-Semites of the World, Unite! People of Europe, Free Yourselves!' His aim, he said, was a 'thorough solution', 'the removal of the Jews from the midst of our people'. That 'thorough solution' was to evolve over the next twenty years into what Nazi terminology called the 'final solution' (*Endlösung*), the murder of six million Jews in Europe.

The anti-Jewish element in the Nazi ideology permeated its programme at every stage. Every development had an anti-Jewish aspect. On 3 August 1921 Hitler set up the SA (*Sturmabteilung*, or Storm Section of the Party), men trained 'to take the offensive at any given moment' and to attack Jews as well as political opponents of Nazism. At their parades and marches, the SA carried high the Nazi emblem, the swastika, which also adorned their uniforms.

Another aspect of the Nazi programme was its attempt to win over German youth. To this end, on 4 July 1926 the Hitler Youth movement was inaugurated. It roused enormous enthusiasm with its sporting and camping activities, its marches and rallies, and with its stress on the purity of the 'German race', the so-called 'Aryans' who were contrasted at every possible moment with the Jews. The Hitler Youth was taught that 'Aryans' were pure, strong, upright, decent, unconquerable, while the Jews were an evil force to be vilified and driven out of Germany.

Violence was an integral part of the Nazi programme. In Berlin, on 1 January 1930, brown-uniformed Stormtroopers – known as Brownshirts – attacked and killed eight Jews in the streets: they were the first Jewish victims of the Nazi era. Henceforth, with increasing ferocity, Jews were molested in cafés and theatres, synagogue services were disrupted and anti-Jewish slogans became the daily calling card of Nazi

above and left
Hitler at a rally in Nuremberg, 1927: Nuremberg rallies were held every year, a central feature of Nazi publicity and propaganda.

thugs. Every area of German society was targeted, one Nazi Party internal directive stating: 'The natural hostility of the peasants against the Jews ... must be worked up to a frenzy.'

In September 1930, as German parliamentarians walked to the Reichstag for its new session, in which the Nazi Party had its first significant representation – 107 seats – crowds of Nazi Youth cried out as the parliamentarians passed: *'Deutschland erwache, Juda verrecke!'* (Germany awake, death to the Jews!).

THE ONE-DAY BOYCOTT

above
Berlin, 1 April 1933. Two Stormtroopers blockade a Jewish-owned shop and urge passers-by not to enter it.

right
'Beware, a Jew! Consultation forbidden!' A boycott placard in the window of a Jewish X-ray specialist in Berlin, April 1933.

On 5 March 1933, five weeks after Hitler became German Chancellor, elections were held throughout Germany under which, following strong Nazi intimidation, the Nazi Party declared itself the winner: eighteen million Germans, 44 per cent of the electorate, had voted for Hitler. Four days later, on March 9, the first mass attacks on Jews took place in the streets throughout Germany. Groups of Stormtroopers, in their familiar brown shirts with swastika armbands, working in groups of between five and thirty, surrounded individual Jews and beat them up. The *Manchester Guardian* reported that many Jews in Berlin were beaten 'until the blood streamed down their heads and faces, and their backs and shoulders were bruised. Many fainted and were left lying in the streets.'

On March 9, terror also found a hidden basis behind barbed wire. For on that day the first Nazi concentration camp was opened, at Dachau, near Munich. Several thousand Communist, Socialist and liberal opponents of the regime, and hundreds of Jews, were sent there in its first weeks. Dachau was to remain a place of brutality, sadism and deliberate killing until the very last days of the Second World War. It was run by the SS (*Schutzstaffel*, Elite Guard), originally set up in 1925 as Hitler's personal bodyguard. Their cruelty was to match, and then to exceed that of the Stormtroopers.

Attacks on Jews continued throughout March. On March 10, in Cassel, Stormtroopers occupied Jewish-owned department stores, and threatened and photographed every customer. On March 15 three Jews were seized by Stormtroopers in the Café New York in Berlin and taken to a local Stormtroop headquarters, where they were severely beaten up.

Accounts of this violence were widely reported in the Western newspapers. As a protest against these critical reports the German newspapers declared in banner headlines: 'Mad Jew Propaganda in London', 'Insolent Jews in America', 'Boycott the Jew!' A boycott of all Jewish shops was organized. The day chosen for the first day of the boycott was 1 April 1933. Boycott committees were set up throughout Germany to plan the event, and to make the boycott permanent.

In protest against plans for a permanent blockade, on March 27 a mass rally in New York's Madison Square Garden threatened a counter-boycott of all German-made goods in the United States, until the German boycott was called off. The Nazi Party back-tracked. Its boycott would be restricted to a single day.

At ten in the morning of April 1, uniformed Stormtroopers, armed with revolvers and rubber truncheons, and carrying pots of paint and brushes, began to smear the walls and doors of Jewish-owned businesses, cafes and doctors' consulting rooms. Tens of thousands of boycott placards were stuck on Jewish-owned premises. Smeared on Jewish-owned buildings were the slogans: 'Perish Judah!', 'Jews Out!', 'Go to Palestine!', 'Go to Jerusalem!' and, simply, 'Jew'. Hitler's Minister of Propaganda, Dr Josef Goebbels, wrote in his diary that it was 'an imposing spectacle'.

Many passers-by who were meant to join in and jeer took no part in this crude racist display. Some deliberately entered Jewish shops, to show their contempt for the boycott. In a number of towns, non-Jews who entered Jewish shops were stopped on their way out, and their faces were marked with a black stamp: 'We traitors bought at Jewish shops.'

Among the signs painted by Stormtroopers on Jewish shops was a yellow Star of David symbol. In the German Jewish newspaper *Jüdische Rundschau*, the editor, Robert Weltsch, wrote on April 4: 'They meant to dishonour us. Jews, take it upon yourselves, that Star of David, and honour it anew.'

top
A German beer mat with the slogan:
'Whoever buys from Jews is a traitor
to the people.'

above
A German newspaper cutting: in
Gailingen, a German village near the
Swiss frontier, Stormtroopers warn two
Swiss visitors not to enter a café owned
by a Jew. On the door of the café (the
Café Biedermann, owned by Gustav
Dreifuss) they have affixed the
medieval sign of a Jew: a yellow spot
on a black background.

left
A boycott placard in a Berlin street:
'Shun Jewish doctors and lawyers.'

PERSECUTION, EXPULSION, BOOK BURNING

A grim future

For the determined Nazis, neither the one-day boycott nor the burning of the books was sufficient for their purpose: they were mere pinpricks, foretastes of what they intended. On 26 June 1933, within seven weeks of the burning of the books, the official newspaper of the Nazi Party, *Völkischer Beobachter*, declared:

'All the suggestions for a lasting status, a lasting regulation of Jews in Germany, fail to solve the Jewish question, in as much as they fail to rid Germany of the Jews ... We must build up our State without Jews. They can never be anything but stateless aliens, they can never have any legal or constitutional status.'

opposite
The burning of 20,000 books in Berlin on the night of 10 May 1933, as Stormtroopers look on.

Not long after the one-day boycott of Jewish shops and businesses, Hitler boasted in a public speech: 'The Jews in Germany had not a hair of their heads rumpled.' In fact, one Jew had been killed: a lawyer by the name of Schrumm, he had been arrested at Kiel after an altercation with a Stormtrooper, taken to Stormtroop headquarters and shot. His death made the headlines in every British newspaper the following day, and was denounced as a 'lynching'.

In the aftermath of the one-day boycott, the isolation, humiliation and persecution of Jews was relentless. The expulsion of Jews from the universities was rapid and total. On learning that the Nobel Prize-winning chemist, Fritz Haber, had been deprived of his professorship, *The Times* commented on the 'irony' that Germany's ability to carry on fighting for four years in the First World War 'was in all probability due to him more than to any other man'. Martin Wolff, the leading German authority on civil law, was driven out of his lecture room by swastika-wearing students.

The German Jewish physicist and Nobel Prize winner Albert Einstein was visiting the United States when Hitler came to power. He called at once for the 'moral intervention of the entire world' against Hitlerism. His property was seized and a reward offered for his capture as 'an enemy of the State'. He became an exile. 'We do not want to be the land of Goethe and Einstein,' declared Berlin's Nazi newspaper, linking Goethe's German cultural genius with Einstein's Jewishness. Within two weeks of the boycott it was announced that no Jewish painter, no Jewish sculptor and no Jewish engineer was to be represented at the annual Academy Exhibition: 'Even Jewish artists who were at the Front,' it was reported, 'have been excluded from exhibitions.'

Throughout Germany, Jews were singled out for violent assault. On 22 April 1933 a newspaper report from Wiesbaden stated that a Jewish merchant, Salomon Rosenstrauch, had been 'shot in his flat'. The following day, at Worms, another Jewish merchant, Mathau Frank, was hanged – six days after his sixty-sixth birthday.

On April 26 the *Geheime Staatspolizei*, or Secret State Police, was taken over by the Nazis. Known (after its abbreviated form) as the Gestapo, it was given powers to shadow, arrest, interrogate and intern, without reference to any other State authority. The apparatus of dictatorship was complete; the brownshirted SA Stormtroopers, the blackshirted SS security service and its SD intelligence arm, the Gestapo secret police, and the concentration camps.

With the SS, SD and Gestapo in place, the law courts, and due process of law, defence lawyers and appeal courts, became of no avail against Nazi tyranny.

The next Nazi assault was on culture, learning and literature. On 10 May 1933, in front of the Berlin Opera House – and opposite the main entrance to the University of Berlin – 20,000 books were burned in a massive bonfire. These were all books that the Nazis judged to be 'degenerate'. Many were by Jewish authors.

Goebbels, who arrived at the Opera House at midnight in an open car to watch the flames, called the books that were burning 'intellectual filth' and described their authors as 'Jewish asphalt literati'. The burning books included some of the finest works of recent German literature, history, sociology, political philosophy, music, art and architecture. Similar bonfires were lit and books burned in a dozen other German university towns.

The burning of books, and the killing of individuals, went on side by side. On the day before the book-burning, Dr Meyer, a Jewish dentist in Wuppertal, was mutilated by Stormtroopers and then drowned. In Dachau concentration camp, in the last two weeks of May, four Jews were murdered: they were Dr Alfred Strauss, a lawyer, on May 15; Louis Schloss, a businessman, on May 25; Karl Lehburger, a businessman, on May 27; and Willi Aron, a lawyer, two days later.

Recalling the names of these early victims of Nazi racism brings home the extent to which, from racism's first year as the dominant philosophy of a government in power, the machinery of destruction was deliberate, cruel and relentless. Human beings, like books, were to be physically destroyed. Life and culture were equally vulnerable to the whim and fury of Nazism.

RACISM IN NAZI GERMANY

On 4 April 1933, three days after the one-day boycott of Jewish shops, the German Boxing Association barred all Jewish boxers from membership. Three days later the first legislative use of the term 'non-Aryan' appeared in an official law. It was a law banning Jews from public service, including teaching. For almost a century Jews had taken an active and constructive part in German public life. Starting on 7 April 1933 they could no longer do so.

A series of laws in 1933 ensured that Jews were increasingly isolated and humiliated. On April 24 people with 'Jewish names' could no longer use them when sending telegrams. A day later Jews were barred from all athletic and sporting associations. On September 22, Jews were excluded from the Reich Chamber of Culture. On October 4 all Jewish journalists were banned from working on German newspapers.

1934 saw further discrimination. From March 5, all Jewish actors were banned from performing on stage or screen. After June 7, Jewish companies could no longer be mentioned on the radio. After July 22, no Jewish student could take a law examination anywhere in Germany. Jewish newspapers could not be displayed or sold publicly after October 1.

In May 1935 Jews were forbidden to serve in the German armed forces. Five months later it was decreed that any new war memorials (and First World War memorials were continually being erected) must not carry the names of Jews who had been killed in action – fighting for Germany.

Then came the Nuremberg Laws. These two sets of laws, promulgated on 15 September 1935, relegated the Jews to second-class citizens. Both laws were signed by Hitler personally. Under the first law, citizenship could only belong to 'a national of German or kindred blood'. Under the second law, all Jews were defined as being not of German blood. Marriages between Jews and 'German nationals' were forbidden.

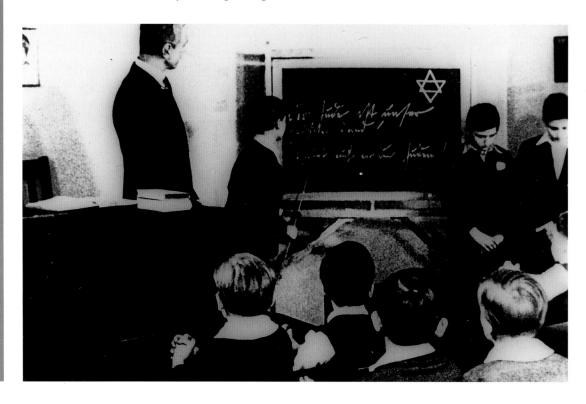

opposite
A lesson in German schools, 'The Jew is our greatest enemy', with two Jewish boys brought to the front of the class to serve as 'life-objects' for the lesson. This photograph was taken in German-annexed Austria in 1938.

left
A bench in a German park, marked 'Only for Jews'. The woman sitting on the bench covered her face when the photograph was taken. Other benches were forbidden to Jews.

left
The moment of expulsion, published in the anti-Semitic magazine *Der Stürmer*, with the gleeful caption: 'The expulsion of the Jews from the Jew-aquarium at Bad Herweck, Mannheim, begins.' The so-called 'Jew-aquarium' was a family swimming pool.

below left
A German town banner, 'Jews are not wanted here'. Towns and villages throughout Germany vied with each other in expelling the Jews, and then declaring themselves 'Jew-free'.

far left
Hitler's signature on the Nuremberg Laws. Signing with him were the Minister of the Interior, Wilhelm Frick, and the Minister of Justice, Dr Franz Gürtner. This, the original signed version of the Nuremberg Laws, was found in the Huntingdon Library in California in 1999. It had been taken from Germany by General Patton at the end of the Second World War, and given by him to the library. Gürtner died during the war. Frick was hanged at Nuremberg on 16 October 1946.

JEWISH EMIGRATION FROM GERMANY

Captain Francis Edward Foley was an extraordinary person in that he felt a genuine compassion for the throngs that day in, day out, besieged his office with their applications, requests and enquiries as to the progress of their case. The winter of 1938 was a harsh one, and elderly men and women waited from six in the morning, queuing up in the snow and biting wind. Captain Foley saw to it that a uniformed commissionaire trundled along the line of frozen misery, and all this despite the clientele, neurotic with frustration and cold, doing little to lighten his task. 'Why had the visa not arrived? Maybe it had arrived and been mislaid. Could *der Herr* have another look?...' Others pleaded, offered bribes, threatened, wept, and threw fits. Captain Foley always maintained his composure.... I learned a lot from him. Where to get genuine fake passports, mainly from South American banana republics; the name of small, helpful print shops willing to produce one-off forms; rubber stamp makers on whose discretion one could rely. And a number of escape routes and procedures, as well as reliable addresses for succour and guidance in the vicinity of certain German frontier crossing points into Belgium, Holland and Switzerland. Most of the addresses were those of lesser dignitaries of the church.

Recollections of **Wim van Leer**, a twenty-five-year-old Dutch Jew then in Berlin

From the very first days of the Nazi regime in Germany, German Jewish refugees found asylum in the countries outside Germany. German Jewish lawyers, doctors, architects and writers were among those finding refuge in more than thirty countries. They constituted a creative array that, had it not been for Hitler and his racist ideology, would have remained in Germany and given its talents to the German nation.

It was a German Jewish refugee in Britain, Berlin-born Ernst Chain, who found a means of turning penicillin into a usable – and revolutionary – life-saving drug, the first antibiotic. As a result, hundreds of thousands of Allied soldiers, sailors and airmen were treated during the war for wounds that would otherwise have killed them. Another German Jewish refugee, the neurosurgeon Ludwig Guttmann, left Germany at the beginning of 1939. Working in Britain, he pioneered the treatment of spinal injuries, reducing the death rate among those wounded in action from 80% to 10%. In 1945 a British government Minister said, with reference to Guttmann: 'Thank you, Hitler, for sending us men like these.'

The United States was the main beneficiary of the exodus of Jews from Nazi persecution: more than 100,000 were given refuge. Many volumes could be written without in any way exhausting their stories. Biographies could be written (and have been written) of many of them, such as the Riga-born Russian Jewish photographer Philippe Halsman, who was forced to flee from his studio in Paris in 1940, went to New York and created 101 covers for *Life* magazine; or Otto Frisch, born in Vienna, who was working in Berlin when the Nazis came to power, emigrated to Britain, and then, during the Second World War, worked in the United States on the atom bomb project; or Henry Kissinger, who left Germany with his parents when he was fifteen, and became Secretary of State and a Nobel Peace Prize winner.

Those German Jews who went to Palestine served as pillars of creativity of the future Jewish State. One of the twenty thousand German Jews reaching Palestine after Hitler came to power in Germany was a teenage student, Stef Wertheimer. Fifty years later he was Israel's leading industrialist and exporter.

Many of the countries that gave sanctuary to the German Jewish refugees eventually fell under Nazi rule. For those 72,000 refugees who had found havens in France, Holland and Belgium, and had begun new lives there, refuge became captivity when the German army struck westward. But it was impossible in 1938, any more than it had been in 1933, to forecast where – if anywhere – German rule would spread.

Among those German Jews who found refuge in Holland in 1933 were the family of Otto Frank. Like so many German Jews of military age, Otto and his brother Herbert had served in the German army in the First World War. Otto's two daughters, Anne and Margot, were born in Frankfurt. When Anne celebrated her tenth birthday in Amsterdam on 12

Refugee havens	
Countries taking in German Jewish refugees from 1933 to the end of 1938	
United States	102,222
Argentina	63,500
Britain	52,000
Palestine	33,399
France	30,000
Holland	30,000
South Africa	26,100
Shanghai	20,000
Chile	14,000
Belgium	12,000
Portugal	10,000
Brazil	8,000
Switzerland	7,000
Bolivia	7,000
Yugoslavia	7,000
Canada	6,000
Italy	5,000
Australia	3,500
Sweden	3,200
Spain	3,000
Hungary	3,000
Uruguay	2,200
Norway	2,000
Denmark	2,000
Philippines	700
Venezuela	600
Japan	300
Total	453,721

June 1939, Europe was still at peace.

Tens of thousands of refugees found havens in lands that were never conquered by Hitler. They were to become an integral part of the countries that took them in. Their children were no longer 'German', but 'British', 'American', 'Israeli' and so on.

Before the outbreak of war on 1 September 1939, almost half of Germany's half million Jews had emigrated. Sigmund Freud had been given asylum in Britain after the German annexation of Austria in 1938.

But in the last year before war came, the willingness of countries to take in refugees had started to change. Most countries, including the United States and Britain, began to put up barriers to immigration. On 5 July 1938 an international conference was held at the French town of Evian, on Lake Geneva, at which many of the countries represented expressed their reluctance to continue with an open-door policy. The Australian delegate at Evian expressed his country's reluctance to take in any more Jews, telling the conference that since Australia had 'no racial problem, we are not desirous of importing one'. His words have echoed ever since in the annals of pre-war anti-Jewish prejudice. They were not, however, echoed by his government: Australia, which had taken in 3,500 Jews between 1933 and the end of 1938, took in a further 5,000 in 1939. Following Arab protests the British government drastically curbed immigration to Palestine, but not before more than thirty thousand Jews, over half of them from Gemany, had been admitted.

GERMAN ANNEXATIONS

German troops entered Austria on 11 March 1938. As they advanced from the German border towards the capital, Vienna, they were welcomed in every town and village by cheering crowds. Austrian democrats and opponents of Nazism stayed indoors. They knew that the new Nazi regime would persecute them mercilessly, as it had persecuted its critics and opponents in Germany for the previous five years.

On 13 March 1938 Hitler formally annexed Austria. Five days later, a Gestapo headquarters was set up in Vienna – in the Hotel Metropol, which had been confiscated from its Jewish owners. That same day the offices of the Jewish community in Vienna, and the Zionist institutions in the city, were closed down, and their officials sent across the German border to Dachau. In all, 444 Jewish societies in Vienna, and 181 in the Austrian provinces, were forced to cease their activities.

From the first night of the German annexation of Austria, Jewish apartments were looted, and tens of thousands of works of art, rugs, pieces of furniture, and valuables confiscated. The two finest Jewish-owned art collections were seized, being taken to Hitler's own private art collection, and to the art museum in Linz (which Hitler wished to make the best in Germany and

Austria). From that first night, Austria's 185,000 Jews were singled out for beatings and humiliation. By March 24, all Jews had been dismissed from their posts in theatres, public libraries and community centres. On March 26 they were thrown out of all university and college appointments.

Hundreds of Austrian Jews committed suicide rather than face the trauma of persecution. Tens of thousands emigrated. The Germans encouraged emigration, and stripped those Jews who left of all their property and possessions. Adolf Eichmann, an SS officer, was sent from Berlin to Vienna to expedite the emigration of Austria's Jews. By the time war broke out in September 1939 – and all borders were effectively sealed by Germany – 126,445 Austrian Jews had left: 15,000 of them were given refuge by countries that were eventually conquered by Germany. They were to be deported to their deaths during the Holocaust. Of those who found safe havens, Britain took 30,850, the United States 28,700, the city of Shanghai 18,120, Latin America 11,500, Palestine 9,190, and Australia and New Zealand 1,880. Canada agreed to take in only 82.

The German annexation of Austria was followed within the space of one year by the occupation of western Czechoslovakia (the provinces of Bohemia and Moravia, which became a German Protectorate) and the Czech capital, Prague. Thousands more Jewish refugees were forced to flee, taking their talents to other lands. Only six months elapsed between German troops entering Prague and the coming of the Second World War in September 1939, which brought with it the sealing of frontiers, with the result that far fewer Jews (34%) were able to leave Czechoslovakia than had left Germany since 1933 (61%) or Austria in 1938 (68%).

Among the Austrian Jews who found refuge elsewhere was William Dressler. Born in Vienna in 1890, he qualified as a doctor of medicine, and specialized in cardiology. He was one of the first advocates of the use of electrocardiology in the early diagnosis of heart problems. Fleeing Austria, he made his home in the United States, publishing *Clinical Cardiology* in 1942 – the authoritative work on diagnosing cardiac illness –

and becoming head of the cardiology clinic of the Maimonides Medical Centre. As a result of his diagnosis, the problems associated with post-myocardial infarction became known as 'Dressler's Syndrome'.

Another Jewish refugee from Vienna, the painter Marie-Louise Motesiczky, born in 1906, fled to Holland in 1938. She held her first exhibition at The Hague in 1939. Shortly afterwards she left for Britain. There are portraits by her in the National Portrait Gallery and the Tate Gallery in London. Her brother stayed in Holland,

joined the Dutch resistance, was captured, and died in Auschwitz. Marie-Louise Motesiczky's last exhibition was in her birthplace, Vienna, in 1994, two years before her death.

As I wrote these words – on 11 October 1999 – a British newspaper has published the obituary of Walter Bor, who had just died at the age of eighty-three. Born in Vienna, educated in Prague, he escaped first to Italy and then to Britain, where he became a leading architect and urban planner.

above and opposite
Jews being forced to scrub the streets in Vienna immediately after Germany annexed Austria, and the Austrian Nazis, previously outlawed or restrained, took control.

KRISTALLNACHT

above
A German Democratic Republic (East German) stamp, issued in 1988, on the fiftieth anniversary of Kristallnacht. It shows the Menorah (the candelabra, the eight-branched version of which is used at the festival of Channukah – the Jewish festival of freedom) below the date of Kristallnacht, 9 November 1938.

above right
A Berlin street on 10 November 1938, the morning after Kristallnacht.

On 18 October 1938, on Hitler's orders, 15,000 Polish-born Jews resident in Germany were declared to be 'stateless' and expelled – taken by train to the Polish border. There they were held for several weeks in harsh conditions, until the Polish government agreed to let them in.

These Jews – more than four thousand families – had been living in Germany for ten, twenty and even thirty years. They were forced to leave their homes in a single night, to go to the nearest railway station, and allowed only one suitcase per person. The rest of their belongings had to be left behind. The Nazis had discovered that even the simplest of possessions – furniture, cutlery, linen, beds, stoves – could be seized and taken over, solely as a result of terror.

One of the 15,000 deportees, Zindel Grynszpan, had been born in 1886 in the Russian Polish town of Radomsko. Since 1911 he had lived in the German city of Hanover. From the severe discomfort of a border village, where several fellow-deportees suffered heart attacks as a result of the harsh conditions, he sent a postcard to his son Hirsch, who was then in Paris, describing the severity of the expulsion and his family's plight at the Polish border.

Enraged by what his father described – 'the SS men were whipping us, those who lingered they hit and blood was flowing on the road' – on November 6 Hirsch Grynszpan went to the German embassy in Paris, where he shot and fatally wounded the first official who received him, a German diplomat, Ernst vom Rath.

On November 9 vom Rath died in Paris. Hitler, who was in Munich when the news was brought to him, gave orders for a night of terror throughout Germany, including German-annexed Austria and the Sudetenland region of Czechoslovakia (incorporated into Germany only a month earlier).

During the night of November 9-10 more than ninety Jews were killed and hundreds of synagogues set on fire. The destruction of Jewish property led to so much broken glass in the streets that the destruction was given the name Kristallnacht.

When the night was over, the German Jewish community was ordered to pay, from its own dwindling

funds, for the cost of the damage.

Immediately after Kristallnacht, 20,000 Jews were seized and sent, some for many months, to the concentration camps at Dachau, Buchenwald and Sachsenhausen (where 25,000 Jews were already being held). In each of these camps several hundred died as a result of the brutality of the guards. Hundreds more committed suicide as the sadistic beatings intensified.

Outside Germany, there were massive public protests as news of Kristallnacht was given wide newspaper coverage. In New York, there was a call for the intensification of the existing boycott on German goods. In Chicago, protesters burned swastika flags.

Hitler had no intention of being intimidated. In a public speech in Berlin on 30 January 1939, he declared that even if Germany found itself at war 'the result will not be the bolshevization of the earth, and thus the victory of Jewry, but the annihilation of the Jewish race in Europe'.

top
A colour photograph taken after Kristallnacht, as Jewish shopowners, having put up bars to prevent looting, begin the work of trying to repair the damage.

above
A postcard of a section of the Berlin Wall, commemorating the fiftieth anniverary of Kristallnacht.

left
Memel: the synagogue set on fire.

A village near Aachen

... suddenly, with one loud cry of 'Down with the Jews', the gathering outside produced axes and heavy sledgehammers. They advanced towards the little synagogue ... burst the door open, and the whole crowd, by now shouting and laughing, stormed into the little House of God.

... three men who had smashed the ark, threw the Scrolls of the Law of Moses out. They threw them – these scrolls which had stood in their quiet dignity, draped in blue or wine-red velvet, with their little crowns of silver covering the tops of the shafts by which the Scroll was held during the service – to the screaming and shouting mass of people which had filled the little synagogue.

The people caught the Scrolls as if they were amusing themselves with a ball game – tossing them up into the air again, while other people flung them further back until they reached the street outside. Women tore away the red and blue velvet and everybody tried to snatch some of the silver adorning the Scrolls.

Naked and open, the Scrolls lay in the muddy autumn lane; children stepped on them and tore pieces from the fine parchment on which the Law was written – the same Law which the people who tore it apart had, in vain, tried to absorb for over a thousand years.

Recollections of **Eric Lucas**, a Jewish teenager from the village of Hoengen, who found refuge in Britain in 1939

JEWISH CHILDREN FIND HAVEN IN BRITAIN

I was born in Hronov, Czechoslovakia and left home in June 1939 when I was five and a quarter years old. I do not remember very much, really nothing, about my departure. I came alone and no other member of my family joined me either before or after the war. While I hoped that my parents had survived, I do not remember anything about my feelings at the end of the war. Sadly my parents did not survive.

Tom Bermann, after the war an Aquatic Microbiologist and director of a research laboratory on the Sea of Galilee, Israel

From the train window at Hamburg Hauptbanhof I saw my parents on the platform, for the last time ever. I was just sixteen.

Eddie Nussbaum, who later left England for the United States

below right

Tom Bermann's 'document of identity', issued by the British Committee for Children in Prague. He had been born in Czechoslovakia on 25 February 1934. On 14 June 1939 his parents, Charles and Lenka Bermann, wrote to Mrs Miller, who had given him a home in Scotland: '… we thank Heaven that has led our only child into the house of so generous and good people. Though we have not known more than your name until now (as well as you of us) upon reading your kind letter we can now form an idea of you, and I need not assure you of our happiness to know that our child is in such good hands.'

Known as the Kinder (children) or Kindertransport (children's transport), more than nine thousand German and Austrian children – between the ages of three months and seventeen years – were brought to Britain after the Kristallnacht. The British government gave permission for the children to come, as an emergency measure to get them out of danger. No regular entry visas were required, only a simple 'document of identity' issued with the automatic approval of the British authorities in Germany. These children came alone. Most were never to see their parents again.

The main task of organizing the collection, travel and resettlement of the children was undertaken by the Central British Fund, a Jewish charitable organization. Many children from Orthodox families were brought over by a young Orthodox rabbi, Dr Solomon Schonfeld, who went to Vienna and other cities to bring the youngsters out; among them was a future British and Commonwealth Chief Rabbi, Immanuel Jakobovits, who had been born in Königsberg.

Non-Jewish organizations – among them the Save the Children Fund, and the Quakers – also made a considerable contribution to the massive effort.

The first children's transport to reach Britain, by train across Europe, and then by sea from the Hook of Holland to the port of Harwich, arrived in Britain on 1 December 1938. After the German occupation of Prague in May 1939, Czech Jewish children from Bohemia and Moravia were also brought to Britain. The last boat reached Harwich on 14 May 1940, as German troops entered Holland.

Otto F. Hutter was fourteen years old when Hitler entered Vienna in March 1939. From 1971 he was Regius Professor of Physiology at the University of Glasgow. He later recalled:

'December 4th 1938 was a fateful day for me. That Sunday afternoon I ventured out into the nearby Quay-Park, a strip of greenery along the banks of the Donau-Kanal. I was on my way home, dutifully before dusk, when crossing the Marienbrücke I met my friend Bobby Mütz (where are you now?). He told me triumphantly that he was soon leaving for England. Upon my questioning, he directed me towards the Hotel Metropole where registration of children for emigration was underway. Though only a stone's throw from home, I turned heel and ran thither to become 359th of 360 children registered that day.

By the time I had been interviewed, photographed and medically examined, it was late evening. In high spirits I ran home, little anticipating my mother's frenzied distress at my failure to return home in good time. Duly, I received instant chastisement. When I explained sobbingly where I had been and what transpired, my at first incredulous mother joined me in tears. However, the British Home Secretary, who barely two weeks earlier had acceded to the rescue of us children, had been correctly informed: Jewish parents were prepared to face the ordeal of parting.

In the next few days I was fitted out with stout boots, a new winter coat and other clothing, each item lovingly embroidered with my name by my heartbroken mother. With all my belongings, not forgetting my *tallith* and *tefillin*, packed into a small case, and with a card bearing the number 359 tied around my neck – a relic I still possess – my parents took me to the Bahnhof late in the evening of Saturday 10th December. Other children were already on the train and –

left
Three German Jewish girls reach Liverpool Street Station, London, on 7 July 1939: they were part of a group of 150 who arrived that day.

below left
Jewish refugee children on the train shortly after crossing the German border into Holland. They then went by boat from the Hook of Holland to Harwich. From there, most of them were taken the two short miles to Dovercourt, where a year earlier a holiday camp had been established by Billy Butlin. A *Jewish Chronicle* reporter noted: '…all the children are given plenty of blankets to keep them warm at night…. Some were playing table tennis, some darts (and it was amusing to watch their efforts at this game, which was entirely new to them)…. In a side room there were several surrounding a piano which was being played by a youngster of about ten…. Closer observation revealed here a group of three little girls, one with a doll clutched to her, seated quite silently in a corner, and there a boy rubbing his eyes furtively.'

below
German Jewish refugee children on the train, leaving Germany on their way to Britain.

thoughtless youngster that I was – I was anxious to join them on what seemed to me more an adventure than a parting. My father, filled with premonition, held me back to bestow upon me the traditional Hebrew blessing. So whenever I now bless my own children, I am comforted by the thought that in that way at least the chain of generations has remained unbroken….

After Victory in Europe, the quest whether my parents, Isak and Elisabeth Hutter, had perchance survived on the continent occupied me. Many evenings were spent helping to compile lists of survivors, but it was a hope in vain; and despite many enquiries over the years I still do not know when and where they perished.'

REFUGEES REJECTED: THE VOYAGE OF THE *ST LOUIS*

Many refugees from Germany, Austria and Czechoslovakia were determined to leave Europe altogether. They did not wish to stay on the same continent as Germany, even in democratic countries such as France, Belgium or Holland. It was to the United States that as many as a quarter of the Jews under Nazi rule sought entry. Thousands did so: more than 100,000 between Hitler coming to power in 1933 and the end of 1938.

The American government set annual quotas, country by country. By the summer of 1939 the annual quotas for the rest of 1939, and for the whole of 1940 and 1941, were full. Those German Jews who were put on the American visa list in 1939 were told that they must wait three years – until 1942 – before they could actually enter the United States.

Undeterred by this rule, 930 refugees left Germany on the *St Louis*, a German ocean liner, which left Hamburg on 13 May 1939. Among them were 734 who held United States immigration quota numbers permitting them entry in three years' time. Reaching the Caribbean, the refugees on the *St Louis* sought entry into a Latin American country where they could wait until the United States would take them in. Cuba agreed to take twenty-four refugees, but no more. Four other South American countries – Colombia, Chile, Paraguay and Argentina – refused to take a single refugee. Steaming off Miami, the refugees appealed, on June 6, direct to President Roosevelt to let them land. They received no reply. Four days later, the United States government formally refused them entry.

The *St Louis* returned across the Atlantic to the Belgian port of Antwerp. It was met by journalists and cameramen who broadcast the story worldwide. As a result of the publicity, and further appeals to governments, none of the refugees had to return to Germany: 619 were admitted by France, Holland and Belgium. A further 287 found haven in Britain: within a year they alone were to be outside German rule, and safe from eventual deportation.

Among those on board the *St Louis* were fifteen-year-old Lisa Mendel, her brother and their mother, from a small town (Kerken) near Düsseldorf. They were hoping to join Lisa's father, who, after his release from Sachsenhausen concentration camp, had reached Cuba. They were refused entry, however, either to Cuba or the United States, and spent the war years in France. After the war they made their way to the United States.

Herbert Manasse, his wife and two young children were also among the passengers given entry to France. After the German invasion in 1940 they escaped to Italy. Following the German occupation of Italy in 1943 they were deported to Auschwitz, and murdered. Among those who found refuge in Britain were several who, after joining the British army, were sent to France six months later. In May 1940 they fought in the retreat to Dunkirk, before being taken back across the Channel to Britain.

The photograph opposite (top) shows Gisela Knepel (on the far left of the picture, with her elbow on the

below
Map showing the route of the *St Louis* to the Americas and back.

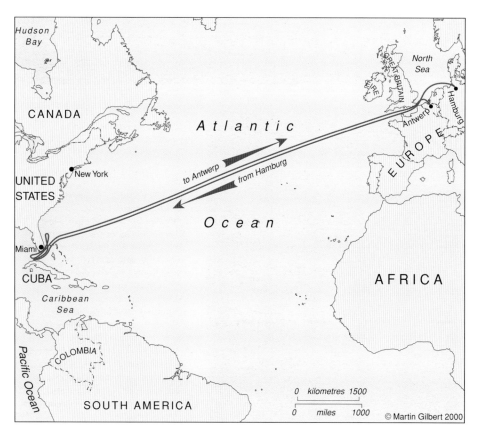

table), her sister Sonja (right, also with her elbow on table) and their mother Chaja (third from the left), on board the *St Louis*. They were among those allowed into Britain, where, Gisela later recalled: 'Life was hard. All you were allowed to do was housework. At fifteen I just was scrubbing floors for a living. I was happy to do it. We were happy to be saved.' After the *St Louis* left Hamburg, Gisela's father, Leo (Leib Yehuda) Knepel, sailed from Germany on board the *Orinoco* with several hundred more refugees. When the *Orinoco* learned that the *St Louis* passengers had not been allowed to land, it returned to Germany. Leo Knepel, who was Polish-born, was then deported by the Germans to Poland. Leo Knepel, his two brothers, their wives and large family, from Rzeszow, in Poland, were killed in the Holocaust. 'We never saw him again,' Gisela recalled.

An estimated 660 of the 930 Jewish refugees who were forced to return to Europe on the *St Louis* were murdered in the Holocaust.

above
A meal on board the *St Louis*. Gisela Knepel is on the far left in the photograph.

left
Two Jewish sisters, the thirteen-year-old twins Renee and Ines Spanier, on board the *St Louis*, photographed after docking at Antwerp. Together with their parents, they were given asylum in Holland. After the German occupation of Holland the family was sent to Westerbork – later a staging post for deportation to Auschwitz. At Westerbork their father, Dr Fritz Spanier, became the chief medical officer in the camp hospital. The family were not deported. After the war, Dr Spanier went to Belsen where he worked to help the survivors back to health. He then made his home in Düsseldorf. The twins emigrated to the United States.

THOSE WHO HELPED

Jews searching for means to leave Germany were helped in many unexpected ways, by people who took great risks to get them out of Europe.

Following the British government's agreement in November 1938 – after the Kristallnacht – to issue visas for up to 10,000 German and Austrian Jewish children, the German authorities initially announced that permission for them to cross the border into Holland would be refused. A Dutch woman, Gertrud Wijsmuller, who was helping organize refugee transports, decided to challenge the German ruling.

Taking the train to Vienna, she insisted on talking to the head of the Central Bureau for Jewish Emigration, Adolf Eichmann, and persuaded him to give her a collective exit permit for six hundred Austrian Jewish children. She then helped to organize a further forty-nine refugee transports to Britain.

In August 1939 Gertrud Wijsmuller travelled from Holland to the Free City of Danzig, a predominantly German city, which had been under League of Nations administration since 1920. In Danzig, she persuaded the local pro-Nazi authorities to let her organize a refugee train. It set off on August 24, serenaded by a brass band provided by the Danzig Gestapo. It was her fiftieth refugee transport. A week later, Hitler invaded Poland. He also occupied Danzig.

Gertrud Wijsmuller continued to organize the transfer of German Jewish refugee children from neutral Holland to Britain. On 10 May 1940 Germany invaded Holland. As German troops approached Amsterdam, she organized half a dozen coaches and assembled two hundred German Jewish refugees, among them eighty children. The refugees were driven to the port of Ijmuiden, where she persuaded the captain of a Dutch freighter to sail with them to England. One of those on board, fourteen-year-old Harry Jacobi, later recalled:

> 'At 7 p.m. we sailed. Far away from the shore we looked back and saw a huge column of black smoke from the oil storage tanks that had been set on fire to prevent the Germans having them. At 9 p.m. news came through, picked up by the ship's radio. The Dutch had capitulated.'

There had been no room on the crowded coaches for Harry Jacobi's grandparents, with whom he had gone to Amsterdam. Neither they, nor his parents – who were still in Berlin – survived the war.

In May 1940, as German troops advanced through France, the Portuguese Consul-General at Bordeaux, Dr Aristides de Sousa Mendes – a devout Catholic – gave visas to 10,000 Jews to cross into Spain and make their way to Portugal, from where they were able to continue across the Atlantic to the United States. Without a Portuguese transit visa, the Spanish government would not allow Jews to enter. De Sousa Mendes issued these visas in defiance of his instructions.

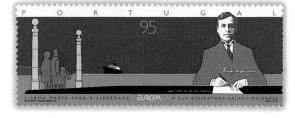

As German troops approached the Spanish border, de Sousa Mendes drove to the border town of Hendaye. There, in the streets, he handed out hundreds of visas – scraps of paper, stamped with his official seal and signed with his name – stating that the bearer had the right to enter Portugal, and requesting Spain to grant the holder unimpeded passage. The scraps of paper were honoured.

On 23 June 1940, the Portuguese ambassador to Spain arrived in Hendaye and, with his higher authority, declared de Sousa Mendes's visas null and void. De Sousa Mendes made one last journey to a remote border area to help refugees with his visas to cross. Then he was recalled to Portugal.

On his return to Portugal, de Sousa Mendes was denied all recognition for his defiant, life-saving act. He died a pauper in 1954. It was with the financial help of the American-based Hebrew Immigrant Aid Society (HIAS) that his children were able to emigrate after the war from Portugal to Belgium, Africa, Canada and the United States.

Another of those who issued documents to enable refugees to leave France for the United States was Varian Fry, the emissary of the American Emergency Committee, a private American relief organization. He and the team helping him – including Bill Freier, an artist who had the skills needed to forge documents – worked from an office in Marseille, constantly having to ignore German attempts to enforce the surrender of political and cultural refugees from Germany, many of them Jews. Article 19 of the Franco-German Armistice of June 1940 imposed a 'surrender on demand' obligation on the defeated French.

Fry worked for thirteen months before being expelled. In that period he was able to secure exit documents for 1,500 people. Among those whom Fry was able to help leave Marseille and reach the United States were the artists Marc Chagall and Max Ernst, the novelist Lion Feuchtwanger and the philosopher Hannah Arendt.

In the Lithuanian capital, Kovno, a Japanese diplomat, Chiune Sugihara, acting on his own initiative, issued 2,400 transit visas – ostensibly to the Dutch East Indies via Japan – to Lithuanian Jews, and to Polish Jews who had fled into Lithuania at the time of the German invasion of Poland in September 1939. As a result of these documents, they were able to travel by Trans-Siberian railway across the Soviet Union, and then by boat through to China (where they could enter Shanghai and stay there without restrictions), or on to the Dutch East Indies, Australia, Canada and the United States.

From Kovno to Vancouver, via Japan, Shanghai, the Dutch East Indies and Australia, was a 17,000-mile journey. It was made by 26-year-old Leon Pommers, born in the eastern Polish town of Pruzana, who was studying in Warsaw to be a pianist when war broke out, escaped to Vilna, and then obtained a visa in Kovno. He was later Professor of Music at Queen's University, New York. The Jews of Pruzana were later deported to Auschwitz.

Also in Kovno, the British Consul, Thomas Preston, issued certificates for Palestine over and above the official British government quota, enabling four hundred Lithuanian Jews to make their way by train to the Black Sea port of Odessa, and then by sea to Istanbul and Haifa.

top left
Varian Fry at his desk in Marseille.

top right
Refugees seeking United States visas, waiting outside the American Consulate in Marseille, 1940.

above
Chiune Sugihara at his desk; and the porch of his consulate in Kovno (photographed in 1997).

The Coming of War

O n 1 September 1939, German troops marched into Poland, while at the same time German aircraft bombed Polish cities, and German warships bombarded naval installations and dockyards on the Polish Baltic coast.

The Second World War had begun. It was to continue, in Europe, for more than five and a half years. Those years would see the spread of armed conflict to almost every European country. Only five European nations were able to remain neutral – Switzerland, Sweden, Spain, Portugal and the Irish Free State. All the other nations of Europe were drawn into the war, suffering military and civilian deaths on an often unprecedented scale.

The victims of the Second World War were numbered in their tens of millions. They included hundreds of thousands of Gypsies, whom the Nazis considered 'impure' – part of the racial language of Nazism that had no basis in genetics. Also murdered, in their tens of thousands, were German citizens, Catholics and Protestants alike – including old people, children and babies – whom Nazi theory judged to be 'unfit for life' because they suffered birth defects or severe mental or physical handicaps, which, in civilized times, are the subject of care and affection, not murder.

Behind the cloak of war and occupation, with all the apparatus of censorship and secret police, crimes were committed on a vast scale against those who were defenceless.

More than eight million Jews lived in Europe on the eve of the Second World War. By the end of the war, six million of them had been murdered, in some of the most barbaric circumstances in recorded history. Even as, inside Germany, the German troops boarded the trains that were to take them to the battlefield, anti-Jewish slogans accompanied them.

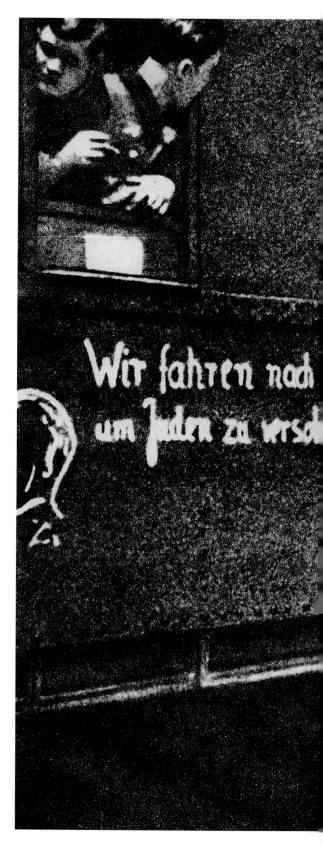

THE GERMAN CONQUEST OF POLAND

top right
A scene in the market square in Krosno, southern Poland, shortly after the German occupation. The Jews in this photograph had been ordered to pull at one another's beards for the camera. A Polish photographer, Stanislaw Leszczynski, writes: 'The picture was taken by some Kraut, who handed it right back to us to be developed. Then we made ourselves copies on the sly. I had no idea they would still be of any use to anyone.' In July 1942 the 1,800 Jews then in Krosno were rounded up in the market square, loaded on to open trucks, driven around the town for the Poles to stare at, transferred to several neighbouring ghettos, and then deported to the death camp at Belzec.

centre right
In the Polish town of Warta, Germans cut the sidelocks of an Orthodox Jew, Hersz Izrael Laskowski. Shortly after this photograph was taken, he was hanged, together with his father Rabbi Eliasz Laskowski and eight other Jews.

bottom right
The back of the Piotrkow synagogue, a photograph taken in 1993.

From 1 September 1939 the Polish army fought with great bravery against far larger and better armed German forces attacking them from the north, west and south. Six weeks after the German invasion, while the Poles were still fighting to halt the invader, the Soviet Union entered Poland from the east. It did so as a result of the secret Nazi-Soviet pact, signed a week before the German attack, under which Hitler's Soviet counterpart, Josef Stalin, was offered eastern Poland in return for his neutrality. On September 17 Stalin's forces advanced to an agreed line that cut Poland in half. After a tenacious defence against the German forces that surrounded it, Warsaw surrendered on September 27.

The Nazi-Soviet partition of Poland left more than a million Polish Jews on the Soviet side of the partition line. They were joined by a quarter of a million Jews who managed to cross the new border from west to east before it was sealed, or who were deliberately pushed over the border by the Germans. The Jews who found themselves under Soviet Communist rule were, in the main, fortunate. Most of them survived the war, having been sent by Stalin to Soviet Central Asia, or to labour camps in Siberia. While the war was still being fought, many of them enlisted in the Polish forces that were created with Stalin's approval, and which then went, via Iran and Palestine, to fight against the Germans in North Africa and Italy. Among the Polish Jews escaping eastward in 1939, who were then sent to labour camps in Siberia, was Menachem Begin. Reaching Palestine in 1943 he remained there as leader of the underground forces fighting against the British. In 1977 he became Prime Minister of Israel. Other Polish Jews who survived the war in the Soviet Union returned to Poland after 1945.

In the battle for Poland, more than sixty thousand Polish soldiers were killed in action. Among them were six thousand Polish Jews. During the German bombing of Warsaw, three thousand Jewish civilians had been among the fifteen thousand civilian dead. Rella Wizenberg recalled the bombing of Radom on 1 September 1939, when many Jews were killed. She

above
A Nazi kicks a Jew in the street of Wloclawek, in German-occupied Poland. Others Germans look on and laugh.

later recalled: 'I remember an old Jew talking to my father that evening. He said that those killed that day were the very lucky ones. They were the chosen ones. I thought he was crazy, but how right he was!'

Rella survived Auschwitz, as did her sister Mania. Their mother Shaindla, and their brother Jacob, were murdered in Treblinka in 1942. Their father Tobias was killed in Mauthausen in January 1945.

As German troops entered Polish towns, there were those who amused themselves by tormenting individual Jews, kicking Jews, cutting off the beards of Orthodox Jews, forcing Orthodox Jews to pull at one another's beards. This was often followed by acts of life-threatening brutality, by severe beatings and by executions. These were carried out by special SS 'operational groups' who roamed through the towns once the army had captured them.

One example of this among many hundreds in the first week of war took place on 3 September 1939, the third day of the German invasion – the day on which Britain and France declared war on Germany – when one of the SS groups entered Wieruszow. The German army had only captured it a few hours earlier. Seizing twenty Jews, the SS took them to the market-place and lined them up for execution. Among them was sixty-four-year-old Israel Lewi. When his daughter, Liebe Lewi, ran up to her father to say goodbye to him, one of the SS men ordered her to open her mouth – for her 'impudence' – and shot her through it. She fell dead on the spot. The twenty men were then executed.

Two days later, on September 5, the German army and the SS units entered the city of Piotrkow. Setting fire to the Jewish-owned buildings in the centre of the city, including the synagogue, they then shot dead all those Jews who sought, desperately, to escape the flames. Finding a house that had not been set on fire, they forced out the six men who were inside it, ordered them to run and shot five of them dead. The sixth, Reb Bunem Lebel, died later of his wounds.

Such acts of barbarity signalled a new and terrible era, when Jewish life was held up to ridicule and contempt by the new German rulers of Poland. Two million Jews were suddenly and terrifyingly at risk.

THE FIRST ONSLAUGHT: RECOLLECTIONS OF TERROR

The murder of Jews that had taken place during the first days of the German conquest of Poland did not abate. Each day saw new executions. The large map opposite shows some of the towns and villages in which groups of Jews were seized and killed.

In the city of Czestochowa, where 30,000 Jews lived, 180 were taken from their homes and shot on the first full day of the German occupation, September 4, known in the annals of Czestochowa Jewry as 'Bloody Monday'. Far bloodier days were to follow – and in 1942 almost all the surviving Jews of Czestochowa were deported to their deaths – but on that 'Bloody Monday', by any contemporary standard, the scale of the killing was high.

A favourite SS 'sport' – for so it was regarded by the perpetrators of these massacres – was to lock Jews in a synagogue and set the building on fire, shooting down anyone who tried to get out. In Bedzin, two hundred Jews were killed in this way; in Mielec, twenty were killed. Men, women and children were all considered legitimate targets of these racial murders.

A German General Staff officer, General Halder, noted in his diary on September 10 that a group of SS men, having ordered fifty Jews to work all day repairing a bridge, had then flung them into a synagogue and shot them. The killers had been brought to trial by the army. In defence of one of the SS men, the army Judge Advocate argued that 'as an SS man he was particularly sensitive to the sight of Jews. He had therefore acted quite thoughtlessly, in a spirit of adventure.' Light sentences were imposed, but even they were overruled by the head of the SS, Heinrich Himmler. The SS men were set free.

In the first fifty-five days of the German conquest and occupation of western Poland, five thousand Jews were murdered. At the same time, the Germans killed

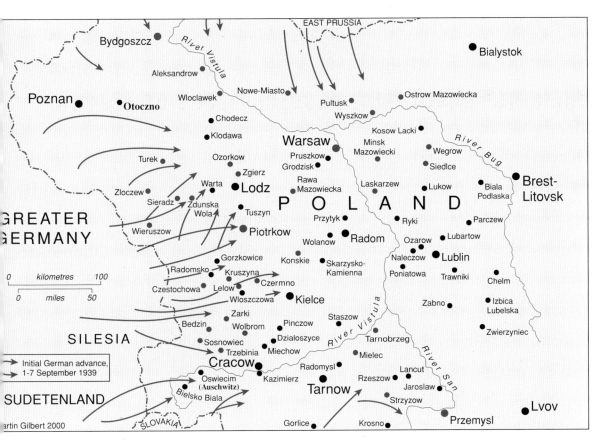

top
The initial German advance into Poland showing (as red circles) some of the towns where Jews were murdered during the first days of German occupation; and (as black circles) other places on Polish soil mentioned in this book.
bottom
The partition of Poland in 1939. The towns named within the German areas were centres of labour camp regions.

more than twice that number of non-Jewish Poles, likewise executed at random, singly and in groups, with the utmost savagery.

The random killings of the first two months of the German occupation of Poland were paralleled by administrative arrangements. Germany annexed parts of western Poland, and transformed the rest into what was called the General Government, ruled from Cracow. The small map shows the new borders. At the same time, Jews were obliged to carry out forced labour, and camps were set up to which they were deported.

In Berlin, William Shirer, an American journalist – the United States was still neutral – was told of this forced labour, and noted down in his diary the wording of the official decree.

Forced labour quickly became slave labour. Beatings were frequent. Labourers could be killed at the whim of the camp commandants, or of the guards.

Any hope the Jews might have had that once Poland was being administered without the pressures of fighting, calm would return, and with it decent behaviour, was in vain. The slave labour camp system was continually extended, with great severity.

THE CREATION OF THE GHETTOS

At a top-secret meeting in Berlin on 21 September 1939, SS General Reinhard Heydrich, Chief of the Reich Security Main Office – responsible for repression – told the commanders of several SS operational groups in Poland that his 'ultimate aim' for Polish Jews must be kept 'strictly secret'. Meanwhile, he wanted large areas of western Poland to be 'cleared completely of Jews', and elsewhere Jews to be confined in special areas of cities and towns. For this, any Jews living outside the designated area would be forced to move into the confined area, which was to be called a 'ghetto'.

Ghettos had existed, as Jewish quarters of towns, hundreds of years earlier. Unlike their medieval predecessors, the new ghettos were to be surrounded by barbed wire, brick walls and armed guards. The ghettos were to be located – Heydrich explained – in cities on railway junctions or along a railway, 'so that future measures may be accomplished more easily'.

The first ghetto was set up in Piotrkow on 28 October 1939. Jews living throughout the town were

forced to leave their homes and move into the ghetto area. It was desperately overcrowded. The Germans kept food and medical supplies to a minimum.

Other ghettos were set up throughout the region. The two largest were Warsaw and Lodz. From fifteen towns and several hundred villages in western Poland, the Germans expelled 40,000 Jews into Warsaw in the course of a few weeks. A further 38,000 were expelled from towns and villages elsewhere in Poland into the Lodz and other ghettos. Their livestock and farm implements were confiscated. It was – thus far – the largest forcible uprooting of the Nazi era. Those expelled from their homes lost their livelihoods, and almost all their possessions, overnight. Jewish farmers, of whom there were many, were forced to leave their farms and move to the designated towns.

Tens of thousands of Jews were also expelled from Germany into Poland, sent to a region – known as Lublinland – where they were left, without resources, to fend for themselves. These expulsions began on 17 October 1939 from Vienna, Prague and the Baltic port of Stettin.

The deportees were sent in locked passenger trains under SS armed guard. Their homes and property were taken by Germans. Many children froze to death on the journey.

Adolf Eichmann, recently promoted to be head of

above right
This cartoon by the British cartoonist David Low was published in a London evening newspaper, the *Evening Standard*, on 20 January 1940, entitled '*Lebensraum* for the conquered' (Living space for the conquered), depicting the deportations from Germany to the Lublin region.

right
The wall of the Warsaw ghetto: Jews can be seen walking and standing on the ghetto side of the wall.

We are cut off from the world. There are no radios, no telephones, no newspapers.

Mary Berg, diary entry, 20 November 1940

The exiles were driven out of their beds before dawn, and the Führer's minions did not let them take money, belongings, or food, threatening all the while to shoot them. Before they left on their exile a search was made of their pockets and of all the hidden places of their bodies. Without a penny in their pockets, or a covering for the women, children, old people or invalids – sometimes without shoes on their feet or staffs in their hands – they were forced to leave their homes and possessions and the graves of their ancestors, and go – whither? And in terrible, fierce, unbearable cold!

Chaim Kaplan, diary entry, 31 January 1941, when the Jews of Pruszkow reached the Warsaw ghetto

the Gestapo's Department of Jewish Affairs, met the deportees on arrival, and told them: 'There are no apartments and no houses – if you build your homes you will have a roof over your head. There is no water. The wells are full of epidemics. There's cholera, dysentery, typhus. If you dig for water, you'll have water.'

German soldiers opened the luggage of the arrivals, and took whatever they wanted. Many other Lublinland deportees died of starvation soon after their arrival. Inside the Warsaw ghetto, deaths from starvation were to reach two thousand a month by the beginning of 1941, a thousand a month in the Lodz ghetto. Six months later, these high death rates had doubled.

above left
Queuing for food coupons in the Warsaw ghetto.

left
Three boys in the Warsaw ghetto, 1940.

EDUCATION AND CULTURE IN THE GHETTOS

With the creation of the ghettos, Jewish communities of tens of thousands of people were cut off from contact with the outside world. With the steady increase in hunger, the preservation of morale found many forms. One of these was education. In every ghetto, efforts were made, in the greatest secrecy and amid continual danger, to continue with the schooling of youngsters.

To maintain the morale of the adults, an enormous effort was put into providing concerts and theatrical performances. In the Lodz ghetto, into which thousands of German Jews were deported, internationally acclaimed conductors and pianists performed amid the privations and hardships. In the Warsaw ghetto, Janusz Korczak, an educator of distinction, ensured that in the orphanage of which he was the director, classes continued as normally as possible, teaching the young children as if the outside world was normal, free and sane.

In the Piotrkow ghetto, a teenager, Ben Giladi – who survived the Holocaust, and went after the war to live in the United States – later recalled:

'Hela Rosenbaum was a lyceum teacher from Warsaw. She rented one of our rooms and, in exchange, I became her student. My curriculum was that of the second year of high school. Soon we were a group of eight students. The studies were based on the 1938/39 educational programme.

The rooftop room was small but spotless, with a curved ceiling and a narrow window – a typical attic. A large table stood in the middle of the room; the small blackboard hung against the teacher's bed, always ready to be removed and hidden in case of a raid. In this tiny room, Hela Rosenbaum opened to us the wide and wonderful world of knowledge. She made us feel equal to all the youngsters who were free. She placed us on the same level as the outside world.

She taught every subject: Literature and History; Latin and Mathematics; Physics and Hebrew. We all felt that such learning added

something important to our understanding, to our capacity for growth and, above all, to our sense of freedom and dignity.

Hela Rosenbaum soon joined forces with two other teachers: Eugenia Rosenzweig, a former pedagogue of the Jewish Gymnasium in Piotrkow, and Madame Eichner from Warsaw. They soon started full-scale education for several classes.

Each one of the teachers taught the subjects that she had taught before the war. An average class of approximately ten pupils went to the teachers' homes on a rotating basis. For example, on Monday to Hela Rosenbaum for Algebra, Geometry, Hebrew, and Latin; on Tuesday to

Eugenia Rosenzweig for Polish Literature, German, and Social Studies; on Wednesday to Madame Eichner for History, Physics, Chemistry, and so on.

The teachers worked all day and succeeded in serving five or six different classes during this time. They also taught students on a public school level – the younger kids who also needed schooling. Their tuition was modest. Some students that could not afford the tuition were taught gratis.

This was the ghetto. Conspiracy was essential. Every false move invited serious consequences. We were told to enter the teaching places one by one, to carry our notebooks under our clothes.

Textbooks were scarce and therefore, cherished and shared. We had to be careful not to say anything to anybody connected with the Germans. Sometimes, we had to stop in the middle of a class session and disperse rapidly when the SS was raiding the block.

In 1942 the older boys faced forced labour. I went to work at the Hortensia glass factory. My world of studies collapsed. Hela Rosenbaum, the teacher, attempted to teach me after working hours. This attempt, however, proved futile. It was impossible. after ten hours of hard work, to study seriously. Until this day, I fondly cherish the memory of a dedicated educator and wonderful human being, who ended her life in Treblinka.'

opposite
A poster announces a theatrical performance in the Warsaw ghetto, in the Eldorado Theatre. The play, in Yiddish, was *The Village Girl*, a musical comedy in two acts by F. Majzels.

above left
Jewish youngsters deported from towns outside Warsaw lived and slept in the women's gallery of a Warsaw synagogue. This, and the two photographs on page 57, were taken by a member of Warsaw's well-known pre-war Forbert Photographic Studio, run by two brothers. One died in the ghetto; the other escaped to Russia, and was filming with the Soviet army when it reached Auschwitz in January 1945.

HUNGER AND DEATH IN THE GHETTOS

In the ghetto

After my recovery from typhoid I was constantly hungry and could not comprehend my mother's loss of appetite. A doctor, an old friend of the family, suggested that she should go to the hospital, but she would not hear of it. She would lie in bed and talk to us about her childhood, and her parents who died before we were born. On one occasion she said that she would die as soon as the weather would get a little warmer. She died a day after my sixteenth birthday, the 10th of March 1941. As it was a Saturday, the funeral took place on the following day.

My uncle made all the arrangements. There was a long queue at the cemetery. Some people were bringing their deceased on handcarts, as the horse-drawn black vans could not cope. The grave diggers would refuse to dig deep enough pits unless they were given bread by the mourners.

Michael Etkind, a survivor of the Lodz ghetto

Despite all their efforts, the Jews could not win the fight against the deliberate German policy of bringing them to death by starvation.

In Warsaw, before the Germans embarked on a policy of deportation to death camps (in mid-1942), almost 30,000 Jews had died of starvation between July and December 1941, and a further 20,000 between January and June 1942.

The second largest Jewish community in Poland was in the city of Lodz. There the deaths from starvation totalled more than 12,000 in the twelve months before the deportations began in January 1942. Jews from more than fifty towns and villages around Lodz had been forced out of their homes and taken to the Lodz ghetto. Jews from Germany, Austria and Czechoslovakia were also deported to Lodz, where space had to be found for them in the already overcrowded and hungry ghetto.

The German ration scales ensured starvation in the

above right
Old man with cane, photographed by Mendel Grossman in the Lodz ghetto in 1940. Two years later, old people were no longer seen in the ghetto: they had been deported to the death camp at Chelmno, and murdered. Grossman himself did not survive.

right
Jewish youngsters in the Lodz ghetto, producing leather goods in one of the German-run factories. This colour photograph was taken by a German official in the ghetto.

ghettos. In the occupied towns, Poles were allowed less than half the daily calorie intake of Germans. In the ghettos that were part of those same towns, Jews were allowed less than half the calories allocated to Poles. The most that Jews were ever allocated – those who were working in the Lodz ghetto workshops – was 1,800 calories a day. A working person needs at least 2,000 calories a day. By the end of 1941 the average intake allowed in the Lodz ghetto had fallen to between 700 and 900 calories. In some ghettos it was even lower.

Rudy Janek – Red-headed Johnny – was a Pole who served the Germans as a ghetto guard. He had also found a way of making money from the Jews. Having smuggled twelve hens into the ghetto, he was paid by the Jews each time the hens laid eggs. When the hens were found by the Germans and confiscated, Janek decided to avenge himself for his loss of revenue by killing two Jews for each hen. An account of what followed was kept by Jozef Zelikowicz, one of the ghetto diarists:

'Let the ghetto know who Janek is, who – two months and two days after the ghetto was closed off – shot 24 Jews to death, for nothing. Like stray dogs.
On July 2, 1940, he shot a 15-year-old girl in the heart.
Three days later, when he was again at his post at the ghetto fence, he killed a 29-year-old man and a woman of 21.
After a pause, on July 10, he shot a 30-year-old woman in the head.
On July 11 a man of 23.
On July 12 he shot the brains out of a 65-year-old man.
On July 16 he hit a 50-year-old woman and a 16-year-old boy.
On July 18 he put a bullet in the heart of a 62-year-old man.
On July 20 he murdered a 20-year-old girl.
With murderous precision he killed five people on one day, July 21: a 17-year-old girl, three young men in their twenties, and a 30-year-old man.
On July 24 two aged women.
On July 26 a 17-year-old boy.
On July 27 a 24-year-old man.
On July 28, his last two victims, a 17-year-old girl and a 50-year-old woman.
Thirty five people were killed by the guards of German justice in the month of July 1940. Rudy Janek killed twenty-four of them. Not one more. Twenty-four – with truly German precision.'

In the ghetto

One day I was standing on my corner – selling cigarettes – when a Gestapo man with a large Alsatian dog appeared. He grabbed hold of me, took all my cigarettes, and said, "Now run". I was terrified. I was sure he was going to set the dog after me. I started running as fast as I could. He used to delight in descending on the ghetto with his ferocious black dog who wreaked havoc on the helpless and terrified victims. On another occasion six Gestapo men caught me with smuggled cigarettes. I thought they were going to shoot me. Instead they formed a circle around me and proceeded to kick me around like a football.

Krulik Wilder, ten years old when the Piotrkow ghetto was set up

The head of a Jewish smuggler is thrust through a hole in the basement of the gutted Post Office. Six guards see him, call over two Jews, and order them to pull the man out. They do it, receiving a blow from the guards in the act. They order the smuggler to crawl back into his hole again, and, as he crawls, pierce his head with their bayonets. His screams ring through the quiet street.

Emanuel Ringelblum, diary entry, Warsaw Ghetto, 27 February 1941

above left
A brother feeds his young sister, photographed in the Lodz ghetto by Mendel Grossman.

The Holocaust Intensifies

The term Holocaust is derived from the Greek word *holokauston*: a devastation or sacrifice, usually by fire. For a quarter of a century after 1945 the murder of six million Jews was usually described as the 'Extermination of the Jews' or 'The Final Solution'. The word Holocaust entered into common usage after 1978, following the American television series *Holocaust*, based on a novel of the same name by Gerald Green.

In Yiddish the word used for the Holocaust is *Churban* (Destruction), and in Hebrew, *Shoah* (Catastrophe).

'None has suffered more cruelly than the Jew the unspeakable evils wrought on the bodies and spirits of men by Hitler and his vile regime. The Jew bore the brunt of the Nazi's first onslaught upon the citadels of freedom and human dignity. He has borne and continued to bear a burden that might have seemed to be beyond endurance. He has not allowed it to break his spirit; he has never lost the will to resist. Assuredly in the day of victory the Jew's sufferings and his part in the struggle will not be forgotten. Once again, at the appointed time, he will see vindicated those principles of righteousness which it was the glory of his fathers to proclaim to the world.'

Winston Churchill, a message to the *Jewish Chronicle*, 14 November 1941, as news of the mass murder in the East reached him

With the German invasion of the Soviet Union on 22 June 1941, the mass murder of Jews began within days, on a scale hitherto unknown.

Before June 1941 the Jews under Nazi rule had been subjected to persecution, humiliation, expulsion and random killing. In June 1941 began the deliberate attempt to destroy all Jewish lives over a vast region of Europe.

In the immediate wake of the victorious German army, advancing swiftly eastward, came the *Einsatzgruppen* (Operational Squads) – in reality, mobile killing squads whose task, for which they had trained since May in the town of Pretzsch, south of Berlin, was to destroy the Jewish communities in regions that had witnessed many centuries of vibrant Jewish life: in eastern Poland, western Russia and the Baltic.

Within twelve months, more than one million Jews had been murdered east of the September 1939 border of Greater Germany. Most were driven from their homes, forced at gunpoint to pits and ravines a few miles away, ordered to undress and then shot. No mercy was shown.

The map shows the areas of operation of the four *Einsatzgruppen* – known as A, B, C and D – which followed in the wake of the German army from 22 June 1941. Jews were murdered in every town shown here, to the very eastern limits of German conquest.

The number of men in each *Einsatzgruppe* was relatively small: 1,000 in *Einsatzgruppe* A, 655 in *Einsatzgruppe* B, 700 in *Einsatzgruppe* C and 600 in *Einsatzgruppe* D. They were helped in carrying out mass murder by German police battalions, and by local auxiliary police battalions made up of local Ukrainian, Belorussian, Latvian and Lithuanian volunteers.

© Martin Gilbert 2000

The eastern border of Greater Germany from mid- September 1939

General direction of the four SS Einsatzgruppen Operation Squads from 22 June 1941

The furthest line of German advance into the Soviet Union in December 1941 (around Moscow and Leningrad) and in November 1942 (North Caucasus)

0 kilometres 150

0 miles 100

Lake Ladoga

Leningrad

Lake Ilmen

Narva

Tallinn (Reval)

Lake Pskov

Luga

Pärnu

STONIA

Tartu

Pskov

Valga

S O V I E T

Rzhev

Moscow

EINSATZGRUPPE A

Riga

Dagda

Nevel

Zarasai

Dvinsk

Polotsk

Yanovichi

Widze

Vitebsk

Lyubavichi

Smolensk

Swiecany

Lepel

Monastyrshchina

Vilna

Wilejka

Orsha

EINSATZGRUPPE B

Oszmiana

BELORUSSIA

Trakai

Lida

Borisov

Mogilev

Bryansk

Orel

U N I O N

Domachevo

Nowogrodek

Minsk

Rogachev

Mir

Baranowicze

Bobruisk

Klintsy

stok

Slonim

Slutsk

Starodub

Kursk

Parichi

Kobryn

David Gorodok

Gomel

Pinsk

Mozyr

Konotop

Belgorod

Brest-Litovsk

Serniki

Lelchitsy

Rokitno

Chernigov

Nyezhin

Stalingrad

Wlodzimierzec

Sarny

Olevsk

Kiev

Priluki

Poltava

Kharkov

Kovel

VOLHYNIA

Radomyshl

Kostopol

Ludvipol

Piryatin

Kremenchug

Lugansk

Vladimir-Volynski

Rovno

Hoshcha

Zhitomir

Pereyaslavl

Artemovsk

rokhov

Dubno

Berdichev

EINSATZGRUPPE C

Pavlograd

Brody

Khmelnik

Smyela

Dnepropetrovsk

Novomoskovsk

EINSATZGRUPPE D

VOV

Kremenets

Vinnitsa

Uman

Kirovograd

Donetsk

ryj

Drohobycz

Stojanow

Tarnopol

Zhmerinka

UKRAINE

Taganrog

Rostov-on-Don

STERN GALICIA

Skalat

TRANSNISTRIA

Zaporozhye

Mariupol

Czernowitz

Hotin

Kamenets-Podolsk

Balta

Nikolayev

Krivoi Rog

Berdyansk

Melitopol

Zabie

BUKOVINA

Ananayev

Sea of Azov

NORTH CAUCASUS

Carpathian Mountains

MOLDAVIA

Dubossary

Kherson

Stavropol

Piatygorsk

BESSARABIA

Kishinev

Dzhankoi

Kerch

Krasnodar

Armavir

Yessentuki

TRANSYLVANIA

Shaumyan

Kislovodsk

CRIMEA

Evpatoria

Novorossisk

Kilya

Bakhchisarai

Feodosiya

Caucasus Mountains

Izmail

Sevastopol

Simferopol

ROUMANIA

DOBRUJA

Odessa

Yalta

Black

Sea

THE GERMAN INVASION OF THE SOVIET UNION

The Germans understood the complex make-up of the regions through which they advanced: they knew of and exploited the historic tensions between Christianity and Judaism, and between the local people and the Jews. As a result, they were able to call on Lithuanian, Latvian, Belorussian and Ukrainian volunteers to participate in mass murder. In some instances, especially in Lithuania, local gangs took the initiative in seeking out Jews and killing them, even before the German army and killing squads arrived.

Almost every town that the German army conquered during the invasion of the Soviet Union, especially in the first months, had a substantial Jewish population. In every city, town and village the Jewish inhabitants were subjected to the same process: the initial slaughter of those seized at random on the streets or arrested because they were leaders in the community; the creation of ghettos strictly sealed off from the outside world and subjected like the ghettos in German-occupied Poland to repeated raids and increasing starvation; and then the deportation of almost all the remaining community to mass murder

sites – deep ravines or specially dug pits – a few miles outside the town.

The names of some of these mass murder sites quickly became synonymous with brutality. One of them, Ponar, in a wooded area outside Vilna, had been a popular picnic resort for Vilna's Jews between the two world wars. It became a site of mass murder, the scene of cruel and relentless destruction.

The head of *Einsatzkommando* 3a, SS Colonel Karl Jaeger, was able to report to his superiors in Berlin on 1 December 1941 that in the former Baltic States of Estonia, Latvia and Lithuania his men had murdered 200,000 Jews. Only 34,000 remained alive, and they were being used as slave labourers. In his report, Jaeger praised the work of the Lithuanian volunteers. As a result of their help in Kovno, he wrote, the city had proved to be 'comparatively speaking, a shooting paradise'.

Brest-Litovsk (which like Vilna and Kovno had been a part of Poland between the wars) was the first city to be overrun by the Germans in June 1941. Jews were half the town's population: 21,519 in 1936, joined by as many as five thousand refugees who had managed to escape in 1939 from German-occupied Poland.

The Jews of Brest (known in Yiddish as Brisk) followed many trades – carpenters, joiners, house painters, tailors, shoemakers, blacksmiths, tinsmiths and taxi drivers. There were Jewish lawyers and doctors, merchants and factory owners. The city had seen five hundred years of Jewish life. A Jewish hospital was built in 1838, a home for Jewish widows in 1866.

When the Germans attacked Brest on 22 June 1941 the Russian commander of the Fortress was on holiday. The defence was taken over by a Jewish officer, Yefim Moiseyevich Fomin. Wounded and suffering from shell-shock, he was made a prisoner of war. Denounced to the new German occupiers by a local informer as both a Communist Commissar and a Jew, he was executed.

The fate of the Jews of Brest was like that of the Jews in every town in the area of the German advance. In the first days, individual Jews were shot at random on the streets. Then, in the first week of July, two hundred Jewish men were seized on the streets, imprisoned in the Fortress, tortured, refused water or medical

treatment, and then shot. Only one managed to escape. On July 10 the first large-scale 'action' (round-up) took place. More than 6,000 – mostly professionals and their families – were seized and taken to a hilly area outside the town, where twelve large pits had been dug. There they were ordered to give up their luggage – they had been told that they were being 'resettled' in another town – before being made to undress. They were then shot. Among those murdered were seven physicians, a neurologist (Bernard Kalvarysky), an economist (Zilberfarb), a woman therapist (Ivanova) and a woman electrical engineer (Zelyonaya).

In the autumn of 1941 a ghetto was established for the remaining 20,000 Jews of Brest. Almost all of them were deported by train in October and November 1942 to a mass execution site at Bronna Gora, seventy-five miles away, on the railway line from Brest to Minsk. A few managed to escape and join the partisans. Fewer than 200 of the 2,000 Jews who were in Brest when the Germans attacked survived the war.

The fate of the Jews of Brest-Litovsk was to be the fate of the Jews of every city, town and village in the area conquered by the German army after the invasion of the Soviet Union in June 1941.

The *Einsatzgruppen* were ruthless in carrying out the task of mass murder. The local volunteer militias and German police battalions were pitiless in assisting in that task.

An eye-witness to mass murder

One afternoon (it was on 12 August 1941) two truckloads of Ukrainian policemen and the Gestapo murderers entered the townlet. Within minutes all the Ukrainian youth, which probably had prepared itself in advance, enlisted itself to assist them. For about two hours some three hundred men, including children aged fourteen, were seized in the streets or driven from their homes....

The Germans did not take part in the abductions. This was carried out with clear conscience by our Ukrainian neighbours who had lived side by side with the Jews for generations.... Within a short time the unfortunate victims, my husband, my brother and my brother-in-law, were assembled in the yard of the militia post where they were kept for several hours.

In the meantime a group of men was led to the Park where they were ordered to dig up a large pit. As soon as the digging was completed they began bringing the unfortunate victims in groups. They were not yet aware of what awaited them. The Ukrainian militia performed its job splendidly. No one among the unfortunates managed to get away. The job of shooting the victims were performed by the German murderers, whose superior training prepared them for it. At six o'clock in the evening the whole thing was over.

An eye-witness of the destruction of the Jews in Horokhov, in Volhynia

THE *EINSATZGRUPPEN*

How are things with your Jews? This place is crawling with them, though I don't think many will be left by the time the war is over, for there's been a lot of clearing up, and I myself have shot down a whole plague of them for what that lot has done over here defies all description....

I only hope to get the chance of leading a group of comrades when we start rooting out the Jew vermin back home: they just won't know what's hit them....

A Dutchman, once a chauffeur from Arnhem, who was serving with the *Waffen SS* on the Russian front, writing from German-occupied Russia in February 1942 to a Dutch SS friend in Holland

Units of the SS and militiamen did or tried to break into houses in groups of four to six men. Whenever the doors and windows were closed and the residents refused to open them, the SS men or the militiamen would break the doors and windows open with iron bars or beams and burst into the house....

A number of families or groups of residents locked themselves in fortified houses, set up barricades and blocked the entrances and openings. In such cases beams or iron bars proved powerless and grenades had to be used to force the entrance.

Herman Graebe, a German engineer, speaking at the Nuremberg Trials, 1946

The killings carried out by the *Einsatzgruppen* continued from the end of June 1941 until the end of the year, and then into 1942 and 1943. One by one the communities that had survived the seventeenth-century Chmielnicki massacres, the nineteenth- and early twentieth-century Tsarist pogroms, the privations of the First World War, and the civil war and famine that followed the Bolshevik revolution of 1917, were each wiped out.

The map on pages 62 and 63 shows some of the cities and towns in which mass killings took place. In Kishinev, where forty-nine Jews were killed in the pogrom in 1903 that shocked the Western world, more than 24,000 Jews were murdered. In Odessa, where three hundred Jews had been killed in a pogrom in 1907, more than 19,000 were killed between 12 January and 23 February 1942. In Kamenets-Podolsk, 14,000 Jews who had been deported from Ruthenia – which had been occupied by Hungary in 1940 – were shot down in cold blood. Everywhere, the scale of the killing was unprecedented.

On 29 September 1941 a three-day orgy of killing took place in the ravine of Babi Yar, just outside the city of Kiev. In those three days, 33,771 Jews were killed, the numbers recorded later by the Germans, when they ordered Jewish slave labourers to dig up the bodies and burn them, to erase the evidence of the crime. After that, only ash and ground-up bones remained. A further 8,000 Kiev Jews – those who had been discovered in hiding, and those who had been kept as slave labourers – were killed in Babi Yar in January 1942.

The name of Babi Yar became synonymous with sudden, vast slaughter. Men, women and children were taken in groups to the ravine, ordered to undress and then shot. Ravines elsewhere were also sites of mass murder. In Minsk, in the Ratomskaya street ravine, 12,000 Jews were shot down in November 1941, a further 25,000 in July 1942, 1,500 in February 1943 and 2,000 in October 1943. In Kharkov, more than 40,000 Jews were killed in Drobitsky Yar.

In Vitebsk, birthplace of the painter Marc Chagall, 7,000 Jews were murdered. In the Crimea – where, as well as Jews living in the towns, there were eighty-six Jewish agricultural settlements, dating back to the early 1920s – a total of 91,678 Jews were killed between January and April 1942. The number was carefully recorded by the killers of *Einsatzgruppe* D, who listed men, women and children in separate columns in their report.

At the very eastern extremity of the advance of the German army, in the foothills of the Caucasus, the killings squads sought out the Jewish inhabitants for slaughter. In Yessentuki, 2,000 were killed on a single day, 9 September 1942. That day, in the spa town of Kislovodsk, 1,800 were taken by train to a neighbouring town and shot. In Piatygorsk, another resort town, 300 were killed.

The scale of the killings was copiously documented. When, in 1943, Jewish slave labourers were forced to dig up the corpses at Ponar, outside Vilna, 58,000 bodies were uncovered. However much the mind may tire at such statistics, or simply fail – for the sake of sanity – to grasp their enormity, they represent real people, people who had committed no crime, people who, in their hundreds of thousands, had not yet reached an age when they could savour life to the full, had not yet had time to add to the sum total of human endeavour and achievement, to marry, to have children

of their own, and to see the growth of succeeding generations. Not only were all these lives destroyed, but those who would have been their descendants were denied the chance to exist.

Ten days before the German invasion of the Soviet Union, Hitler had summoned the Roumanian dictator, General Ion Antonescu, to Berlin, and explained to him the imminent destruction of the 'Jews of the east'. Roumanian troops were active alongside the Germans during the advance into Bessarabia (with its capital at Kishinev) and Bukovina (the main town of which was Czernowitz). Roumanian gendarmes and soldiers rounded up Jews, imprisoned them and carried out mass executions in which 160,000 Jews were killed. Antonescu then ordered the eastward expulsion of the 150,000 Jews who remained. As they were driven eastward into Transnistria and northward into Podolia, tens of thousands were killed, either shot by their Roumanian guards, or dying of thirst, disease, ill-treatment and exhaustion. In all, 90,000 of those deported died. In Transnistria and Podolia they were put into concentration camps under SS control. Within Ukraine, Roumanian soldiers and gendarmes joined the Germans in killing Ukrainian Jews.

above

Dubossary, Transnistria, 14 September 1941. Two thousand Jews were killed in this execution.

opposite

A list compiled in Kovno – Kauen in German – and sent to *Einsatzgruppe* A headquarters in Riga, of executions in Lithuania. Colonel Jaeger, responsible for the killings, has noted, in the last line, the number of women (55,556) and children (34,464) in the total murdered (138,272).

DEPORTATIONS FROM GERMANY TO THE EAST

above

After the war Gertrude Schneider became a distinguished scholar in the United States, and the author of five books. She recorded her considered judgement of the action of the Riga Jews in 1979 in her book *Journey Into Terror: Story of the Riga Ghetto*. She later wrote, in a letter to me (on 17 February 2000): 'I have thought about the largesse vis-à-vis those little German, Austrian and Czech children, and I included these thoughts, perhaps to show the world that humanity was still there, despite our enemies' branding us as subhuman.'

right

Cities and towns from which Jews were deported to the east, starting on 19 October 1941 and continuing until 6 February 1942. The map shows the routes eastward, and the destinations.

By the third week of October 1941 the killing squads in the east had completed four months of uninterrupted killing, seen by thousands of German soldiers, but far from the gaze of the German population. Not since the Kristallnacht three years earlier had the German public – or the diplomats of neutral countries whose embassies were in Berlin – seen violence in the street; even then it had been minor and short-lived compared to what was happening in the east.

With the 'success' both of the killing squads in the east and the starvation in ghettos in German-occupied Poland, a new prospect presented itself to Hitler, Himmler and the SS: blood need not be shed in any German street, or risk taken of local protests at violence done to the Jews of Germany. Instead, those German

Jews who had not managed to emigrate before the outbreak of war would be deported to the east: either to the ghettos on Polish soil, where they would be left to suffer and starve with the local population, or to killing sites in the east.

Tens of thousands of Jews had been murdered between June and October 1941 in the Ratomskaya ravine on the outskirts of Minsk, in the Rumbula forest outside Riga, and in the nineteenth-century Tsarist forts surrounding the city of Kovno – principally the Ninth Fort. German Jews would be sent to these destinations: they would never be seen again in the streets of Greater Germany, and their distant fate could be kept secret.

The first eastward deportations began on 16 October 1941. German Jews were rounded up in a dozen cities and sent to three ghettos – Warsaw, Lublin

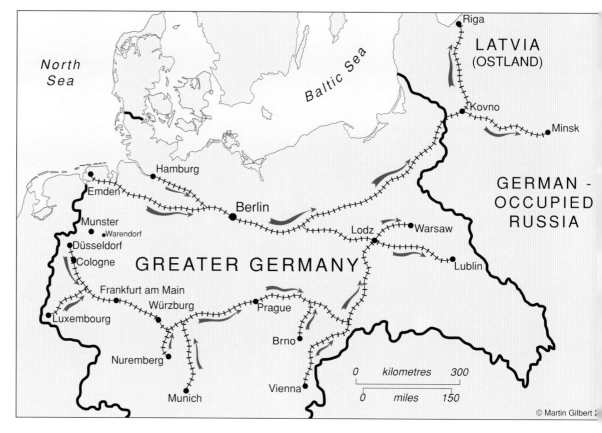

© Martin Gilbert

and Lodz – and to three eastern cities – Minsk, Kovno and Riga. By 29 November 1941, more than 24,000 German Jews had been deported, including 5,000 from Vienna and more than 4,000 from Berlin. From Luxembourg 500 Jews were deported, as were several thousand Czech Jews from Prague and Brno. The map opposite shows the eastward routes.

Most of those deportees who reached Minsk and Kovno were killed on arrival at Ratomskaya ravine and the Ninth Fort; a few were selected for slave labour. Those reaching Riga were sent into a ghetto (known as the 'German ghetto') set up next to the existing ghetto for Riga Jews. From there many were sent to slave labour camps in the region, others to their death. Of 20,000 German deportees reaching Riga, less than a thousand survived the war. In the adjacent ghetto (in a part of the city known as the Moscow suburb) 33,000 Riga Jews had been confined. On 28 November 1941 more than 15,000 of them were taken to the Rumbula forest and killed.

The killings at Rumbula were supervised by SS Major Rudolf Lange, who had a pre-war German university degree as a Doctor of Jurisprudence. He and members of his SS killing squad provided the expert knowledge of procedure; the actual shooting was done by local Latvian SS troops. After the war, the senior SS officer in Riga, SS General Friedrich Jeckeln, praised the Latvians for their 'strong nerves for executions of this sort' – shooting thousands of human beings in such a way that they fell from the edge of the pit to which they had been driven, directly on to the bodies below.

The eastward deportation of German, Austrian and Czech Jews continued until February 1942. Small towns were combed for Jews. From Munster – near the Dutch border – and from the smaller towns around it, 403 Jews were deported to Riga and killed.

The last six Jews living in Warendorf were also among those rounded up in December. Their small community dated back to 1387. In 1933 there had been forty-four Jews in the town. All but six managed to emigrate before 1939. In the December 1941 deportation, the remaining six Jews of Warendorf were deported to Riga, and killed. In less than fifty days, thousands of Jewish homes had been emptied of their inhabitants. After their disappearance 'to the east' their property and possessions were seized.

above left
The entrance to the Ninth Fort at Kovno. This photograph was taken in 1996, when the Fort was being prepared as a memorial site.

above
Part of the deep moat around the Ninth Fort: tens of thousands of Jews were driven into it and shot.

The deportees to Kovno, 1941

15 November 1,000 from Munich, killed on 25 November

17 November 943 from Berlin, killed on 25 November

22 November 991 from Frankfurt, killed on 25 November

23 November 1,000 from Vienna, killed on 29 November

23 November 1,005 from Breslau, killed on 29 November

THE WANNSEE CONFERENCE

On 20 January 1942 thirteen senior Nazi and German officials met at a secluded lakeside villa on the shore of the Wannsee, a few miles from Berlin. They had been summoned by SS General Reinhard Heydrich, who told them that he had just been appointed 'Plenipotentiary for the Preparation of the Final Solution of the European Jewish Question'.

The aim of the meeting, Heydrich explained, was to coordinate the work of Hitler's Chancellery, the SS Race and Resettlement Office, the Ministry for the Occupied Eastern Territories, the Ministry of the Interior, the Justice Ministry, the Foreign Office and several other government departments. Also brought into the discussion, having made the journey from Cracow by train, were senior officials of the General Government.

Also present at Wannsee were the head of the German Four Year Plan, responsible for the disposing of Jewish property; and Adolf Eichmann, in charge of the Gestapo's Jewish affairs section, together with his chief, the head of the Gestapo, Heinrich Müller.

Heydrich told the meeting: 'In the course of the practical implementation of the Final Solution, Europe will be combed from east to west.'

Eichmann presented the gathering with a list of countries, setting out the number of Jews living in each, whom it was intended to deport to their deaths. Estonia (Estland) was marked as being *Judenfrei* (Jew-free), as almost all Estonia's 1,000 Jews had already been murdered. There were two figures for France: one for the area, including Paris, that had been occupied by Germany since June 1940. The other, much larger figure, was for 'Unoccupied France' still under French rule (with its capital at Vichy), which included the Jews of Morocco, Algeria and Tunisia.

During the meeting, Dr Josef Bühler, who had come to the meeting from Cracow, said: 'Jews should be removed from the domain of the General Government

L a n d	Zahl
A. Altreich	131.800
Ostmark	43.700
Ostgebiete	420.000
Generalgouvernement	2.284.000
Bialystok	400.000
Protektorat Böhmen und Mähren	74.200
Estland – judenfrei –	
Lettland	3.500
Litauen	34.000
Belgien	43.000
Dänemark	5.600
Frankreich / Besetztes Gebiet	165.000
Unbesetztes Gebiet	700.000
Griechenland	69.600
Niederlande	160.800
Norwegen	1.300
B. Bulgarien	48.000
England	330.000
Finnland	2.300
Irland	4.000
Italien einschl. Sardinien	58.000
Albanien	200
Kroatien	40.000
Portugal	3.000
Rumänien einschl. Bessarabien	342.000
Schweden	8.000
Schweiz	18.000
Serbien	10.000
Slowakei	88.000
Spanien	6.000
Türkei (europ. Teil)	55.500
Ungarn	742.800
UdSSR	5.000.000
Ukraine 2.994.684	
Weißrußland aus-	
schl. Bialystok 446.484	
Zusammen: über	11.000.000

Country	Number	
A. Germany (the Old Reich)	131,800	
Austria (renamed Ostmark)	43,700	
Eastern Territories	420,000	
General-Government	2,284,000	
Bialystok	400,000	
Protectorate of Bohemia and Moravia	74,200	
Estonia – Free of Jews –		
Latvia	3,500	
Lithuania	34,000	
Belgium	43,000	
Denmark	5,600	
France / Occupied territory	165,000	
Unoccupied territory	700,000	
Greece	69,600	
Netherlands	160,800	
Norway	1,300	
B. Bulgaria	48,000	
England	330,000	
Finland	2,300	
Ireland	4,000	
Italy, including Sardinia	58,000	
and Albania	200	
Croatia	40,000	
Portugal	3,000	
Roumania, including Bessarabia	342,000	
Sweden	8,000	
Switzerland	18,000	
Serbia	10,000	
Slovakia	88,000	
Spain	6,000	
Turkey (in Europe)	55,500	
Hungary	742,800	
USSR	5,000,000	
Ukraine	2,994,684	
Belorussia,		
without Bialystok	446,484	
Total: More than		11,000,000

as fast as possible, because it is precisely here that the Jew constitutes a substantial danger as carrier of epidemics.... Moreover, the majority of the two and a half million Jews involved were not capable of work.' Bühler then asked the meeting for 'only one favour', that ' the Jewish question in this territory be solved as rapidly as possible'.

With the concluding of the meeting at Wannsee, which took less than a day, a new phase of the mass murder of Jews was about to begin. To mass slaughter and starvation was to be added a third method of killing: murder by poison gas. Two months before Wannsee, 1,200 German political prisoners had been taken from Buchenwald concentration camp to the town of Bernberg, just south of Berlin. There, at a euthanasia institute where thousands of Germans had already been murdered, the new arrivals were put to death by gas.

far left
The list of countries presented by Eichmann to the Wannsee Conference, with the number of Jews who it was intended to deport to their deaths. England is in the list, with 330,000 Jews, and the Republic of Ireland with 4,000. The total number of Jews marked out for death is more than 11 million. Almost half of them (including those of England, Ireland, Spain, Turkey and Russia east of the German military advance) did not come under German rule or control.

left
Translation of Eichmann's list. List A gives the countries under direct German rule or control; list B gives countries allied to Germany, neutral or (as in the case of Britain and the Soviet Union) at war with Germany. The Lithuanian figure shows that more than 100,000 Lithuanian Jews had already been killed. The USSR figure is far too high: less than a million Jews were still alive in the German-occupied regions of the Soviet Union, where as many as a million had already been murdered in the previous six months. Less than a quarter of a million Jews were still alive in the Ukraine, Belorussia and western Russia. A further quarter of a million lived in areas that Germany was still to overrun, mostly in southern Russia and the Caucasus. A million more – as well as a quarter of a million Polish-Jewish refugees – lived in areas, including the Urals and Soviet Central Asia, as well as in Leningrad and Moscow, that Germany was never to conquer.

MASS DEPORTATION

Early morning we were rounded up and taken to a kiln (a brick factory), where we spent three days, after which the Germans opened the gates and started screaming: 'Everybody out'. At the same time we heard shooting, I saw it through a little window, I naturally thought that they were killing us all so I got hold of my mother, sister and brother and pushed us forward, as I couldn't bear to watch the shooting and thought that the sooner it would be over the better.

Fortunately we weren't being shot, they were only shooting the people whom they found in hiding and brought them back to this place. We were put in groups of one hundred and dragged to the trains, but I was pulled out of the group to bury the dead ones. I heard that my mother, sister and brother were taken to Belzec which was an extermination camp and I never heard from them again. Each group consisted of ninety Jews and ten Gypsies.

I was then alone in the ghetto. People were being taken away everyday and at that time we did not know where they were being taken to. Killing and shooting became a normal everyday event, you constantly heard shots being fired, one here, two there, four somewhere else, it is very difficult to say, but that is how it was and you got used to the idea that killing meant nothing. You just got used to it, everyone had one thing in mind and that was to survive.

Harry Balsam, aged twelve in 1942, recalling the Gorlice ghetto

Starting in December 1941, with the deportations to the Chelmno death camp, and reaching a crescendo in the summer and autumn of 1942, no day passed in German-occupied Poland without one, and even more, communities being deported. Sometimes a whole community was taken away on a single day. At other times five or six deportations were needed to clear (to 'liquidate' in the German parlance) the whole ghetto. Very few people, mostly young able-bodied men and some women, were kept back, as slave labourers.

Each deportation saw scenes of barbarity, episodes that have remained seared in the minds of those who saw them. In Piotrkow, during eight days in October, 22,000 Jews were deported from the ghetto and killed at Treblinka. Two thousand managed to hide, and escape deportation. Repeated searches were made for them. Those caught were taken outside the town, to the Rakow forest, and shot. On 25 November 1942 those still in hiding were offered the chance of staying in the ghetto 'legally' if they surrendered. Many did so.

They were taken to the synagogue and locked in. The synagogue was then surrounded by uniformed Ukrainian volunteers, who shot into the building at random. Those who survived the shooting were taken to the Rakow forest and killed.

In the Zwierzyniec ghetto lived Luba Krugman Gurdus. Her son Bobus was three years old. She later recalled how, night after night, trains from other ghettos would pass through Zwierzyniec – on their way to the death camp at Belzec :

'At night the rumbling of the train woke me up. I rushed to the door and found it wide open, with father watching the dark monster, which had only one brightly illuminated car window behind the locomotive.

"It's a real Cyclops," I said.

"I can't hear you," replied Father.

Our voices were drowned out by the clatter of the wheels and the penetrating whistle of the

engine. The train was of gigantic proportions and its load stupendous. I counted sixty-two cars. Father was breathing heavily, and his temples were moist with sweat. He wiped his forehead and opened his shirt.

"Please, close your shirt," I implored. "It's bitterly cold." He did not hear; his eyes were fixed on the train.

A few windows opened. Our Gentile neighbours were awakened by the noise. The train passed, leaving behind a cloud of smoke. Windows were closing when one harsh voice came through loudly: "Those damned Jews – they won't even let one sleep at night."'

Luba Gurdus and her son avoided deportation as her father had work papers issued by the local Forestry Administration. Her recollections continued:

'After the deportation, Bobus developed a greater interest in the boxcar trains, which resumed their route in front of our windows. One Tuesday morning, he joined me at the kitchen window to watch the death train, which suddenly appeared on the horizon. He grabbed a pencil and a piece of paper and drew his interpretation of the steaming and puffing monster rolling along the tracks. The drawing, produced in minutes

with spontaneity and an instinctive grasp of essentials was excellent. It left us all speechless.

Proud of his achievement, Bobus raised the drawing and exclaimed: "This is the train, you see – the train passing over there," and pointed to the box cars slowly moving along the tracks.

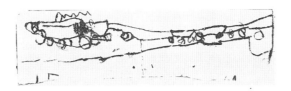

Bobus created this drawing on the morning of his birthday. On 24 August 1942 my son was four years old. Grateful to God for still being alive, we celebrated his birthday with a small afternoon party.... Several days later, Bobus contracted a serious case of diphtheria. I summoned the only Polish physician in Zwierzyniec, who came in spite of German restrictions forbidding him any contact with Jews. His prognosis was grim, and the lack of medicine sealed my son's fate.'

above
A painting of the Ten Commandments, in the study house next to the Piotrkow synagogue. It was riddled with bullets during the killings in the building in December 1942. Today the building is a public library. The Ten Commandments are usually covered by book shelves. The painting was done by a well-known painter and sculptor, Professor P. Willenberg (whose son Samuel was one of the few Jews to escape from Treblinka). Professor Willenberg survived the war in Warsaw, pretending to be a Pole who could not speak, and offering German soldiers sketches of themselves.

above far left
A deportation to Chelmno: the deportees had been ordered to board the open railway carriages, ostensibly for a journey to another ghetto.

above left
Lodz: the moment of deportation.

opposite
In the Lodz ghetto, a parting kiss for a deportee: those about to be deported have been separated behind a wire fence.

DEATH CAMPS

Eye-witnesses

That afternoon the work lasted till six. Nine vans, each of sixty Jews from Klodawa, were buried; five hundred people from Klodawa in all.

My friend Getzel Chrzastowski screamed terribly for a moment when he recognized his fourteen-year-old son, who had just been thrown into the ditch. We had to stop him, too, from begging the Germans to shoot him.

Yakov Grojanowski, recalling 12 January 1942 at Chelmno

Very frequently I awake at night with a terrible groan.... I see thousands of skeletons stretching out their bony hands to me, begging for their lives and for mercy.... I sit bolt upright, then rub my eyes and am glad to find that it was only a dream.... The spectres of death move about me. Children, children, and more children. I sacrificed all of my nearest and dearest. I myself led them to their execution. I myself built death chambers for them....

I want to report everything faithfully. Let people know....

Let millions find out. That is why I stay alive. that is my sole purpose.

Recollections of **Jankiel Wiernik**, who had escaped from Treblinka during the uprising of slave labourers there on 2 August 1943

The deportation of Polish Jewry that began in December 1941 was to four death camps: Chelmno, Belzec, Sobibor and Treblinka. In each of these camps almost every deportee was murdered. A fragment, a few hundred people in each death camp, was kept alive as slave labour, to sort the clothes of the victims, and to service the SS facilities. The rest, including all the able-bodied deportees – men and women – were sent from the railway sidings to their deaths in the gas chambers.

At Chelmno, between 8 December 1941 and the late summer of 1942, 360,000 Jews, many of them from the Lodz ghetto, were murdered, as were several thousand Gypsies. The ghettos around Chelmno were systematically emptied, and their inhabitants sent, by truck and by train, to the brick mill at the hamlet of Zawadki. At the mill they were forced, in groups of up to sixty at a time, into a large van (there were two vans in the camp). By the time each van reached the death camp site, all those inside it were dead – killed by poison gas. A small group of deportees, a dozen at a time, were saved from this final journey, and forced to pull the dead bodies out of the vans. Those Jews were then shot: several hundred in all. Only two managed to escape: one of them, Yakov Grojanowski, brought details of the whole terrible procedure to the Jews of Warsaw.

At Belzec, starting on 17 March 1942 and continuing for almost a year, 600,000 Jews from throughout

Galicia were killed. Many thousands of Jews from Lublin and Lvov, vibrant centres of pre-war Jewish creativity, were among those murdered at Belzec.

Also sent to Belzec, and killed on reaching the camp, were several thousand Jews brought by train almost a thousand miles from Germany. They included 320 from Würzburg and 224 from Fürth on March 24; 650 from Nuremberg on April 24; 2,100 from Dortmund on May 1; and 260 from Düsseldorf on July 22. They were first kept in a camp sixty miles from Belzec, at Izbica Lubelska – in a camp where hundreds were killed by sadistic guards – and the remainder taken on by train to Belzec. Many died in the trains. The rest were murdered on reaching Belzec.

At Sobibor, starting in early April 1942 and continuing for a year, more than 250,000 Jews were killed, mostly from central Poland. Several deportation trains of Dutch Jews were also brought from Westerbork to Sobibor; all the deportees were killed on arrival.

At Treblinka, in less than a year, an estimated 750,000 Jews, half a million of them from Warsaw, were killed by gas. The first deportation took place on 22 July 1942. Treblinka was set up in a secluded wood, just over forty miles from Warsaw. A spur railway line was built from the village station into the wood. In the first month, 66,701 Warsaw Jews were deported to Treblinka, and killed.

There was a fifth camp where everyone was murdered on arrival: Maly Trostinets, near Minsk, in German-occupied Belorussia. Jews were deported there across Europe by train, then murdered in gas vans during the drive from a wayside railway station to the camp. The first deportation train reached Maly Trostinets on 10 May 1942. Most trains came from the Theresienstadt ghetto (see pages 80–1). The train that arrived from Theresienstadt 4 August 1942 took six days and nights on its journey – the normal journey took two days and nights. Forty of the thousand deportees were taken off the train at Minsk to be used as slave labourers. The rest, 960 German, Austrian and Czech Jews, were murdered. Of a thousand Jews deported from Theresienstadt on 25 August 1942, all but twenty-one were killed: the twenty-one had been taken off at Minsk to work on an SS farm. Only two survived, escaping to join the Russian partisans: one was killed in action against the Germans, the other survived the war. At least 26,000 Jewish deportees – mostly from Theresienstadt but also from Holland – were murdered at Maly Trostinets, as well as 39,000 Jews brought from the Minsk ghetto.

More than a third of the Jews murdered in the Holocaust were murdered in the five death camps: Chelmno, Belzec, Sobibor, Treblinka and Maly Trostinets.

opposite, top
Two SS men: SS Major Heinrich Gley (left), who worked at both Sobibor and Belzec, and SS Major Gottlieb Hering, camp commandant at Belzec, enjoying a moment of relaxation.

opposite, centre
SS guards pose for a photograph behind the commandant's house in Belzec.

opposite, bottom
To reach Chelmno, the deportation trains, and trucks, went to the village of Powierce. From there the deportees were made to walk a few hundred yards to a mill at the hamlet of Zawadki, by the river Warta. From the mill they were taken in a sealed van to a clearing in the wood near the village of Chelmno. The vans were gas vans. When they reached the wood, all of the people inside them were dead.

below
The left-hand map shows some of the routes of deportations to the death camps. The right-hand map gives the timetable of a single deportation, from Wloszczowa to Treblinka.

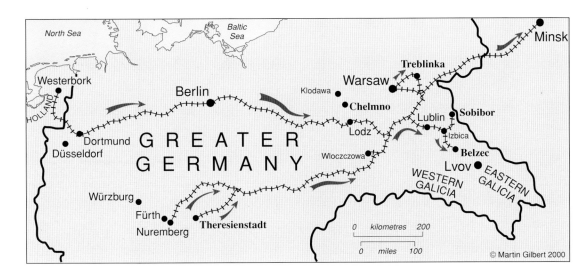

THE BEGINNING OF AUSCHWITZ

right
Auschwitz: the inside of the gas chamber, Crematorium I.

below
Maps showing the routes of the first deportations to Auschwitz, in March 1942 (left), and in May 1942 (right).

A deportation

The timetable of the first Paris deportation to Auschwitz
27–30 March 1942

27 March

Bourget-Drancy	depart	17.00
Compiègne	arrive	18.40
	depart	19.40
Laôn	arrive	21.05
	depart	21.23
Reims	arrive	22.25

28 March

Reims	depart	9.10
Neuberg (frontier)	arrive	13.59

30 March

Auschwitz	arrive	5.33

Starting in the summer of 1942, the concentration camp at Auschwitz, which had until then been principally a place where Poles had been held – and killed – was turned by the SS into a killing place for Jews. Across the railway from the main camp, at Birkenau, a vast area of barracks was created, and four gas chambers built. Experiments in murder by gas had been carried out on Soviet prisoners of war during the spring.

The first Jews to reach the barracks at Birkenau were 2,000 Slovak Jews deported from Bratislava on 26 March 1942, and 1,112 mostly Polish-born Jews deported from France on the following day. On that first (of more than seventy) deportation trains from Paris, there were Jews who had been born in London, Marrakech, Haifa, Istanbul and Copenhagen. They had been living in France when war came. French police rounded them up for deportation.

The first Jews to be 'selected' at Birkenau to be murdered by gas were taken from the sick bay by an SS Medical Officer on 4 May 1942. They were loaded on to a truck and taken to the gas chamber (known also as Bunker I, or Crematorium I) at Auschwitz main camp. More than a thousand exhausted, sick Jews – condemned to death because they were 'incapable of working' – were killed by gas that May.

Between 5 May and 11 May 1942 more than 10,000 Polish Jews were brought by train from the nearby ghettos of Dabrowa Gornicza, Bedzin, Zawierce and Gliwice, in German-annexed Poland. Of these deportees, 5,200 were gassed on arrival. This set the pattern for the coming two and a half years.

From May 1942, deportation trains began to arrive at Auschwitz with increasing regularity. All old people, women with children, babies, young people, and children with or without their mothers, were taken from the railway siding, mostly in trucks, direct to the gas chambers. Most of the able-bodied men and women among the deportees were not sent to the gas chambers, but tattooed with a number on their forearm, and sent to the barracks at Birkenau. There they formed a vast force of slave labour, numbering by late 1944 more than 30,000 in Birkenau and the nearby slave labour camps.

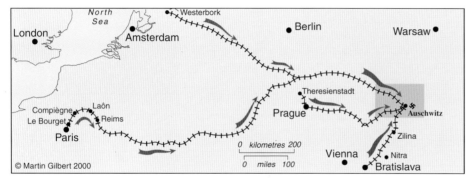

above
Birkenau: Crematorium IV (two chimneys) under construction. The gas chamber is on the far left; the three small windows visible just below the roof are where the poison gas was dropped in. The administrative section and undressing chamber is in the central sector; the crematorium is below the two chimneys.

above left and far left
Birkenau: construction of gas chamber and Crematorium II (single chimney).

left
Crematorium II, as recalled immediately after the war by a Czech deportee, Alfred Kantor. The trees were planted to shield the building from the rest of the camp.

On 27 May 1942, 3,000 Jews from Theresienstadt and 2,000 from Prague were brought to Auschwitz by train and gassed. A second deportation from Paris to Auschwitz took place on June 5, followed by three more from Paris before the end of the month. That June, 3,831 Jews from France were gassed on arrival. By the end of June, 52,000 Slovak Jews had been killed by gas. They had been brought from more than twenty towns in Slovakia.

Henceforth, deportees to Auschwitz were brought from two main areas: from Western Europe, and from the Silesian and Zaglembia regions of German-annexed south-west Poland. Methodically, ghettos in south-west Poland were combed for deportees. In June they were brought from Krzepice, Chrzanow, Olkusz, Sosnowiec and Bielsko-Biala. From these five ghettos, 16,000 people were gassed on arrival.

In July 1942 the first deportations from Holland reached Auschwitz: seven trains, from which 5,978 Dutch Jews were taken straight to the gas chambers. That month, on July 10, the first hundred Jewish women, then in the barracks at Birkenau, were taken by the SS for medical experiments, including sterilization. Those carrying out the experiments were German doctors, trained in medical schools in Germany, who had decided to cast in their lot with the SS: the much-feared Dr Mengele joined them, as an SS Captain, in May 1943. Standing at the head of the line of deportees, Mengele, immaculately dressed in SS uniform, with white gloves, would indicate with a flick of his finger where the person in front of him must go: to the left or to the right. One way was to the gas chambers, the other to the barracks.

SLAVE LABOUR CAMPS

When we entered the women's barracks we were appalled. The scene before us was so horrifying that it didn't seem real. From the filthy yellow pallets, yellow-green ghouls looked out and in screeching voices invited us to draw near them. The goods they had for sale were arranged on the edge of their pallets.

Yellow eyes peered out at us from all sides. With what profound envy, what amazement, these ugly wrinkled women with rusty-coloured hair stared out at us! We were still dressed in coats and shoes, while they were wrapped in rags or paper with wooden clogs on their feet. We still looked young and fresh, while they looked old, bitter, gnawed to the bone by the yellow picric acid.

Maria Lewinger, recalling Skarzysko-Kamienna camp

The German war machine used Jewish and non-Jewish forced labour as one of its principal means of producing armaments, and – in the absence of so many able-bodied German men at the front – to maintain agricultural production. 5,500,000 forced labourers (non-Jews) were brought to Germany from every occupied country. A further 2,500,000 prisoners of war were put to forced labour. Conditions of labour varied: they could be harsh in the extreme. One quarter of all munitions – rifles, artillery pieces, grenades – sent to the war fronts was produced in German-owned factories by Russian, Polish, French and other deportees.

Jewish slave labourers were among those forced to make munitions, and a vast range of other goods, including German army uniforms. Many of these Jews were treated as if they were totally expendable. Their lives were less important than the work they did. Most were subjected to repeated beatings, and given less food and less medical attention (if any) than the foreign labourers. At least half a million Jews died while slave labourers. Many of them were worked to exhaustion, or beaten to death as they worked.

In the period after the mass deportation of Jews from the ghettos to the death camps and slaughter pits, almost all those still in the ghettos were used as slave labourers – both inside the ghetto walls and outside them – until the deportations and killings were renewed in the spring and summer of 1944. Slave labour camps were also set up inside Germany, as the badly bombed war industries were forced to move underground.

In some ghettos – principally Lodz and Kovno – the slave labour system kept tens of thousands of Jews alive for more than two years after the first deportations and killings. Work seemed the way to survive. In the Bialystok and Vilna ghettos, work permits, and the rations that they ensured, were regarded as 'the road to life' for tens of thousands of people.

In some slave labour camps, the chance of survival was small. At the explosives factory at Skarzysko-Kamienna, in one section, Work C, where the explosives were made, almost none of the labourers survived. Of 20,000 Jews taken to Skarzysko-Kamienna from the surrounding ghettos, 14,000 (70%) were killed: when

above right
A drawing done immediately after the war by Alfred Kantor, showing a scene he had witnessed at Auschwitz: Jewish women being used as slave labourers.

right
A drawing by Alfred Kantor, done immediately after the war, showing a scene at Auschwitz which he witnessed. He captioned it: Sunday morning 'sport'. Under the picture he wrote: 'Labour had no use since there were no roads. Primary target was to weaken the prisoners' resistance.'

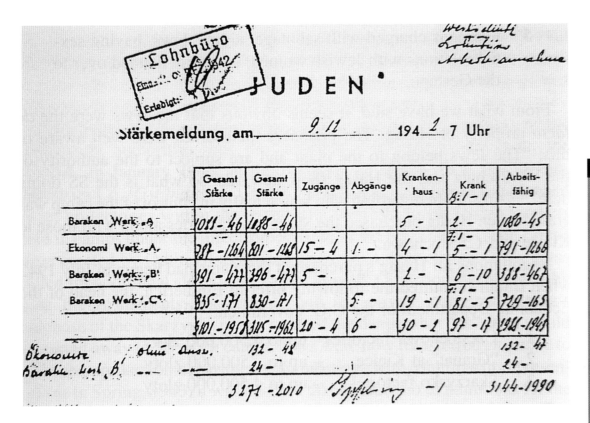

they became too weak to work, they were taken to the camp's firing range, and shot.

Skarzysko-Kamienna was one of 1,750 labour camps (*Arbeitslager*) in the General Government, of which 437 were for Jews (*Judenlager*). In the rest, more than five million Poles toiled for their captors. The owners and operators of Skarzysko-Kamienna were the Hasag (Hugo Schneider Stock Company) industries: in 1943 80% of the stock was held by three leading German banks. Hasag had other factories in the General Government including one in Czestochowa.

The largest slave labour camp region was set up around Auschwitz. Jews not selected for the gas chambers were sent to arms factories, coal mines, and the synthetic rubber and oil production plant of Buna – located at Monowitz, a few miles from the gas chambers of Birkenau. This plant, known as Auschwitz III, was specially set up by the German industrial giant, I.G. Farben, in order to make use of slave labour. The Nuremberg Trials concluded that Buna was 'financed and owned by Farben' and that what took place there was 'a crime against humanity'.

German industry's use of concentration camp labour was central to its manpower needs. On 20 October 1942 SS Lieutenant-General Pohl (Chief of the SS Economic and Administrative Department) informed

Himmler that the German industrial firm of Siemens was building new barracks at Ravensbrück concentration camp to house 2,500 women who would work on telecommunications equipment for the army. The commandant of Auschwitz, Rudolf Höss, provided 1,200 women workers to Siemens in 1943 and about 1,500 in 1944. They each bore a tattoo number, and worked in a factory manufacturing electrical switches for aircraft. The factory was located at Bobrek, five miles from Auschwitz. When Hermann Göring complained to Himmler that not enough concentration camp inmates were being used for aircraft production, Himmler referred in his reply to the Siemens factory at Auschwitz.

Siemens also used concentration camp labour elsewhere: 550 Jewish women, bearing tattoo numbers 55,740 to 56,290, were sent to the Siemens factory in Nuremberg; 1,200 women were taken from Sachsenhausen to Siemens-Berlin. When those works were bombed, Siemens moved the operation to Buchenwald. Inmates from Buchenwald also worked for Siemens in Bavaria; inmates from Gross Rosen worked for Siemens in Brandenburg.

Freddie Knoller, born in Vienna, a slave labourer at Buna, later recalled: 'I had to carry twenty-five kilogrammes of cement bags on my back, day-in, day-out … People dropped like flies.'

A survivor remembers

Of medium height, blond, with steel-cold colourless eyes and the glossy gaze of one accustomed to heavy drinking, Feix appeared restless. His expression was one of undisguised rancor, cruelty his strongest facial characteristic. Standing erect with legs apart, wearing polished boots, a pistol in an open holster, and a Mauser hanging from his neck, he seemed ready to make the welcoming address.

'You are fortunate to have come here. This is a good camp. Here you will work and get fed. Of course, if you expect to eat, you will have to work for it and as long as you work, you will get along fine. Now, it is prohibited to possess any silver, gold, money, or jewelry – therefore, if you turn it in now, you will not be punished.' Just at this moment, someone moved in the ranks. Feix whipped out his gun and shot him on the spot, then resumed without a pause: 'Now, when I finish speaking, I want you to turn in your valuables, such as gold, silver, diamonds, and currency.'

George Topas, recalling SS Sergeant Reinhold Feix, camp commandant at Budzyn slave labour camp

above left
The daily report (headed *Juden* – Jews) of the number of slave labourers at Skarzysko-Kamienna. This report is dated 9 December 1942. The notorious Work C lists 729 men and 165 women working, and 86 sick.

THE THERESIENSTADT GHETTO

The eighteenth-century Austro-Hungarian town of Theresienstadt, part of Czechoslovakia since 1918, was known as Terezin in Czech. In October 1941 the 3,700 Czech inhabitants of the town were ordered to leave by the Germans, who turned it into a ghetto. More than 96,000 Jews were brought there from all over Europe (*see map far right*). Conditions were harsh, dominated by overcrowding and hunger. More than 33,000 Jews died in the ghetto, mostly of starvation.

Among those deported to Theresienstadt were artists, writers, musicians, scholars and teachers. Under Jewish leadership, several orchestras were founded there, as well as an operatic and a theatrical troupe. Lectures were organized, and a library of 60,000 volumes opened. Jewish studies played a major part in cultural activities. Classes were held for the children, who had to carry their benches into the classroom, under the protective eye of Jewish guardians, who, like all adults in the ghetto, were obliged to wear the yellow star. The drawing on the right was done in Theresienstadt by the twelve-year-old Helga Weiss, in Czech, Weissova.

From January 1942 the Germans began to deport Jews from Theresienstadt to death camps in the east, including Auschwitz and Maly Trostinets (*see page 75*). In all, 88,000 were deported from Theresienstadt to their deaths.

From 1942 to 1944, a group of thirteen- to fifteen-year-old boys in Theresienstadt produced, in greatest secrecy, a weekly magazine. It was called *Vedem* (In the Lead). Each issue was copied out by hand in the attic of the building used for their equally secret schooling. The editor was fourteen-year-old Petr Ginz, who was later deported to Auschwitz and killed.

One of the few survivors of those who produced *Vedem*, Kurt Kotouc, later recalled Petr Ginz at work: 'I can still see him, sitting cross-legged on his lower bunk, surrounded by pens, pencils, engravers, brushes and paints, and sheets of paper of all sizes, along with what was left of a parcel from his parents. "Well, here you are, Petr, *Vedem* is coming out again. But it took us a long time, didn't it?" Petr is smiling ... "Well, get on with it," he'd say. "Go round to all the boys so we get it out on time" ...'

Alfred (known as Fredy) Kantor, who was eighteen, and an art student, when he was deported from Prague to Theresienstadt in December 1941, later recalled: 'There were times when life even assumed a deceptive normalcy. Many Jews still believed Terezin to be a work camp where they would be safe until the end of the war. There were moments that seemed strangely magnified

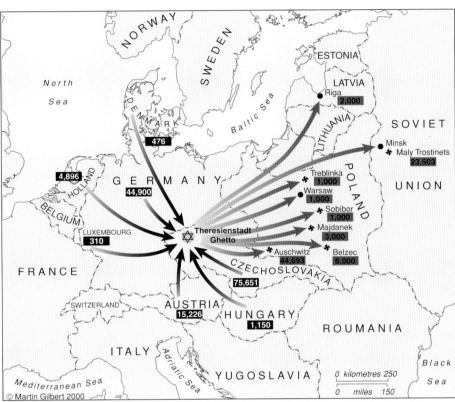

Life, Terezin's first underground production. This was a stinging political cabaret, and one of our own men stood guard at the door in case any SS appeared.'

On 15 March 1943 a fifty-two-year-old woman, Trude Neumann, died of hunger in Theresienstadt. She was the daughter of Theodor Herzl, founder of the Zionist movement. From 1918 she had been a patient in a mental institution in Vienna: in 1942 all the patients were deported to Theresienstadt.

On 17 August 1943, 1,260 children under thirteen were rounded up in the Bialystok ghetto and deported to Theresienstadt. After a month, volunteers were asked for to accompany them to neutral Switzerland (another rumour said to Palestine). Fifty-three doctors and nurses offered to accompany them. Their destination was Auschwitz, where all the children and most of their helpers were killed.

by a feeling of blissful make-believe amidst an otherwise cold reality. I remembered how overjoyed we were one day by the music of an accordion that someone had smuggled into the barracks. Everyone huddled together in the poorly lit, freezing room; and for a while we forgot our hurt as we listened to the tunes. Or I remember how we gathered at night in a cramped cellar to watch Karel Svenk's *Cheers to*

above

Map showing the deportation of Jews into Theresienstadt (black arrows), and the deportations out of Theresienstadt to the death camps in the east (red arrows). The numbers sent to Theresienstadt are shown in black boxes. The numbers murdered after deportation to the east are shown in red boxes (the largest numbers were killed at Auschwitz and at Maly Trostinets).

above left

A drawing by Helga Weiss (Weissová) done in Theresienstadt. She noted on her drawing that she was twelve years old, and was living in the Dresden Kaserne. This was one of the former Austro-Hungarian army barracks being used as living space – desperately cramped – in the ghetto.

HOLLAND – WESTERBORK

The German technique of deportation from the occupied countries of Western Europe was to take Jews from their homes in the cities and towns in which they lived, and to confine them in an internment camp. There, they would be forced to remain, cut off from contact with the outside world, deprived of their possessions, without access to all that had been homely and familiar to them, until they were taken away by train – normally in groups of about a thousand – across Europe to what they were told was a new camp, somewhere to help with the harvest of 1942 (or 1943), a place of permanent resettlement, even a 'Jewish State' set aside for them in the East – but which was in fact death for all but a very few.

During 1941 the Jews of Holland had been relatively unmolested. On 12 February 1941 the German occupation authorities had set up a Jewish Council, headed by two Jewish 'Presidents', to supervise all Jewish institutions. By the autumn of 1941 all Jewish children had been forced by German order to leave school and to study only at special schools under the supervision of the Jewish Council. That August, the Germans confiscated all Jewish funds and property:

20% of their value was given to the Council, 80% was kept by the Germans as booty. At the same time all Jewish businesses were seized, and more than 5,000 Jewish men were sent to forced labour camps throughout Holland. On 2 May 1942 every Dutch Jew was forced to wear the yellow Star of David.

On 14 July 1942, several thousand Jews were arrested in Amsterdam, and sent to a camp near the north-eastern town of Westerbork. The next day, one thousand were sent to Auschwitz. A new German slogan then burst upon the harassed, bewildered Jewish community: 'Work in the East'. The aim, it was declared by the German occupation authorities, was to make all Holland *Judenrein* – rid of Jews.

On 2 October 1942, in a single round-up throughout Holland, 13,000 Jews were seized and taken to Westerbork. Thousands had to sleep on the floors with neither matresses nor blankets. But despite the deprivations, concerts were given by the inmates, some by famous German musicians who had fled to Holland from Germany before 1940. There was a camp orchestra, a hospital with 120 surgeons – themselves internees about to be deported – a pharmacy,

right

Dutch Jews being loaded on a train at Westerbork, for Auschwitz. Having been told that they were being resettled 'somewhere in the east', they were allowed to take with them no more than they could carry.

above

A stamp issued by the Dutch government in 1992, on the fiftieth anniversary of the first deportation from Westerbork. It lists those who were killed: grandfather, grandmother, father, mother, brother, sister, uncle, aunt, nephew, niece, neighbour, friend.

above left

Westerbork: inmates celebrate Channukah, the Festival of Lights, recalling the victory of the Maccabees over the Seleucid Greek occupiers of Jerusalem, who had looted the Temple, forbidden the practice of the Jewish religion, and sought to force the Jews to worship pagan gods.

left

Westerbork: children at a concert.

workshops for the repair of clothes and shoes, a bathhouse, a post office, schools and a playground. These activities were continuous. So too were the deportations. Within two years, 93 trains, each made up of precisely twenty wagons, took between one and two thousand Jews from Westerbork to Auschwitz: of the 60,000 deported to Auschwitz, only 500 survived.

A total of 1,700 letters and postcards was received in Amsterdam from Auschwitz between July 1942 and the autumn of 1943, a thousand of which arrived in the spring of 1943. So small a total from so large a number of deportees began to worry the remaining Jews, forced to live only in Amsterdam, and themselves continually rounded up and despatched to Westerbork for the rail journey east.

In the autumn of 1943 the Dutch Government-in-Exile in London received a report from a Dutch Jew still in Holland, in which the writer asked: 'But what are 1,000 letters when there are 60,000 deportees? Where are the letters from the rest? And why, above all, is there no sign from all the children, the old and the sick?'

There was another destination in addition to Auschwitz: 34,000 Dutch Jews were deported to Sobibor. Only nineteen survived.

The railways from Holland transported 106,000 Jews to the east. Some of them were already refugees from Germany and Austria. More than 100,000 of those deported were never to return. At the end of the war, there were only 900 Jews in Westerbork. 24,000 Dutch Jews were hidden during the German occupation. Of those, 8,000 (like Anne Frank and her family) were betrayed and deported. Those Dutch Jews who survived the war, mostly in hiding, were saved by Dutch citizens who, at great personal risk, gave them food and shelter.

Recollection

The fact that the Germans had perpetrated atrocities against Polish Jews was no reason for thinking that they behaved in the same way towards Dutch Jews, firstly because the Germans had always held Polish Jews in disrepute, and secondly because in the Netherlands, unlike Poland, they had to sit up and take notice of public opinion.

Professor D. Cohen, joint-President of the Jewish Council

FRANCE – DRANCY

After several days and nights the doors were opened. We arrived worn out, dehydrated, with many ill. A newborn baby, snatched from its mother's arms, was thrown against a column. The mother, crazed from pain, began to scream. The SS man struck her violently with the butt end of his weapon over her head. Her eyes haggard, with fearful screams, her beautiful hair became tinted with her own blood. She was struck down by a bullet in her head.

Albert Hollender, one of only eight survivors of a thousand Jews deported from Paris to Auschwitz on 28 August 1942

In France it was Frenchmen, members of the *Milice française*, who took the main part in the round-up of Jews. Between 1941 and 1944, a total of 73,853 Jews were seized in France, taken to holding camps – principally Drancy, a suburb of Paris – and then deported, mostly to Auschwitz. There were only 2,500 survivors.

Of the deportees from France who were murdered in Auschwitz, 11,400 were under the age of sixteen. Many of these children were deported without their parents.

A French law of 4 October 1940 made it legal for the French police to arrest 'any foreigner of the Jewish race'.

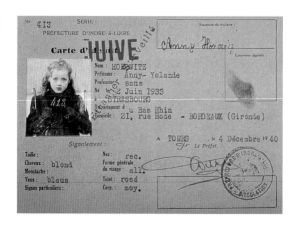

above right
The identity card of Anny-Yolande Horowitz, together with her signature and fingerprint. She was born in Strasbourg on 2 June 1933, and deported to Auschwitz on 11 September 1942, three months after her ninth birthday. The registration card, issued at Tours on 4 December 1940, notes that she is Jewish (*juive*), and that she is under police surveillance as a foreigner – (*Etranger surveillé*) – although Strasbourg, her birthplace, was part of France when she was born.

right
A deportation train leaves Paris. The railway wagon is a standard French goods wagon of the SNCF (*Societé Nationale de Chemins de Fers*) French railways. Many of those boarding are children.

Camille Himelfarb-Sarnacka, born in Paris on 10 June 1940. In 1942 she was arrested with her mother in front of the Goncourt metro station in Paris. On 16 September 1942 she was deported to Auschwitz and murdered there on reaching the camp. She was two years and three months old.

In France at that time there were about 12,000 German Jews and 5,000 Austrian Jews, who had found refuge there before the outbreak of the Second World War. There were also tens of thousands of Polish-born Jews, who had emigrated to France between the two world wars, and had worked, married and raised families in France.

The first round-up of foreign-born Jews – 3,700 in all – took place in Paris on 14 May 1941. They were taken by train from Austerlitz station to two specially created internment camps, at Pithiviers and Beaune-la-Rolande. Most had been born in Poland, a few in Czechoslovakia and Austria. Later they were deported to Auschwitz.

The first deportation from Paris to Auschwitz had taken place on 27 March 1942 (*see page 76*). These deportations were accelerated after a special request on June 11 from Berlin to the Vichy French authorities. In a two-day round-up that started on 16 July 1942, 13,000 Jews were seized in Paris and its suburbs, among them more than 4,000 children, some arrested in the

apartments where they were living, others seized in the streets. Between July 17 and the end of September 1942, more than 33,000 Jews were deported from Paris – in 34 trains ('convoys') of goods wagons. The deportations continued even after the Allied forces had landed in Normandy in June 1944.

top left
The round-up of 14 May 1941: foreign born Jews at Austerlitz station in Paris, about to board the train for internment camps. They were allowed to take with them only what they could carry.

above left
A memorial plaque to 112 people, of whom forty were small children, deported to Auschwitz in 1942 from the Fondation Fernand Halphen (their wartime home) on the Ile St. Louis, Paris.

BELGIUM – MALINES

The story of Mala Zimetbaum

Among the Belgian Jewish girls in the barracks at Auschwitz-Birkenau was nineteen-year-old Mala Zimetbaum. She became known for her attempts to comfort new arrivals, one of whom later recalled: 'She was the one who tried to make it easier for us when we arrived.' At the beginning of June 1944 Mala, having become too weak to work, was taken to Block 25, the 'death hut', all of whose inmates were to be taken to the gas chambers. They were kept locked in the hut, naked and without food, until they were too weak to offer any form of resistance. Mala and a few others managed, however, to escape through an air vent in the ceiling. She returned to the women's barracks and became an interpreter (she was fluent in French, German and Polish, the language of her parents). Later she escaped from Auschwitz with a Pole, Edward Galinski, who had managed to steal an SS uniform for himself and the uniform of a woman SS guard for Mala. They walked out of the main gate side by side. Two weeks later they were caught. Taken back to Auschwitz they were tortured, and Galinski was hanged. Mala tried to kill herself. A survivor, Lena Berg, wrote of the next moments: 'The SS men knocked her down and shot her. Then they dumped her in a hand cart and several women were ordered to pull the cart round the camp so everyone could see it. Thousands of women stood there in the setting sun saying farewell to Mala. Later it was said that she was still alive when they threw her into the crematorium furnace.'

From the earliest days of Nazi rule in Germany, 2,000 German Jews found refuge in Belgium. When Hitler acquired the Saar in 1935 as a result of a League of Nations plebiscite, all 5,000 Jews chose Belgian or French citizenship, and left the enlarged confines of the Reich. Belgium also took in a quarter of the refugees from the *St Louis*.

Germany invaded Belgium on 10 May 1940. Eighteen days later Belgium capitulated. German military rule was imposed: it remained in force until liberation in September 1944.

Almost seven hundred years earlier, in 1261, the Jews of Belgium had faced a deathbed order by Duke Henry III of Brabant, to be 'totally extirpated until not one remains'. They managed to replace this by manual labour. With the expulsion of Jews from Spain in 1492 the Jewish communities in Belgium were revitalized. Antwerp became a centre of Jewish life and prosperity, centring around the diamond trade. With the German occupation, all prosperity ended. From October 1940, Jews were forbidden to practise in their professions. On 10 May 1941 all Jews had to give up their radios. On August 29 they had to be indoors from eight in the evening to seven in the morning. On 27 May 1942 all Jews were ordered to wear the yellow Star of David. At the beginning of July 1942 all Jewish unemployed were ordered to report to Dossin de Saint-Georges camp, at Malines (Mechelen) – halfway between Brussels and Antwerp – for what they were told would be 'work in the east'. Insufficient numbers of volunteers having presented themselves, on 22 July 1942 the Germans instituted the first of a series of mass round-ups, known as *razzias*. On 2 August 1942 the first train left Malines for the east, with a thousand Jews. Its destination was unknown to those on board. It was in fact Auschwitz.

At first only foreign-born Jews were deported: as many as 70% of Belgian Jews had emigrated to Belgium from Poland between the wars. The Queen Mother, Elisabeth, and the Roman Catholic Cardinal, van Roey, persuaded the Germans to exempt Jews of Belgian nationality from deportation. This exemption lasted a year. On 3 September 1943 those Jews with Belgian nationality were

rounded up and deported. One train to Auschwitz had Belgian Gypsies on board. They too were murdered.

On 15 January 1944, among the Jews deported from Belgium to Auschwitz were the Polish-born Meir Tabakman and his wife Raizl. Tabakman had already been deported some months earlier, but had jumped off the train. Later he had been caught. Branded as a *flitzer* – one who had tried to flee – he was locked into a special goods wagon with many other former escapees. At

above
A commemorative stamp issued by the Belgian Post Office in 1997, after the opening of the Museum of Deportation and Resistance at Malines.

far left
Jewish orphans in Brussels shortly after liberation. They had survived the war in hiding. Their parents had been deported through Malines to Auschwitz. This drawing was done by a former inmate at Malines, Irene Awret, who had been an art student in Germany before Hitler came to power, when she fled to Belgium.

left
Paul Halter, born in Geneva in 1920, of Polish-born parents. He studied philosophy in Belgium. After the Germans invaded he was active in resistance activities. He was arrested, imprisoned and then deported to Auschwitz on 16 June 1943 (in a train with 1,400 Jews, of whom only nineteen survived). In January 1945 he escaped from a death march and reached the Russian front line. In 1980 he created the Auschwitz Foundation to perpetuate the remembrance of the Holocaust and the camps.

a German-born painter who had lived in hiding in Brussels from 1940 to 1944. He and his wife were arrested while trying to change their attic hiding place; it is believed that they were betrayed. Both were killed on reaching Auschwitz.

By 31 July 1944, thirty-one trains had left Malines for Auschwitz. In all, 25,257 Jews were deported. Of them, only 1,207 survived the war. Among those murdered were 5,000 children under the age of sixteen, and 150 infants less than two years old. The youngest of the deportees was thirty-nine days old, the oldest ninety-one years old. Both were murdered on reaching Auschwitz.

In 1996 the Museum of Deportation and Resistance was opened at Malines, situated in Dossin camp. In the museum's underground remembrance hall, a voice recites the names and ages of the five thousand murdered children.

Auschwitz, his wife later recalled, 'not one of them entered the camp'. All were taken direct to the gas chamber.

Even after the Allies had landed in Normandy on 6 June 1944, and were advancing towards Belgium, the deportations to Auschwitz continued. From the last deportation train, which left Belgium on 31 July 1944, 564 Jews were murdered on arrival at the camp eight days later. Among them was Felix Nussbaum,

Chapter Five

Survival: Hope, Resistance, Refuge

The 'will to live'

In the evenings people would talk about politics.... Listening to these conversations I became aware of everybody's strong will to live despite fatigue, mood of depression, lack of certainty what tomorrow would bring. They would console themselves by saying that soon the Russians would come and liberate them despite the fact that at that time the Russians were beyond Rostov, at Stalingrad, with Moscow and Leningrad under siege and all of Russia imperiled.

A **survivor** of the Rovno ghetto

It was the cold winter of 1944 and although we had nothing like calendars, my father, who was my fellow prisoner there, took me and some of our friends to a corner in our barrack. He announced that it was the eve of Channukah, produced a curious-shaped clay bowl, and began to light a wick immersed in his precious, but now melted, margarine ration. Before he could recite the blessing, I protested at this waste of food. He looked at me – then at the lamp – and finally said: 'You and I have seen that it is possible to live up to three weeks without food. We once lived almost three days without water; but you cannot live properly for three minutes without hope!'

Hugo Gryn, recalling the festival of Channukah at the Lieberose slave labour camp. He was then fourteen years old

right
Four Jews in the town of Chelm, executed on 28 May 1942.

The hope of all Jews in ghettos and slave labour camps was to survive, to live through the time of torment, to stay alive until Hitler, Nazism and Germany were defeated. The Yiddish verb *uberleben* (to live through) had a powerful resonance in every ghetto and camp.

Opposing the chances of survival was the strength of the German war machine – the German military mastery of Europe – and Hitler's determination that Jewish life should be wiped out wherever the power of Germany reached. All the captive peoples of Europe suffered from the rigours of the forced labour system, the suppression of all manifestations of independent thought, and the day-to-day workings of totalitarianism: the confiscation of radios, the total control of the newspapers and the all-pervading reach of the Gestapo, with its ability to imprison, torture and execute all whom it regarded as hostile to Nazism.

For the Jews, there was the added terror that they had no means of acceptable subservience: hard work could not save them, compliance with the whim of the occupier could not save them, conversion to Christianity could not save them (even devout Christians of Jewish origin were sent to the death camps as Jews). The fate of the Jews was confinement, deportation and death. Reprisals were ever-present: for a single German soldier killed, a hundred Jews – sometimes many more – would be shot. But despite the omnipresence of persecution the instinct to survive was strong; the flame of resistance never died.

Against overwhelming odds, in every ghetto, in every death camp, acts of individual and collective bravery took place. Throughout Europe, Jews prayed, hoped, fought, hid, and joined national resistance movements. Some Jews were saved by the goodwill of neighbours and of nations.

WARSAW GHETTO REVOLT

above right
On the pavement lie the bodies of those who had thrown themselves out of the windows in an attempt to escape the flames. Many were shot dead even as they were falling, or – injured and in agony – were killed where they fell. In Stroop's official report, this photograph was captioned: 'Bandits who jumped.'

Between 22 July and 3 October 1942, 310,322 Jews had been deported from the Warsaw ghetto to Treblinka, where almost all of them had been killed. Between 18 and 22 January 1943 the round-up was renewed, with a search for 16,000 slave labourers required in the Lublin region, but after 6,000 had been seized, Jewish resistance fighters opened fire and the round-up was halted: the SS left the ghetto.

On the night of 18 April 1943, the Jews in the Warsaw ghetto learned that the Germans planned to renew the deportations. Since January, plans had been made to resist the next German incursion. One of those who intended to fight, Zivia Lubetkin, later recalled: 'Even though we were prepared, and had even prayed for this hour, we turned pale. A tremor of joy, mixed with a shudder of fear, passed through all of us. But we suppressed our emotions and reached for our guns.'

On the morning of 19 April 1943 the Germans entered the Warsaw ghetto in force. They were met by arms fire. The Germans had 135 machine guns, the Jews had two. The Germans had 1,358 rifles, the Jews had fifteen. The Jews also had five hundred pistols, but these were of little use in street fighting, or against artillery, of which the Jews had none. The main Jewish weapon was several thousand grenades, supplemented by petrol-filled bottles.

The fighting lasted for a month. On the first day, the Germans beat a hasty retreat. The Jews had made use of the cellars to prepare hundreds of fortified bunkers. But incredible bravery could not survive a sustained military onslaught, or the savagery with which it was accompanied. On April 20, the German forces broke into the Jewish hospital: they killed all the sick and wounded as they lay in their beds. Then they set the building on fire: those patients, doctors and nurses who had managed to reach the cellars of the building, in search of safety, died in the fire.

Systematically, the German military commander, SS Brigadier-General Stroop, ordered the buildings of the ghetto to be set on fire, and their inhabitants with them. As building after building burned, all who managed to escape the flames were rounded up and marched to the

Umschlagplatz – the collecting point for deportation to Treblinka. As thousands of unarmed Jews – women and children among them – were being marched to the Umschlagplatz, the ghetto fighters continued with the battle from cellars and attics.

On May 8 the Germans attacked the command post of the insurgents, a fortified bunker at 18 Mila Street. When artillery fire failed to dislodge the defenders, the Germans used gas. A few fighters escaped into the sewers. Most were suffocated by the gas. Among the hundred who were killed at Mila 18 was the commander of the uprising, Mordechai Anielewicz.

On May 16, Stroop reported to his superiors that the Warsaw ghetto 'is no longer in existence'. Street by street, his men then dynamited the buildings, reducing the whole ghetto area to rubble.

In all, 7,000 Jews – fighters and unarmed ghetto dwellers alike – had been killed in the fighting. A further 30,000 were deported to Treblinka, where they were murdered. Others were deported to Majdanek, Poniatowa and Trawniki, where most of them were later killed. A total of 631 bunkers were destroyed.

For crushing the Warsaw ghetto uprising, Stroop was awarded the Iron Cross, First Class. In September 1943 he was sent to Greece to fight the growing partisan movement there. In 1951 he was hanged in Warsaw for war crimes.

top
A Jew surrenders, and comes out of the rubble.

left
German soldiers stand in the ghetto, next to the wall, watching as the ghetto burns, and the pall of smoke drifts to the Polish side.

left
German artillerymen fire into ghetto houses, which are systematically reduced to rubble.

above, left stamp
A Polish stamp issued in 1948, on the 5th anniversary of the Warsaw ghetto uprising.

above, right stamp
An Israeli stamp, issued in 1988, on the 45th anniversary of the first day of the Warsaw ghetto uprising: the day chosen by the government of Israel for the annual Heroes and Martyrs Memorial Day (*Yom Hazikaron l'Shoah v-l'Gvurah*). The stamp shows the leader of the uprising, Mordechai Anielewicz.

Days of revolt

What we have experienced cannot be described in words. We are aware of one thing only: what has happened has exceeded our dreams. The Germans ran twice from the ghetto…

Keep well, my dear. Perhaps we shall meet again. But what really matters is that the dream, of my life has come true. Jewish self-defence in the Warsaw ghetto has become a fact. Jewish armed resistance and retaliation have become a reality. I have been witness to the magnificent heroic struggle of the Jewish fighters.

Mordechai Anielewicz, in a letter to Yitzhak Zuckerman, shortly before Anielewicz was killed in the fighting

We sat in the dark, scores of Jewish fighters, still carrying our weapons, surrounded by thousands of eager and expectant Jews. Was it not May Day? The feeling of responsibility lay heavy on our hearts, on our conscience, and gave no respite.

The crowded, cowering masses of Jews huddled around us waited for a word of hope from the fighters' lips. We were bewildered and lost. What should we say to them? What could we say to ourselves? How terrible was this feeling of helplessness! How grave the responsibility we felt as the last desperate Hebrew warriors! We could not hold out against the Germans' consuming fire for long without water or food or weapons.

Zivia Lubetkin, recalling 1 May 1943

WARSAW GHETTO: AFTER THE REVOLT

right
A girl with arms raised, drawn in the Warsaw ghetto in 1943 by Halina Olomucki. Her drawings, although scorched at the time, were smuggled by friends to the 'Aryan' side of Warsaw. Born in 1921, Halina Olomucki was deported to Majdanek after the uprising, and from there taken to Auschwitz. She survived the war, returned to Warsaw and then studied at the Lodz Academy of Art before emigrating to Paris in 1957, and to Israel in 1972.

opposite, top
Jews from the Toebbens factories in the Warsaw ghetto being taken on 21 April 1943 to the Umschlagplatz deportation railway sidings.

opposite, bottom
A Jewish boy surrenders.

In the Warsaw ghetto, at noon on 20 April 1943 – the third day of the revolt – a German industrialist Walther Toebbens (from Bremen) ordered the 10,000 Jewish labourers in his military uniform factories to assemble at the Umschlagplatz railway deportation sidings the next morning. Their destination, he told them truthfully, was not the dreaded Treblinka, but factories that he had set up a hundred miles away, near Lublin, at Trawniki and Poniatowa. On April 21 his workers set off. They could take with them whatever they could carry. Also leaving that day were the workers employed by another German industrialist, Fritz Schultz. Both men had enriched themselves, and their shareholders, by the exploitation of Jewish labour, charging their Jewish workers large sums of money for the work certificates that had protected them from deportations.

As Toebbens had promised, the deportees worked at Trawniki and Poniatowa. But starting on 2 November 1943 and continuing without interruption for three days, almost all of them were killed – 8,000 at Trawniki and 14,000 at Poniatowa. This killing was part of what the SS callously called the 'Harvest Festival'.

A further 18,000 Jews had been deported from the Warsaw ghetto to Majdanek concentration camp immediately after the uprising. They too were killed in the executions starting on November 2. Like many dates when mass killings took place, this one was deliberately chosen by the Germans. It was part of what was known as the 'Goebbels calendar', significant dates of the Jewish religion or history. In this case, the day chosen was that on which the British government had issued the Balfour Declaration in 1917, promising the Jewish people a 'National Home' in Palestine. (In 1993 a fiftieth anniversary memorial meeting of the 'Harvest Festival' killings was held in London, in the House of Lords – of which both Lord Balfour, who made the promise, and Lord Rothschild, to whom it was made, were members.)

During and after the Warsaw ghetto uprising, several thousand Jews managed to escape to the 'Aryan' side of the city. There they hid, dependent for the most part on the goodwill of those Poles who were prepared to give them shelter, and were willing to take the risk of sheltering them. Some of those in hiding, among them

the historian Emanuel Ringelblum, his wife and son, were betrayed to the Germans and killed. Others managed to survive in hiding until the end of the war.

A few small groups of Jews survived within the ghetto area, hiding in the few underground bunkers that had not been detected. But one by one almost all these bunkers were found, and those hiding in them killed. In September 1943 the Germans sent in Polish forced labourers to demolish whatever walls and structures were still standing. A survivor of the uprising, Israel Gutman – who after the uprising had been sent first to Majdanek and then to Auschwitz, and who later published a history of the Warsaw ghetto – has written: 'Those who still remained in hiding evidently met their deaths during these demolition activities, although a few individuals continued to live in dug-outs, totally cut off from nature, light and human company.'

When news of the Warsaw ghetto revolt reached the Vilna ghetto there was a sense of wonderment. On 1 May 1943, while the battle was still raging in Warsaw, a twenty-two-year-old poet, Hirsh Glik, brought a poem he had just written to a group of writers who had gathered for one of their regular evening discussions on Yiddish literature. 'Now listen carefully,' he told his friends, 'I'll sing it to you.' A fellow-poet recalled: 'He began to sing it softly, but full of excitement. His eyes glowed with little sparks. "The hour for which we yearned will yet arrive." Where did he get his faith? His voice became firmer. He tapped out the rhythm with his foot, as if he were marching.'

Hirsh Glik's song was soon to be widely heard in the Vilna ghetto, in other ghettos, and among the Jewish partisans hiding and fighting in the forests. It became a song of hope, the battle hymn of oppressed Jewry. Itself inspired by the Warsaw ghetto revolt, the song was to inspire tens of thousand of Jews in their efforts to survive.

In 1944, Glik was deported from the Vilna ghetto to a slave labour camp in Estonia. There all trace of him was lost. His song, known as 'The Partisan Song', continues to be sung at Jewish gatherings worldwide that commemorate the Holocaust and Jewish resistance.

THE PARTISAN SONG (1st stanza)

Yiddish:
Zog nit keynmol az du geyst dem letstn veg
Chotsh himlen blayene farshteln bloye teg
Kumen vet noch undzer oysgebenkte sho
S'vet a poyk ton undzer trotmir zenen do!

English:
Never say that you have reached the very end
Though leaden skies a bitter future may portend
The hour for which we yearned will yet arrive
And our marching step will thunder: 'We survive!'

A survivor recalls

The Germans stopped us on the road near the new huts, and ordered us to pull off our shoes. I said loudly: 'It seems to me that we are being led to the grave.'

I looked around and saw naked women in a circle with arms raised aloft... I could see a naked woman calling to her mother-in-law, 'Mother, till we meet again in the next world!' In one of the rooms of the hut, three women were sorting out the clothing. It occurred to me that I could join them and take part in the sorting, but I could not leave my child....

We undressed quickly and, our arms uplifted, we went into the direction of the ditches we had dug ourselves. The graves which were two metres deep were full of naked bodies.

My neighbour from the hut, with her fourteen-year-old, fair-haired and innocent looking daughter seemed to be looking for a comfortable place. While they were approaching the place an SS man charged his rifle and told them: 'Don't hurry.' Nevertheless we lay down quickly, in order to avoid looking at the dead. My little daughter was quaking with fear and asked me to cover her eyes. I embraced her head; my left hand I put on her eyes while in my right I held her hands. In this way we lay down, our faces turned downwards.

Shots were fired; I felt a sharp pain in my left hand, and the bullet pierced the skull of my daughter...

One of only very few **survivors** of the Poniatowa massacre

GHETTO REVOLTS

Survivors are often asked, 'Why did you not resist?' Their answer: How can civilians resist soldiers? How can unarmed and starving people resist? How can those who saw as their first duty to stay with elderly parents resist? How can parents of young children resist, rather than guard their children as best they could? Why should people resist when they are told they are to be deported to somewhere where they will have work and food? How can people resist who know that as a result of taking up arms they will provoke reprisals of the most savage sort: the killing of hundreds of defenceless people? Why should people resist whose hope is to survive in hiding?

There is also another set of questions in reply to the question, 'Why did you not resist?' They are: Did you know that there were revolts in many ghettos, not just the Warsaw ghetto? (*see map below*). Did you know that tens of thousands of Jews escaped from the ghettos to the forests, to protect Jews in hiding, and to fight the Germans? (*see pages 100–1*). Did you know that thousands of instances of individual acts of defiance and courage have been recorded? Did you know that Jews were active in the partisan movements of every conquered country? (*see pages 112–13*). Did you know that there were even revolts in the death camps, including Auschwitz? (*see pages 126–7*).

above right

Gole Mire. A lifelong Communist, she was sentenced to fifteen years in prison by the Polish authorities in 1933. In September 1939 she escaped from prison, and in September 1942 helped unite the Jewish political groups in Cracow into a single resistance organization of some 300 members. Imprisoned after the Cracow uprising, she was among a group of Jewish women prisoners who attacked their guards while being marched from one prison to another. During the struggle she was killed by German machine-gun fire.

right

Map showing some of the ghettos in which Jewish revolts took place.

The will to resist was everywhere stronger than the ability to prevent the slaughter. The fighting appeals that were pasted up in the ghettos offered no real chance of survival through resistance, but advocated putting up a fight to show that the instinct of self-defence was not dead, even if there was no possibility of 'victory'. The appeal posted up inside the Bialystok ghetto by the Jewish Self-Defence Organization included the phrase: 'Fight for life to the last breath.'

Traditionally, Jews have always defended themselves when they had the arms to do so. The Jews of Zamosc, in Poland, took part in the town's successful defence against the Chmielnicki massacres in the seventeenth century. The Jews of Starodub, in Russia, drove away the pogromists in the nineteenth century. In the 1930s, Polish Jews beat off repeated attacks by anti-Semites.

Because of the strength of the German occupation forces, resistance could be crushed before it could acquire strength of its own. On 22 December 1942 members of the Jewish Fighting Organization in Cracow, led by Adolf (Dolek) Liebeskind, attacked a

café used by the SS and Gestapo. Yitzhak Zuckerman, who had come from the Warsaw ghetto that day, at great risk to himself, took part in the attack, in order, he later wrote, 'to save what could be saved – at least honour'. Zuckerman managed to return to Warsaw. The other members of the Organization were tracked down by the Germans. One of them, Judah Tenenbaum, snatching a pistol from a German, killed one soldier before he was shot by bursts of machine-gun fire. Liebeskind was also killed. A few weeks before his death he had remarked: 'We are fighting for three lines in the history books.'

A few of Liebeskind's group survived, intending, as his wife Rivka later recalled, 'to set up hide-outs, to work in forest, and to enable Jews to hide' because they hoped they would be able 'to save at least someone to relate our story'.

The story of Czestochowa illustrates the near-impossibility of making a stand, and the terrible consequences that could ensue. In the Czestochowa ghetto, on 4 January 1943, several young men and women, members of the Jewish Fighting Organization,

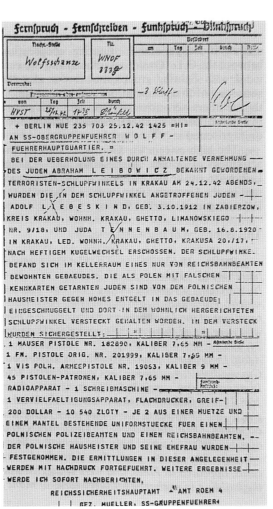

were caught up in a 'selection' for deportation. They possessed only a single pistol and one knife. Their leader, Mendel Fiszlewicz, used the pistol to attack and wound the German commander of the 'action'. After the first shot, Fiszlewicz's pistol jammed, and he was killed by one of the guards. As a reprisal, the Germans took twenty-five men out of the line-up for deportation, and shot them on the spot. As a further reprisal, 300 women and children were sent to nearby Radomsko, where the deportation to Treblinka was actually taking place; all 300 were gassed on arrival at Treblinka.

left
A telegram sent to Hitler's headquarters, describing the defeat of the Jewish Fighting Organization in Cracow. It reads: 'Berlin, 25.12.42 – to SS Lieutenant-General Wolff – Führer's headquarters. In searching a terrorist hiding place in Cracow which became known to us during continuous interrogations of the Jew Abraham Leibowitz, the Jews who were found there on the evening of 24 December, 1942 – Adolf Liebeskind, born 3.10.1912 in Zabierzow, Cracow district, residing in the Cracow ghetto, 9/18 Limanowskiego, and Juda Tennenbaum, born 16.8.1920 in Cracow, single, residing in the Cracow ghetto 20/17 Krakusa, were shot after heavy fire exchange. The hiding place was located in the cellar of a building, occupied only by German railway officials. The Jews, possessing forged identity cards, appeared as Poles, and were smuggled into the building in exchange for large sums of money by the concierge, who hid them there in the hiding place, which was arranged as a dwelling. In the hiding place were confiscated: 1 Mauser pistol, Nr 182890, calibre 7.65 mm, 1 FN pistol orig. Nr 201999, calibre 7.65 mm, 1 Vis. Polish army pistol, Nr 19063, calibre 9 mm, 45 bullets for 7.65 mm calibre pistol, 1 radio, 1 typewriter, I duplicating machine, 1 small printing press, 200 dollars, 10,540 zlotys, 2 uniforms of a Polish policeman and of a German railway official, each consisting of a hat and a coat. The Polish concierge and his wife were arrested. The investigations in this matter are being continued with emphasis. I shall report immediately further results.
Reichs-Security Head Office, (signed) Mueller, SS-Major-General.'

above, far left
Adolf (Dolek) Liebeskind, leader of the Jewish Fighting Organization in the Cracow ghetto.

THE KOVNO GHETTO

right
Soup distribution in the ghetto. This and the two photographs opposite were taken by Zvi Kadushin (later George Kadish) who survived the war. He took hundreds of photographs, risking his life each time: photographing by Jews was strictly forbidden by the Germans. Most of his outside pictures were taken through a buttonhole in his overcoat.

opposite, above
Even newborn babies wore the yellow star – on their swaddling clothes.

opposite, below
Selling bread illegally in a ghetto street. This man was shot a few days after this photograph was taken.

More than 30,000 Jews lived in Kovno on the eve of the Second World War. With the German invasion of Poland, several thousand Polish Jewish refugees found sanctuary there. In 1940 the city came under Soviet rule. On 21 June 1941 – the day of the German invasion of the Soviet Union – several hundred Jews were seized in the streets of Kovno by Lithuanian mobs, and murdered. Two days later the German army arrived. The killings continued, both by Lithuanians and Germans. A Lithuanian mob burst into the suburb of Slobodka, across the river from Kovno, on June 25, killing a thousand Jews, among them Mordechai Yatkunski, a leading Lithuanian Zionist. For several weeks, Jews were taken almost daily to the forts surrounding the city, and killed there. The Ninth Fort become synonymous with mass murder.

On 10 July 1941 two senior Lithuanian officials, Kovno's mayor and its military commander, announced, with German approval, the establishment of a ghetto in Slobodka, where – after the June slaughter – 5,000 of Kovno's remaining 35,000 Jews lived. All 30,000 Jews living in the main city were forced into the ghetto. Each Jew had to wear two yellow stars, one on the left side of all visible clothing, and the other on the back.

The ghetto was divided into a Small and Large Ghetto, separated by a footbridge. A Jewish Council sought to regulate life as normally as possible, and a Jewish police force kept order. A distinguished physician, Dr Elchanan Elkes, became head of the Council. He worked tirelessly to mitigate the hardships of ghetto life.

On 4 October 1941 the Germans surrounded the Jewish contagious diseases hospital, locked the doors, barred the windows and set the building on fire. All

sixty-two people who were there at the time – Dr Dawidowicz, two nurses and all the patients – were killed. That day, the patients in the ghetto's General Hospital and the inhabitants of the Small Ghetto, were taken to the Ninth Fort and killed.

On October 28 the senior SS officer in Kovno, Helmut Rauca, ordered all the ghetto inmates to Democracy Square. There, during the course of a whole day – in what was known as the 'Great Action' – he selected 10,000 Jews, all of whom were sent to the Small Ghetto for twenty-four hours, and then to the Ninth Fort, where they were killed. By December 1942 only 16,000 Jews were still alive in the ghetto: 19,000 had been killed.

The Kovno ghetto – like the Warsaw ghetto until the uprising of 1943, like the Lodz ghetto until the final deportations of 1944 – relied for its survival on work done for the German-run factories in the ghetto workshops, which employed 2,000 Jews, and at the nearby airport, a transit point from Germany to the Russian front, where 8,000 Jews were employed. Those 10,000, who had work permits, also had rations on which they and their families could survive. Those without work were in danger of starvation, arrest and execution.

The Jewish Council, led by Dr Elkes, made strenuous efforts to ameliorate hunger and hardship, feeding 2,000 Jews, mainly women and children, of whom the Germans were told nothing. Had they known about them, they would have been sent to the Ninth Fort. The Council also organized cultural events, concerts, debates, lectures and sports activities in an attempt to maintain morale. Religious and Zionist gatherings took place. A physician, Dr Moses Brauns, organized a medical system that had as its prime task the control of contagious diseases, lest the Germans used the excuse of disease to destroy the ghetto altogether.

Deportations from Kovno to slave labour camps in Estonia began on 26 October 1943. That day, the first train with children and old people locked into its wagons was sent to Auschwitz. The 'status' of the Kovno ghetto was officially changed: it became a concentration camp. The chance of 'living through' the German occupation

was dwindling. On 25 December 1943, however, sixty-four slave labourers escaped from the Ninth Fort.

In March 1944, after a tenacious German search, 1,200 Jews in hiding – those of whom the Germans had earlier known nothing – were found and killed. Fewer than a hundred remained in hiding. Between 8 and 11 July 1944, as Soviet forces approached Kovno, the surviving 8,000 Jews still working in the ghetto were sent westward, the women to Stutthof, the men to Dachau. Dr Elkes died in Dachau. Dr Brauns, who was also deported to Dachau, survived.

An estimated 200 Jewish children from Kovno survived the war, hidden by Lithuanians in the city and in the nearby countryside.

DEFIANCE, A PAINTER AND THREE SONGS

Defiance took many forms. In large ghettos, Jewish uprisings led to days and even weeks of fighting. In smaller ghettos, Jewish fighting units were crushed within a single day, even in a few hours. Acts of individual defiance might last a few minutes, yet each one represented the determination of a people marked out for death not to die without a struggle, despite the overwhelming military might of the conqueror, despite the fierce ideological determination of the Nazi machine to blot out Jewish life in its entirety.

Thousands of individual acts of Jewish resistance, defiance and courage are recorded: by Jewish eye-witnesses, by local bystanders and by the Germans themselves. These acts did not only involve taking up arms, or wielding a knife against the enemy. On 22 July 1942 the chairman of the Jewish Council in Warsaw, Adam Czerniakow, was ordered by the Germans to assemble 6,000 Jews a day for deportation. He took his own life rather than comply.

When – also in the Warsaw ghetto – the order reached Janusz Korczak for his orphans to be deported, he refused offers of a place in hiding for himself. He would go with his children wherever they were being taken. Earlier he had written, 'Children are not the people of tomorrow, but people today. They are entitled to be taken seriously. They have a right to be treated by adults with tenderness and respect, as equals. They should be allowed to grow into whoever

right
The road to the Ninth Fort, with its line of tall trees, painted from an upstairs window in the ghetto by Esther Lurie: Jews can be seen walking along the road uphill towards the Ninth Fort.

above
Esther Lurie, a self-portrait drawn in the ghetto, 1941.

they were meant to be – the unknown person inside each of them is the hope for the future.' Korczak went with his children to Treblinka, and was killed with them there.

Acts of individual defiance took many forms. In the Kovno ghetto, Zvi Kadushin had taken photographs at risk of his life so that some photographic record might survive. Also in the Kovno ghetto, Esther Lurie did a series of paintings and drawings of Jewish life and fate. She was living in Palestine, but was visiting Kovno when war came, and was unable to return home. In 1944 she was among the women deported from Kovno to Stutthof concentration camp on the Baltic. There she was liberated by Soviet soldiers and made her way back

to Palestine. After the war she was refused permission by the Communist authorities in Lithuania to go back to look for her paintings. The secretary to the Jewish Council, Avraham Tory, who had escaped from the ghetto, had managed to smuggle out several dozen originals, and photographs of others. They were first exhibited in Tel Aviv in 1951.

Another form of individual – and collective – defiance was song. Jewish songsters had always had an ear for the tragic and the absurd. The Yiddish language rang out in the ghettos with their compositions. To sing was to show that the human spirit refused to be daunted. Even songs of sorrow could end with defiance – and hope.

THE OLD MOTHER

An old mother sits and ponders,
It's already late at night,
But still she sits by the window, grief-stricken,
And waits for her child.

The good old days are gone now,
Seems like eternity;
But don't give up hope,
Courageous Jewish nation!

refrain:
A ghetto song rings through the night,
An old Jewish mother anxiously cries:
Where is my child?
Cast to the wind.
Tell me, please: Where is my child?

Oh, mother-dear,
You'll find no rest here,
Everything you see is dark,
Suffering and torment weigh on your heart,
Mother-dear.

But now be brave,
Things will improve –
The day will arrive
When you will be free,
Free from tyranny's yoke.

IT SOON WILL BE A YEAR GONE BY

It's only been a few short days,
Untold numbers dragged away;
From here to there in dead of night,
It isn't far to the Ninth Fort.
They rip and tear us limb from limb,
They never tire out, the fiends;
When will this horror ever stop?
They capture us without a thought!

No more strength is left in us,
Every hour seems the worst;
But surely there will come the day,
When from the ghetto we'll be free.
Have courage, brothers, don't despair,
This dark night will disappear;
The sun will then shine brightly down
And call to us: 'Come out now, come!'

YIDDISH TANGO

Play a tango for me about peacetime,
Let it be real peacetime, not just dreamtime,
So Hitler and his state
Get the punishment they rate,
Oh, what a little dance for us we'd make!

above
A songster in the Kovno ghetto: a photograph taken by Zvi Kadushin.

left
(far left) lyrics by Percy Haid, born in Dortmund, a pianist and accordionist at Café Monika in Kovno in the 1930s. He wrote this song after 1,300 children were murdered in March 1944. Surviving Dachau, he became a composer in Chicago; (left) the last stanzas of a song whose lyricist is unknown; (left, below) the lyricist of 'Yiddish Tango', Ruven Tsarfat, died in Dachau.

A ghetto diary

The people, bit by bit, create, notate, and express the pain of Jewish life in songs. Here, the ghetto dweller's life is recounted and sung about. Every song is a slice of life from a very special era. A ghetto song begins with pain and misfortune and ends with the hope of better things to come, of a bright and happy future.

Ilya Gerber, aged eighteen when he wrote this diary entry in the Kovno ghetto on 4 December 1942. He did not survive the war

ESCAPE TO THE PARTISANS

right
The Bielski 'family camp' in the Nalibocka forest, a photograph taken in the summer of 1944, shortly before liberation. A year earlier the Germans had launched a major assault on the Bielski partisans, causing heavy losses, but from the spring of 1944 German patrols were reluctant to leave the main roads and towns. The smaller towns were by then in partisan hands.

Many Jews tried to escape from the ghettos, to join partisan groups in nearby forests. Jewish partisan groups were among the first organized adversaries of the German army, disrupting communication and destroying German military stores.

Three Jewish brothers – Tuvia, Asael and Zus – from a village a few miles from Nowogrodek, where they and their family were the only Jews, formed a Jewish partisan group in March 1942. Tuvia was the leader. By December 1942 the group was 150 strong, with nineteen rifles and two machine guns between them. In an ambush at the end of the year, nineteen members of the group – including four women – were killed. Tuvia Bielski's wife and nephew were among the dead.

By mid-1943 the Bielski group was sheltering and protecting more than 1,200 Jewish women and children who had escaped from the ghettos of western Belorussia. Their camp, built below ground in the Nalibocka forest, included a flour-mill and bakery, a cattle shed, sausage factory, leather works, and shoe- and watch-repair workshops. The largest underground dwelling sheltered fifty people.

Captured German weapons were repaired at a metal workshop. There was a hospital for contagious diseases – principally cholera – and a clinic. At the centre of the camp were a kitchen and bread distribution hut. There was also a school. Tuvia Bielski later wrote that it was set up 'primarily to separate the children from the atmosphere of fighting'.

Another Jewish partisan group, based a few miles from the Bielski group, was led by Shimon Zorin. He sheltered 800 elderly Jewish men, women and children.

Jewish partisan groups existed throughout central and eastern Poland. They were repeatedly attacked by the Germans, who used substantial military forces, even aircraft, against them. Near Vilna, Jewish partisan groups, active in the Narocz and Rudnicka forests, were joined by Jews escaping from the Kovno and Grodno

ghettos, and from smaller ghettos and labour camps throughout the region.

Small Jewish partisan groups were active in the Bialystok region. In southern Poland, Jews who had escaped from the Cracow ghetto struggled to survive in the Niempolomicka and Dulcza forests. Those in the Dulcza forest were joined by Jews who escaped from the Radomysl ghetto. Almost all were tracked down and killed. The same fate befell most of the Jews who escaped from the Pinczow ghetto to join the two partisan groups in the Kozubowski forest.

During 1942 as many as 40,000 Jews escaped from the ghettos of central Poland to the forests. They had hardly any weapons, brackish water, almost no food – except what the forests could provide – and they faced the ravages of fierce heat and insects in summer, violent autumn storms, and sub-zero temperatures in winter. Fewer than a thousand survived the war.

Some local villagers helped Jews. But many betrayed

them to the Germans, who knew that a small monetary reward, or even extra food – a pound of sugar, a litre of vodka or a carton of cigarettes – could be sufficient incentive to betray.

In the Parczew forest, two 'family camps' were established by Jewish partisans at the time of the deportations of 1942. But of more than 2,000 people being sheltered there, only 200 survived the repeated German attacks and two consecutive winters. During the final year of the war a Polish partisan battalion, commanded by a Jewish officer, Alexander Skotnicki, used the Parczew forest as its base to attack German rail communications.

Skotnicki had one entirely Jewish company under his command, led by Yehiel Grynszpan. At first this company had only two rifles and one pistol. After raiding German military outposts, they acquired seven rifles, ammunition and a number of grenades. As many as 150 of Grynszpan's Jewish partisans survived the war.

Among the many small Jewish groups who fought in the forests was one in the Skorodnica forest. It had a hundred members, with fewer than a dozen pistols between them. When the Germans attacked, seventy-five partisans were killed, but the survivors fought on, and were even able to hide in their midst a number of Jews whom they had helped to escape from nearby ghettos. Few of these partisans survived. One of them, Hershel Zimmerman (later known as Harold Werner), told the story of this group in his memoirs.

Conversation among partisans

Did you study, in High School?

I did.

Did you study at University?

I did.

So what does it give you. Can you make a thicker soup out of it?

No.

above
A map showing some of the forests to which Jews escaped from the ghettos, hid, and fought the Germans.

panel of four photographs, left
(top left) Tuvia Bielski, who survived the war: he lived first in Israel and then in the United States; (top right) Zus Bielski, in charge of intelligence operations in the forest: he survived the war and emigrated to the United States; (bottom left) Asael Bielski, second in command of the group, who joined the Soviet army after the liberation of the Nalibocka forest, and was killed in action against the Germans in January 1945; (bottom right) two of Bielski's partisans: Yankel Abramovitch (left) and Yudel Levin, both of whom survived.

HIDDEN CHILDREN

A million and a half Jewish children were murdered in the Holocaust. An estimated twenty to thirty thousand children survived the war in hiding. These 'hidden children' were those, under the age of fourteen, many of them babies, whose parents managed to find someone – a non-Jewish person or family, or a Christian institution – with whom they could live without their Jewishness becoming known. Many hidden children led the life of a Christian child, saying Christian prayers, attending church and school, becoming part of a Christian family circle, taking on a Christian-sounding first name.

A few hidden children survived alone, in forests and barns, living from day to day with the threat hanging over them of capture and execution. All of those in hiding had to make daily efforts to hide the fact that they were Jewish. One slip could mean betrayal, arrest and deportation. After the war, most hidden children discovered that their parents had been murdered, that they were the sole survivors of once large families.

A peasant woman in a Polish hamlet heard her neighbours say, of four- or five-year-old Renée Lindenberg (now Kuker): 'Throw her into the well.' The peasant woman replied: 'She's not a dog after all,' and Renée was saved. Some children were hidden by many different families and individuals: '22 different places' writes Lotty Heymans (Rozendaal) of Utrecht; '2 German soldiers' writes Susan Blum (Bendor) of Budapest; 'Various Poles' writes Joseph Kutrzeba of Lodz; 'Nuns' writes Batia Friedman (Gortler) of Przemysl.

It was not until forty-five years after the end of the Second World War that the lives of the hidden children became widely recognized as an integral part of the Holocaust. In 1991 a meeting was held in New York, organized by those who had survived the war as children in hiding. A second such meeting was organized two years later in Jerusalem. More than a thousand hidden children came to the first of these meetings. On notice boards at both, those who attended pinned up appeals for people who might have known their parents, or known the children themselves in hiding.

Under the auspices of the American-based Anti-Defamation League, whose president Abraham Foxman was himself a hidden child, the Hidden Child Foundation was set up in New York, to organize meetings, publish a newsletter and coordinate hidden child activities throughout the world. Each year saw new revelations: in 1999 it was learned that the head of the Munich Jewish community, Charlotte Knobloch, was a hidden child. Born in Munich in 1932, she survived the war in hiding with local farmers.

Stella Tzur, who was hidden in a barn in a Polish village, was sixteen in 1942. Recalling the farmer who first allowed her to live in his barn, she later wrote:

'I lay down in my hole and he covered it from above with bundles of straw. It was impossible to find me

there. They liked my knitting and I asked him to bring me more wool. I felt so secure. From behind my hiding place I could see the lovely landscape, fields and forests. The air was transparent and full of light, heaven and earth seemed to harmonize and prove the existence of a Creator.'

The farmer and his wife who hid Stella Tzur and her mother later also hid four Jews under their cowshed – for two years. Stella and her mother were then hidden by Lucyna and Marian Piechowicz.

Gisele Naichouler Feldman, born in Paris, was eleven when she was taken in by a children's sanitarium at Chavaniac, the former castle (and birthplace) of the Marquis de Lafayette. She later recalled: 'A very difficult thing for me was having to attend a Catholic Church every Sunday. I pretended to be a Catholic also, and even sang in the choir. I excused my ignorance of prayers and so did my brother by the explanations that our parents were not religious. I memorized all the necessary prayers, but couldn't take the wafer. Still, every Sunday, I felt like a fraud and had guilt feelings pretending to be someone I was not.' As a teacher in the United States after the war, in Michigan, Gisele Feldman used her personal story to introduce her pupils to the Holocaust.

In 1998 Miriam Winter told the story, in her book *Trains*, of how, when she was eight, her parents gave her to a stranger in the Polish town of Ozarow, near Lublin. She had to endure, in addition to the daily fear of discovery and capture, the abuse and exploitation of her rescuers. In 1945 she realized she was the sole survivor of her family. She emigrated to the United States. Reviewing her book in 1999, *The Hidden Child* journal wrote: 'A successful writer, teacher, director and actor, Winter continues to wrestle with the demons of a child trapped in the Holocaust. Mostly, she still tries to remember her mother's face.'

In 1993, following the collapse of Communism in Eastern Europe, a Czech Hidden Children association was formed, with a hundred members. They decided to compile a list of those non-Jewish families who had taken them in and saved their lives. More than thirty families were identified and honoured.

In 1999 the World Conference of Hidden Children

above
Abraham Foxman with Bronislawa Kurpi, his Polish Catholic nanny who hid and saved him.

above right
Robert Krell (then Robbie Munnick) as a hidden child, photographed with a neighbour's dog.

opposite, above and below
The barn where Stella Tzur was hidden by the Piechowicz family (a photograph taken in the 1990s) and the view from the one window through which she dared to look.

was held in Prague. Recalling the first conference that had been held in New York eight years earlier, Eva Benesova of Prague reflected: 'Only there could I rid myself of the burden of having been a hidden child.' Ann Shore told the Prague gathering: 'We are here to remember the past, celebrate our survival, and help each other heal.'

Abraham Foxman was hidden as a young boy in Vilna. He was later head of the Anti-Defamation League in the United States. He told the first Hidden Child conference in 1991: 'We hidden children have a mission, a mission to proclaim and recognize goodness. For the first fifty years after the Holocaust survivors bore witness to evil, brutality and bestiality. Now is the time for us, for our generation to bear witness to goodness. For each one of us is living proof that even in hell, even in that hell called the Holocaust, there was goodness, there was kindness, and there was love and compassion.'

'RIGHTEOUS GENTILES'

Saving Jewish lives

Many non-Jews put forward plans to help Jews escape from Nazi-dominated Europe. On 3 September 1944, as the result of a suggestion first put forward by Winston Churchill's son Randolph, the evacuation began, by air, of 650 German, Austrian and Czech Jews from the partisan-held areas of Yugoslavia to Bari, in Allied-occupied Italy.

Also in Italy in 1944, in the German-held port of Fiume, the Germans arrested a senior Italian police officer, Giovanni Palatucci, who had helped more than five hundred Jewish refugees who had reached Italy from Yugoslavia, giving them 'Aryan' papers and sending them to safety in southern Italy. Palatucci was sent to Dachau where he died.

Jan Zabinski, director of the Warsaw Zoo, sheltered Jews in the zoo's abandoned animal cages. After hiding them in the cages, he and his wife Antonina found them permanent places of refuge in 'Aryan' Warsaw: 300 Jews were saved in this way. The Zabinskis also hid twenty Jews in their house in the zoo's grounds. When Zabinski was taken prisoner by the Germans after taking part in the Warsaw uprising of 1944, his wife continued his work, and helped bring food to Jews hiding in the ruins of the city.

Many thousands of non-Jews risked – and in many cases lost – their own lives to save a Jewish life. Some non-Jews – Christians, Muslims, atheists, men and women of all nations – saved more than one life: there were those who saved whole families and even several families.

Non-Jews who were caught helping Jews faced execution. The Polish Jewish historian Szymon Datner, who had escaped from the Bialystok ghetto to fight with a Jewish partisan unit, recorded after the war just how severe reprisals could be: 'In thirty-eight cases of Jews being saved by Poles, as established on the basis of one source, the Nazis murdered ninety-seven Poles, including thirty women, fourteen children and one infant.' From other documents and enquiries, Szymon Datner established that 343 Poles had been shot in the Bialystok region for helping Jews. Among those shot were forty-two Polish children under the age of thirteen.

At Belzec, the monument to the 600,000 Jews murdered there also honours 1,500 Poles 'who tried to save Jews', and were killed at Belzec.

On 19 August 1953 the Israeli Parliament – the Knesset – passed a law making it the duty of the State of Israel to recognize the work done by non-Jews in saving Jewish lives during the Second World War. An 'expression of honour' was awarded, in the name of the Jewish people, to every non-Jewish person or family who took the risk of hiding and saving Jews. The Hebrew phrase chosen for those to be honoured was *Sderot hassidei umot haolam* (the Righteous among the Nations of the World). They became known as 'Righteous Gentiles'.

A committee of eighteen Israeli judges and experts examines the evidence of rescue activity. This evidence has to be put forward, where possible, by the individual who was saved. At the Israeli Holocaust memorial, Yad Vashem, in Jerusalem, an Avenue of the Righteous was begun in 1962. Every non-Jew honoured for helping Jews escape deportation and death plants a tree, or has a tree planted in his or her name. Righteous Gentile medals and diplomas are both awarded.

One of the four Righteous Gentile awards given to Norway was a collective one, in honour of all the

top
A stamp issued by the Czech Republic on 1 February 1995, to honour Premysl Pitter, a Czech Protestant educator, social worker and author who, between the two world wars, founded a school in Prague for poor children. During the German occupation of Prague, he took in Jewish children. When questioned by the Gestapo he claimed that they were not Jewish, and then smuggled them out of Prague to a children's home in the village of Myto. In all, Pitter, and his assistant Olga Fierz, saved a hundred Jewish children from deportation; thirty-five of them live today in Israel. On 13 October 1964, Pitter (who after the war went to Switzerland as a refugee from Communism) was presented with Israel's Righteous Gentile medal. Olga Fierz received a Diploma of the Righteous.

above
A Belgian stamp issued in honour of Yvonne Nevejean, as part of a stamp series with the theme 'famous women'. More than 4,500 Belgian Jewish children were found safe homes with Christian families, convents, boarding schools, orphanages and sanatoriums, many as a result of her efforts as director of the National Works for Childhood, of which she became the director in 1940. On several occasions she was able to rescue children (of whose whereabouts the Nazis had been alerted) a few hours before they were to be deported.

members of the Norwegian resistance movement, which was active helping Jews escape across the border to Sweden. The medals given to Danish citizens included one that was made to the King of Denmark in honour of the whole Danish nation, for enabling almost all Denmark's Jews to be taken across the sea to Sweden

all Denmark's Jews to be taken across the sea to Sweden on the eve of their intended deportation to the death camps. The Danish wartime underground also asked that members who participated in the rescue of Jews should be honoured as a group, not individually.

Inspired by their pastor, André Trocmé, the French Protestant villagers of Le Chambon-sur-Lignon gave sanctuary to more than three thousand Jewish adults and children, and helped disperse them to other hiding places, and to safety in Switzerland. André Trocmé's cousin Daniel, who was caught hiding Jews, was sent to Buchenwald, where he died in April 1944.

In Holland, 250 families in the town of Nieuwland acted collectively to take in Jews, and feed, house and hide them until liberation.

When, in July 1944, the Germans rounded up all 1,500 Jews on the island of Rhodes, the Turkish Consul-General on the island, Selahattin Ulkumen, presented the local German commander with a list of fifty Jews whom he claimed were Turkish nationals, and demanded their release. The commander agreed, not wishing to antagonize neutral Turkey. Ulkumen was recognized as a Righteous Gentile in 1990. Also made a Righteous Gentile was Princess Alice of Greece, a great-granddaughter of Queen Victoria – and the mother of HRH Prince Philip – who hid and saved Jews in her home in Athens.

The total number of Righteous Gentiles honoured between 1962 and 1999 was 16,552. Not shown on the map are three Armenians, two Chinese, one Brazilian, one Portuguese – Consul de Sousa Mendes – and one Japanese – Consul Sugihara.

The phrase 'Righteous Gentile' has sometimes been seen as patronizing. For Jews, the word 'gentile' has the simple connotation of 'non-Jew'. In order not to sound patronizing, or specifically Christian, the phrase 'Righteous Gentile' was replaced in 1998 by 'Righteous Person' in Yad Vashem's publications.

top right
Towns and villages in Belgium where Jewish children were hidden by Christian institutions and families.

right
The number of 'Righteous Gentile' awards, country by country, granted by Israel between 1953 and 1999.

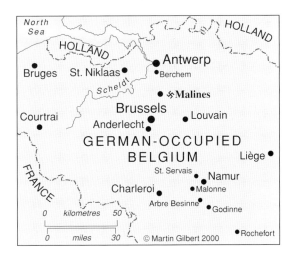

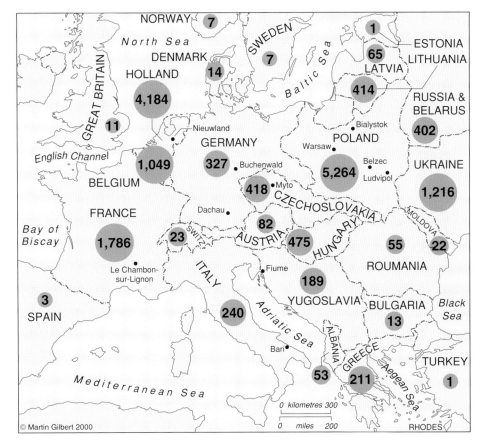

A survivor from Ludvipol

Next morning, when the peasant entered the barn he found us nearly frozen to death. Without thinking twice he brought all of us into his home. With tearful eyes he looked at his children and then pointed at ours and said: Oh, Lord, what was the sin of this little Jewish child?!... He told his wife to fix us a warm meal and invited us to climb up (on the stove) so that we could warm ourselves. Soon the warm meal was before us; we spent the whole day in his cottage.

EUROPEAN GOVERNMENTS THAT SAVED JEWS

above right
Danish Jews being rowed to safety.

Five countries refused all German pressure to deport the Jew living in their midst. As a result – in two cases only until direct German military intervention – they were successful in saving their Jewish populations. The German ability to put pressure on sovereign States, even those that were linked to them by alliances or ideological sympathies, thus had its limitations. In the last resort, it required the arrival of a German army of occupation to enable the deportation of the Jews to be put into effect.

FINLAND

In August 1942, while on a 'private unofficial holiday visit' to Finland, Himmler persuaded the Finnish leaders to deport all two thousand Jews then in Finland. Most were refugees who had left Germany and Austria before 1939. In February 1943 the first eight Jewish deportees were sent from Helsinki to Auschwitz, a journey of more than twelve hundred miles. Only one survived.

When news of the deportation of the eight Jewish refugees became known in Finland there were public protests by the opposition Social Democratic Party, by several Lutheran clergymen and by the Archbishop of Helsinki. As a result, the Finnish Cabinet refused to allow any further deportations.

DENMARK

Following the German occupation of Denmark in the spring of 1940, the Germans embarked on a policy of co-operation with the Danish authorities. But growing Danish resistance to the German occupation led the Germans to declare martial law on 28 August 1943 .

The SS hoped to use martial law to deport all Denmark's Jews, and also 'half-Jews' (whom the Nazis designated Jews because they had one Jewish parent). Opposition to the deportation was voiced publicly by King Christian X and by the heads of the Danish churches, who used their pulpits to urge the Danes to help the Jews. All Danish universities were closed down to enable students to help in the rescue effort.

The deportation was planned for the night of 1–2 October 1943. Warned in advance, Danish sea captains and fishermen ferried the endangered Jews across the sea to neutral Sweden: 7,906 were saved in this way.

There were 5,919 Jews, 1,301 'half-Jews' and 686 Christians who were married to Jews.

On searching for deportees, the Germans found only 500 Jews, mostly old people too frail to make the sea journey. They were sent to the Theresienstadt ghetto. Each month the Danish authorities asked about them, insisting they should not be harmed. As a result of this sustained scrutiny, 423 of the 500 survived the war. The Danish Jews who had been ferried to Sweden survived unmolested, as did a further 3,000 Jewish refugees who had reached Sweden before the outbreak of war, from Germany, Austria and Czechoslovakia.

ITALY AND ITALIAN-OCCUPIED REGIONS

As long as Mussolini ruled Italy, no Jews were deported to the death camps on Polish soil. They were protected, at times by Mussolini himself, but mostly through the determination of his military commanders in Italian-occupied Croatia, Greece, Albania and the Italian-occupied areas of the South of France. Only when Germany occupied Italy in 1943 were SS units able to move in, and the deportations to Auschwitz began.

THE VATICAN

On 16 October 1943 the Germans searched Rome for the Jews of the city – more than 7,000 – to be deported. A few days before the search, Pope Pius XII had personally ordered the Vatican clergy to open the sanctuaries of the Vatican to all 'non-Aryans' in need of refuge: 477 Jews were given shelter in the Vatican itself and in its sovereign enclaves in Rome; a further 4,238 Jews were given sanctuary in more than a hundred monasteries, convents and Church institutions throughout Rome. On the morning of October 16, when the round-up began, 5,615 of Rome's Jews could not be found. The 1,015 whom the Germans did discover were deported. The Vatican's Secretary of State, Cardinal Maglione, then asked for a meeting with the German military commander in Rome, General Stahl. After this meeting, Stahl sent a message to Himmler, warning that any further round-up of Jews in Rome would disturb Stahl's military plans to reinforce the German troops fighting the Allies in southern Italy. Himmler thereupon ordered a halt to the deportations.

BULGARIA

Starting on 10 March 1943, as a result of German pressure, 12,000 Jews from the Bulgarian-occupied zones of Thrace (formerly Greece) and Macedonia (formerly Yugoslavia) were deported to Treblinka and murdered. On 22 February 1943 Eichmann's emissary from the Reich Chief Security Office in Berlin, SS Captain Theodor Dannecker, had signed an agreement with the Bulgarian Commissioner for Jewish Affairs, Alexander Belev – who had already instituted a series of anti-Jewish measures in Bulgaria – for the deportation of the 48,565 Jews of pre-war Bulgaria. Several thousand had already been interned. But when the deportation order became known there was an outcry from the Bulgarian people, including many Orthodox church leaders.

In northern Bulgaria, farmers threatened to lie down on the railway tracks to halt the deportation trains. The King of Bulgaria, Boris III, also intervened. Although he was German, from the royal family of Coburg, he was opposed to the anti-Jewish measures then in force in Bulgaria. All Jews in custody were released, and the government rescinded the deportation order.

One influence on King Boris in his opposition to German demands had been the former Apostolic Delegate in Sofia, Cardinal Angelo Roncalli, the godfather to Boris's son. He urged the King not to allow the Jews of Bulgaria to be sent to Germany. From 1958

to 1963 he was Pope, as John XXIII. King Boris, summoned to Berlin by Hitler, died on 29 August 1943, three days after his return, in mysterious circumstances. He was forty-nine years old.

Bulgaria was the only country in Europe whose local Jewish population in 1945 – 49,172 – was larger than it had been before the war.

HUNGARY

On 17 April 1943, a month after Bulgaria's refusal to allow Bulgarian Jews to be deported, Hitler summoned the Hungarian Regent, Admiral Horthy, to Salzburg, and urged him to allow the Jews of Hungary to be 'resettled'. Horthy refused. 'The Jews cannot be exterminated or beaten to death,' he insisted. Hitler then set out his own virulent anti-Semitic perspective, telling Horthy:

'Where the Jews were left to themselves, as for instance in Poland, the most terrible misery and decay prevailed. They are just pure parasites. In Poland this state of affairs had been fundamentally cleared up. If the Jews there did not want to work, they were shot. If they could not work, they had to succumb. They had to be treated like tuberculosis bacilli, with which a healthy body may become infected. This was not cruel, if one remembered that even innocent creatures of nature, such as hares and deer, have to be killed, so that no harm is caused by them. Why should the beasts who wanted to bring us Bolshevism be spared more? Nations which did not rid themselves of Jews, perished. One of the most famous examples of this was the downfall of a people who were once so proud – the Persians, who now lead a pitiful existence as Armenians.'

Horthy rejected Hitler's arguments and pressure and returned to Budapest. The Jews of Hungary remained in Hungary. Horthy's refusal had been effective. But when the German army occupied Hungary in March 1944, bringing in its wake Eichmann and the SS, the 750,000 Jews then living within Hungary's extended borders were in immediate danger. Horthy's earlier refusal to deport them could not protect them from direct German and SS intervention.

JEWISH RESISTANCE MOVEMENTS

In every country under German rule, there were Jews who formed entirely Jewish resistance groups. Many fought in the forests, to which they had escaped from the ghettos and deportation round-ups.

In 1942, the Jewish resistance groups in German-occupied France united to form the *Armée Juive* (the Jewish Army). Its members attacked German military trucks and trains, and sabotaged factories making war equipment. In 1944 an enlarged Jewish resistance group, *Organisation Juive de Combat* (Jewish Fighting Organization), took part in the liberation of two French towns, Castres and Mazamet.

In French Algeria, a group of Jews, organized under the guise of a sports club, seized strategic positions in several cities in November 1942, helping the Allied landings in North Africa.

In Belgium, a Jewish defence organization, the

Comité de Défense des Juifs (CDJ – Jewish Defence Committee) was set up in September 1942. Communists and Zionists worked together, making contact with the Belgian resistance, initiating rescue and resistance operations, and working closely with the Belgian Catholic Church to find hiding places for Jewish children. The committee's most dramatic success was on the night of 19–20 April 1943, when a deportation train on the way to Auschwitz was derailed while still on Belgian soil, and many deportees escaped.

Members of the *Zydowska Organizacja Bojowa* (ZOB, the Jewish Fighting Organization) were active throughout German-occupied Poland, despite having to confront the military strength of the German army. Their actions inspired other Jews to feel it was possible to make a stand.

In Cracow, a group led by Heshek Bauminger carried

out acts of sabotage inside and outside the ghetto. After being caught in his hiding place, he turned his pistol on the Germans before killing himself with his last bullet. In Bedzin, Frumka Plotnicka worked on behalf of the Jewish Fighting Organization to set up a resistance group, and then took up arms with them. She was killed in battle with the Germans on 3 August 1943.

In the Bialystok ghetto, Haika Grosman was among the organizers of resistance. With five other Jewish women she was able to pose as a Pole and travel to other ghettos to co-ordinate resistance efforts. Her group – Antifascist Bialystok – also helped Jewish partisans in the forests. In Israel, from 1969 to 1981 and 1984 to 1988, Haika Grosman was a member of the parliament (Knesset). One of her colleagues in Antifascist Bialystok, Bronka Klibanski, became a leading Israeli historian of the Holocaust.

In Lublin, Jewish prisoners of war, captured while fighting in the Polish army in 1939, managed to escape from their prisoner-of-war camp, and formed a partisan unit, commanded by Shmuel Jegier.

In the Vilna ghetto, *Fareynegte Partizaner Organizatsye* (FOP, the United Partisan Organization) founded on 21 January 1942, stimulated resistance throughout the region. One of its leaders, Abba Kovner, appealed openly for armed struggle against the Nazis. After the destruction of the Vilna ghetto, Kovner commanded a Jewish partisan unit in the Rudnicka forest. After the war, in Israel, he helped create the Tel Aviv Museum of the Jewish Diaspora.

In the Kovno ghetto, Chaim Yellin, a writer and Communist, established the Anti-Fascist Struggle Organization in 1941. He later formed a united force of all resistance groups in the ghetto, including the Zionists. Over a period of several months he led 350 young Jews out of the ghetto to fight alongside the Soviet partisans in the Rudnicka forest, ninety miles east of Kovno. On 4 April 1944, while on a mission outside the ghetto, he was ambushed by the Germans, and later executed. Elsewhere in Lithuania, as many as 800 Jews fought as a unit alongside 3,000 Lithuanian anti-German partisans. A third of these Jews were killed in battle.

Jewish units were among the first partisan groups to fight behind German lines on Soviet soil. As many as 8,000 Jews fought in partisan units in Belorussia, and 3,000 in the Ukraine. When the slave labour camp at Skalat, in Eastern Galicia, was reached by Soviet partisans, the liberated slave labourers formed an all-Jewish partisan company, serving under experienced Soviet Jewish partisan commanders. In the Nalibocka forest in eastern Poland, as many as 3,000 Jews, in all-Jewish units, were among the 20,000 partisans active against the Germans.

At the outbreak of the war in 1939 seven hundred young Berlin Jews were employed in the Siemens Electrical Works. During 1940 a resistance organization was set up in the works under the leadership of Herbert Baum. In 1940 it had thirty members. At night, they pasted up leaflets calling for resistance against the Nazi regime. Members of the group also painted anti-Nazi slogans on the walls.

On 18 May 1942, Baum and his wife Marianne, and five of their group, including two non-Jews, Suzanne Wesse and Irene Walter, went to the Lustgarten, in the centre of the city only a few yards from where the Nazi burning of books had been organized in May 1933. There, they set fire to an anti-Bolshevik and anti-Jewish exhibition.

Four days later the Gestapo arrested Baum and his wife and three others. Within a week, Suzanne Wesse and Irene Walter had been arrested. In reprisal for the fire at the exhibition, the Gestapo rounded up five hundred Berlin Jews. Half were shot in prisons in the city. Half were sent to Sachsenhausen. Herbert Baum was tortured, but betrayed no one. According to his torturers he killed himself. Prisoners said he was tortured to death.

One of those arrested, Sala Kochmann, afraid lest she break down under torture, threw herself out of a window. She survived her fall, and with a broken spine was taken on a stretcher to her execution. Eighteen others were executed with her. Edith Fraenkel, another member of the group, who was twenty-one years old at the time of her arrest, was sent to Theresienstadt, and then to Auschwitz, where she died.

above
The memorial stone in the Berlin Jewish cemetery to the members of the Baum group executed in 1943, or killed in Auschwitz, giving their ages at the time of their execution. The inscription at the bottom reads: 'They fell in the battle for victory and freedom.'

JEWS IN THE ALLIED ARMIES

Before the Second World War, Martin Spitzer lived in the Czechoslovak town of Zilina. When, in 1942, the town was part of independent Slovakia, he managed to hide just before a round-up for deportation to Auschwitz. Of Zilina's 3,000 Jews, 2,900 were murdered, including his parents and brother. He escaped by train to Switzerland in an open goods wagon, hiding in a consignment of timber. Crossing into France, he was interned, and then released – and made his way to Gibraltar. Reaching England by sea, he joined a Czech Armoured Brigade attached to the Canadian forces then in England. About twenty per cent of the men in his unit were Jews. In 1944 they took part in the liberation of northern Europe; Spitzer lost a leg in the fighting. After the war he settled in Australia.

above right
Jewish soldiers in many Allied armies were issued prayer books with Jewish prayers, just as Christian soldiers had Christian prayer books. Some of these prayers were specially devised for those who would be going into action. In 1940 the British government's Stationery Office, with the authority of the Chief Rabbi, published its Prayer Book for Jewish members of the British Armed Forces; it was issued to every Jewish soldier. The book included the traditional prayers for the daily and Sabbath services, for the New Year and Day of Atonement, and for the Passover, Channukah and Purim festivals. It also contained special prayers, in Hebrew and English, for the sick and wounded, for the dying, and for those fallen in battle, as well as the 'prayer before a battle' shown here.

Jewish soldiers, sailors and airmen fought in all the Allied armies. Jewish doctors and nurses carried out their healing duties in every war zone.

Polish Jews fought from the first day of the war in defence of Poland. French, Dutch and Belgian Jews fought alongside their fellow-defenders when German troops attacked westward in May 1940. Yugoslav and Greek Jews were in action against the Germans in April 1941. British Jews served in all the branches of the armed forces, in Britain and overseas. Canadian, South African and American Jews fought in North Africa, Italy and Western Europe.

Among the Jews who fought in the Soviet army was General Semyon Moiseyevich Krivosheyn. At the time of the German invasion of Russia in June 1941, his forces held up German tanks near Gomel for a whole month. In 1943 he commanded a mechanized Corps in the decisive battle of Kursk, which halted the last German offensive. In 1945 he commanded a mechanized Corps that broke through the German defences east of Berlin. For his courage in battle he was made a Hero of the Soviet Union, the highest Soviet award for bravery. He was one of 133 Soviet Jews to receive this honour.

Among the Jews who had emigrated to Palestine before the war, several thousand volunteered to fight, and were in action against the Germans in Greece, Crete, North Africa and Italy: 734 were killed in action. Thirty-two of these volunteers were parachuted behind German lines. Seven of them were caught by the Germans and executed, including two women, Haviva Reich and Hannah Senesh. Another of the parachutists who was captured and killed – Peretz Goldstein – had fought for two months alongside the Yugoslav partisans before being captured.

A Jewish Brigade was established as part of the British army in 1944: it fought in Italy, identified by its Star of David insignia; 83 of its members were killed in action or died of their wounds. Later its members worked to smuggle Jewish refugees to Palestine.

Jewish soldiers fought on all the fronts, from the first day of the war on 1 September 1939 to the very last day of the war on 8 May 1945. They were also among the

PRAYER BEFORE A BATTLE.

אָבִינוּ שֶׁבַּשָּׁמַיִם . עֲשֵׂה רְצוֹנְךָ בַּשָּׁמַיִם מִמַּעַל .
וְתֵן נָחַת רוּחַ לִירֵאֶיךָ מִתָּחַת . וְהַטּוֹב בְּעֵינֶיךָ
עֲשֵׂה . בָּרוּךְ אַתָּה יְיָ שׁוֹמֵעַ תְּפִלָּה :
בְּיָדְךָ אַפְקִיד רוּחִי . פָּדִיתָה אֹתִי יְיָ אֵל אֱמֶת :
שְׁמַע יִשְׂרָאֵל יְיָ אֱלֹהֵינוּ יְיָ אֶחָד :
בָּרוּךְ שֵׁם כְּבוֹד מַלְכוּתוֹ לְעוֹלָם וָעֶד : אָמֵן :

Unto thee, Heavenly Father, I lift up my heart in this hour of trial and danger. Pardon all my sins and transgressions before thee; and, I beseech thee, extend thy loving care over the lives of those near and dear unto me. Give me the strength to do my duty this day as a true and loyal Israelite in this War for Freedom and Righteousness. Fill me with the faith and courage of those who put their trust in thine everlasting mercy; and lead us through victory unto peace. May thy will be done.

Blessed art thou, O Lord, Who hearest prayer.

Into thy hand I commend my spirit; thou hast redeemed me, O Lord God of truth.

Hear, O Israel, the Lord our God, the Lord is One. Blessed be his name, whose glorious kingdom is for ever and ever. Amen.

left
A snapshot, found in Poland after the
war, of two Jewish soldiers holding
matzah (unleavened bread) during
Passover 1939, five months before the
outbreak of the Second World War.
This photograph was taken at Biala
Podlaska. Those in this photograph
were killed, as were 6,000 other Jewish
soldiers on the battlefield, and 60,000
other Polish Jewish soldiers, killed by
their German captors.

opposite, bottom
Peretz Goldstein, one of the seven
Jewish parachutists from Palestine,
who was sentenced to death and
executed in 1944.

liberators of the concentration camps in the last months
of the war.

From the first days of the war, Jewish prisoners of
war were singled out for ill-treatment. Of the 400,000
soldiers taken prisoner when the Polish armies
surrendered in 1939, 61,000 were Jews. They were
separated from their Polish comrades-in-arms and sent
to camps in Germany, where they were denied the basic
rights of prisoners of war (rights that the Germans were
later to deny to all Soviet soldiers whom they captured).
Employed at forced labour – forbidden under the inter-
war Geneva conventions on prisoners of war – these
Polish Jewish soldiers were sent to work without shoes,
and half-naked. Many froze to death during the winter
of 1939–40. Some of the first 'death marches' of the
war involved captured Jewish soldiers. Of 1,200 about
to be marched from Zambrow, 250 were shot down
before the march began. Of 880 who were marched
from Lublin to Biala Podlaska, six hundred were killed
on the march, and two hundred died in the prisoner-of-
war camp in Biala Podlaska, mostly of typhus, having
been denied medical attention by their German captors.

JEWS IN NATIONAL RESISTANCE MOVEMENTS

opposite, top
Boris Yochai, a Jewish partisan in a Soviet partisan unit, sets an explosive charge on a railway line near Vilna. He was credited with blowing up twelve German military trains.

opposite, bottom
The result of partisan activity in German-occupied eastern Poland. Among the derailed wagons is one from the Munich depot of the German railways.

Under the harsh conditions of German occupation, every conquered country faced the challenge of forming resistance groups. Across Europe, in addition to forming their own entirely Jewish groups, Jews also participated in every national resistance organization.

In the first partisan unit formed in Slovakia, in 1942, of twenty-five partisans, eighteen were Jews. The only one of the twenty-five who had battle experience was Ernest Lipkovic, a Slovak Jew, who had fought in the International Brigades in the Spanish Civil War five years earlier. Of the next three Slovak partisan groups that were formed, each had Jewish members, and one was commanded by a Jew.

When the Slovak national uprising broke out in August 1944, 2,500 Jews fought alongside 57,000 Slovak soldiers and partisans. Five hundred Jews were killed in the fighting. Among the Jewish partisan commanders was Edita Katz. She fell in battle, covering the retreat of her group with machine-gun fire until her ammunition ran out. She then used her hand grenades to hold off both the German troops and the Hlinka (Slovak Fascist) Guards until she was killed.

After the Slovak rising had been crushed by the German army, the Slovak fighting force fell to 15,000. Of these 2,000 were Jews. In severe winter conditions the whole force made its way through the Carpathian mountains, broke through the German front line, and joined the Soviet army. It was helped in this by several Soviet partisan detachments, one of which was commanded by a Russian Jew, Leonid Berenshteyn.

In the German-occupied areas of the Soviet Union, many Jews who escaped from the eastern ghettos of Pinsk, Slutsk and Minsk joined Soviet partisan groups in the forests. One of these Jews, Hana Ginzberg, from Brest-Litovsk, was regarded throughout the Soviet partisan movement as an outstanding fighter. One of the first Soviet partisans to be executed in Minsk was a Jewish woman, Marina Bruskina.

Many thousands of Jews were active within the Soviet partisan movement. Vladimir Epshteyn, a Soviet soldier, was captured by the Germans on the battlefield and sent to Auschwitz. From there he managed to escape, with two fellow Soviet prisoners of war.

Travelling by night for almost a month, they reached the forest area north-east of Cracow, where they established a partisan group made up of escaped Soviet prisoners of war like themselves, and local Poles and Jews. During their activities, they killed 120 SS men, whose identity papers Epshteyn handed over to the first Soviet troops whom he met on 15 January 1945. After the war he returned to Moscow, where he helped run a restaurant.

Another Soviet prisoner of war, Colonel Yosif Feldman, organized anti-Nazi activity inside several prisoner-of-war camps in Germany. His organization, *Bratskoye Sotrudnichestvo Voyennoplennych* (BSV – the Brotherhood of Prisoners of War) had several Jewish officers in its leadership. Feldman was discovered by the Germans and died under torture on 10 March 1944. Two of his Jewish co-conspirators, Captain Mikhail Zinger and Lieutenant Boris Groisman, survived.

Jewish doctors were also prominent among the Soviet partisans. The Belorussian partisan leader, Colonel Fyodor Markov, had six Jewish doctors in his brigade group. Dinah Mayevskaya was chief medical officer and surgeon of the Kovpak partisans. On several occasions she used her machine gun to prevent the wounded under her care from falling into German hands. A senior Soviet partisan, General Pyotr Vershigora, wrote: 'If in any of us, who have survived despite everything, there remains a feeling of respect and gratitude towards that most humane of sciences, medicine, it is forever linked with the image of that girl.'

In Yugoslavia, Jews were among Tito's partisans from the first days of the armed struggle. One of Tito's closest colleagues in the fighting was a Jew, Mosha Pijade. Most of the doctors with Tito's partisans were Jews. Three thousand Yugoslav Jews managed to find their way, evading German searches, to the partisan areas: 1,318 of them were killed in action. Ten Jews received the National Hero award, Yugoslavia's highest decoration. After the war a former Jewish partisan, Voja Todorovic, became commander of the Yugoslav land forces. The first woman general in the Yugoslav army was Jewish, a former partisan, Dr Rosa Papo.

In Bulgaria, several thousand Jews were active in the

national partisan movement. In Greece, Greek Jews fought with all the partisan groups in the mountains. Some had been soldiers in the Greek army before it was demobilized by the Italians. In Italy, Jews were to be found in all the partisan groups. A street in Verona is named after Rita Rosani. An Italian Jew, she was killed by the Germans leading a small Italian partisan group. Primo Levi, a young Jewish chemist born in Turin, had been on his way to join a partisan unit in northern Italy when he was caught by Fascist militia and deported to Auschwitz, of which he later became an eloquent witness.

In the six months before the Allied landings in Normandy, more than 250 Jews were executed in France for their part in the French resistance. More than half of them had emigrated to France between the wars, or had come as refugees before the war, when France offered both work and a safe haven. Nineteen of those executed had been born in Warsaw, and five in Berlin. Mandel Langer had been born in 1903 in the then Austro-Hungarian town of Auschwitz. Haim Matem had been born in Jerusalem in 1898, when it was part of the Ottoman Empire. Victor Rubinstein, sixty-seven years old when he was executed, had been born in New York.

On 27 June 1944, near Lyon, the Germans executed the Jewish resistance leader, David Donoff, known as 'Dodo'. He was twenty-four years old. Four months earlier they had shot twenty-year-old Moise Fingercwajg, the leader of another Jewish resistance group which was an integral part of the French struggle. In all, more than eleven hundred Jews were executed in France for their resistance activities.

Among Albanian Jews – a small community of thirty-three families, who were saved from deportation by local efforts – several fought against the Germans with the Albanian partisans. Among them were Dario Zhak Artiti, David Koen and Ruben Zhak. Another Jewish partisan, Pepe Biro Kantos, remained in the Albanian army after the war, becoming a senior army officer. The only Jewish family killed by the Germans in Albania – the Ardet family – was killed as a reprisal because one of its members was a partisan.

Chapter Six

The Deportations Continue

Defiance at Auschwitz

On 23 October 1943 a group of 1,750 Polish Jews who had been held at Belsen, ostensibly to be exchanged for German citizens held by the Allies, were deported to Birkenau. Driven towards the undressing section of the gas chamber by SS Sergeant-Major Josef Schillinger, they were ordered to undress. As they did so the SS guards seized rings from their fingers and watches from their wrists: a final act of looting. When Schillinger ordered one of the women to undress completely, she threw her shoe in his face, seized his revolver, and shot him in the stomach. She also wounded SS Sergeant Emmerich. According to some reports she was a dancer from Warsaw, named Horowitz. After her act of defiance, other women began to strike the SS men, at the very entrance to the gas chamber, severely injuring two of them. The SS men fled. Shortly afterwards they returned, armed with grenades and machine guns, with the camp commandant, Rudolf Hoess. One by one the women were removed from the gas chamber building, and shot.

Report of **Jerzy Tabau**, a non-Jewish Polish prisoner at Auschwitz who escaped shortly after this episode, and who included it in his report (which reached the Allied governments in the summer of 1944, and was published in Washington and London)

On 20 January 1943 Himmler wrote to the Reich Minister of Transport about 'the removal of Jews' from every area to which German rule or authority then extended. To complete this task, Himmler explained, 'I need your help and support. If I am to wind things up quickly, I must have more trains for transport.'

'I must have more trains....' In his letter Himmler went on to express his understanding of the Minister's problems, at a time when the German army, just defeated at Stalingrad, was having to rush extra troops and munitions to the Eastern Front by train, to prevent the Soviet forces pushing the Germans back. 'I know very well,' Himmler added, 'how taxing the situation is for the railways and what demands are constantly made of you. Just the same, I must make this request of you: help me to get more trains.'

Himmler's wish was the Transport Minister's command. Not that there had been any relaxation of deportations that winter. On the day after Himmler wrote his letter, and while the Minister was still studying it, a deportation train left Holland. Locked into its wagons were all 1,100 adults from the Jewish mental home at Apeldoorn, and 74 boys and 24 girls from the nearby home for seriously physically and mentally handicapped children. Their destination was Auschwitz. Their fate was to be sent to the gas chambers on arrival. Fifty nurses accompanied the patients. They were put in a separate carriage at one end of the train, and offered the choice of returning to Holland after delivering their patients, or working in a 'really modern' mental home in the east. All of them were murdered at Auschwitz.

As Himmler had requested, extra trains were found. They were, indeed, already being found. 'Action Tiger', the seizure of 4,000 Jews in Marseille, and their deportation, first to Paris and then to Auschwitz, was carried out two days after Himmler's letter.

CHARLOTTE SALOMON'S STORY

top

Charlotte Salomon and her father on the balcony of their Berlin apartment, in the late 1920s.

above

Charlotte (top right) with five of her classmates in Berlin before the war. She entered the school, a grammar school for girls, in 1927, at the age of ten.

Charlotte Salomon was born in Berlin in 1917, during the First World War. Her father, Professor Albert Salomon, was a surgeon. In 1933 he lost his professorship, and soon afterwards, in common with all Jewish doctors, was deprived of the right to practise as a medical doctor. In 1935 Charlotte was admitted as a student to the Berlin Academy of Fine Arts (which allowed in a small number of Jewish students whose fathers had served in the German army in the First World War, as Charlotte's father had done, as a military doctor at the front). Her first professor there, Ernst Böhm, a commercial artist, was later dismissed because his wife was Jewish.

After the Kristallnacht, in November 1938, Professor Salomon was held briefly in Sachsenhausen concentration camp. In January 1939 he and Charlotte were given permission to emigrate. They decided to make their home at Villefranche, in the South of France, a thousand miles from Berlin. Charlotte was twenty-one years old. Briefly, she was interned at Gurs, in the Pyrenees, but then allowed back to Villefranche. In May 1943 she married Alexander Nagler, an Austrian Jewish refugee.

On 8 September 1943, after Italy signed an armistice with the Allies, German troops occupied the South of France. At Villefranche, as throughout the coastal region, both the police headquarters and the town hall were taken over by the Gestapo. On the evening of 21 September 1943 (at seven o'clock) a Gestapo truck drew up outside the house where Charlotte and her husband were living. They were dragged out of the house and thrown into the truck. Charlotte was four months pregnant.

On 7 October 1943 Charlotte and her husband were deported by train to Auschwitz. They were both murdered on arrival at the camp, on 12 October 1943.

Charlotte's father survived the war. In 1971 he gave the Jewish Historical Museum in Amsterdam more than 1,300 paintings that his daughter had done, constituting a dramatized autobiography that she had called *Life? or Theatre?* She had painted them in the South of France in the three years before her deportation to Auschwitz.

left
One of the 1,300 paintings by
Charlotte in her series *Life? or Theatre?*
She is sitting on a suitcase amid
packing up for the journey from Berlin
to the South of France, singing, for the
last time, a farewell song to
the land of her birth. The portrait on
the wall is a self-portrait of her as a
young girl.

opposite, top right
Charlotte painting in the South of
France.

opposite, bottom right
Alexander Nagler, Charlotte's husband,
deported with her to Auschwitz,
and killed.

FURTHER DEPORTATIONS TO AUSCHWITZ

The conditions under which these victims of German barbarism were transported were terrible. The trucks into which men, women and children, healthy and sick alike, were loaded, were of the type normally used to transport coal and wood, and had only one entrance which closes hermetically with an iron bar, and a small railed window at the top corner. The Germans closed even this small window with barbed wire, thus making impossible any communication with the outside. These Jews had to remain two whole days in the trucks which remained at the railway station before the train started on its journey. During this time one died, and a woman gave birth to a child without any medical assistance. No food or water was given to these Jews during this time.

When informed of what was happening the Greek Red Cross immediately sent to the railway station some lorries with food to be distributed to the Jews by nursing sisters, but the officers in command of the guard refused to open the doors of the railway trucks, saying they had orders to forbid any communication with the Jews under transport. The only concession made was to remove temporarily the barbed wire of the windows, through which the nursing sisters threw whatever they could into the trucks.

News bulletin issued by the Greek Information Office of the Greek Embassy in London 6 June 1944 (the day of the Allied landings in Normandy)

Himmler's letter seeking 'more trains' for the deportation of Jews was dated 20 January 1943. A month later, Dr Goebbels – after Hitler the most vociferous anti-Jewish Nazi leader – determined to rid Berlin of its Jews. On the night of February 27 he ordered a raid on the city's munitions factories. The factories were surrounded by SS troops, who kept 7,000 Jewish slave labourers inside the factories until trucks arrived to take them away to the Grunewald railway station, in the suburbs. There the deportation trains were waiting. The operation was called the 'Factory Action'.

Goebbels was not satisfied, writing in his diary: 'The better circles, particularly the intellectuals, do not understand our Jewish policy and partly side with the Jews. As a result, our operation was revealed prematurely, so that quite a few Jews slipped through our hands. But we'll catch them yet. At any rate I won't rest until at least the capital has become completely Jew-free.'

Several thousand Berlin Jews were in hiding. Searches were carried out for them, and during March five more trains left Berlin-Grunewald, taking 7,752 Jews to Auschwitz. On 19 May 1943 Berlin was declared 'Jew-free'. Goebbels called this his 'greatest political accomplishment'.

© Martin Gilbert 2000

above
Stamp issued in Italy in 1993 in memory of the Rome deportees of October 1943.

left
This map shows the main deportation routes to Auschwitz, the most destructive of the concentration camps. From each of the towns shown on this map, and from hundreds of other towns and villages, Jews were forced from their homes, interned in local camps (such as Gurs and Rivesaltes in Vichy France, Malines in Belgium and Westerbork in Holland), or forced into ghettos. They were then deported by train – or in the case of Oslo, Helsinki, Rhodes, Kos and Corfu initially by boat – across Europe to Auschwitz. More than a million of the Jews who were deported to Auschwitz were murdered there, most of them – including all children and old people – being killed in the gas chambers within a few hours of their arrival. Tens of thousands of others – able-bodied men and women – were forced to work as slave labourers. Most of them were killed when they became too ill or too weak to work. Fewer than ten thousand survived.

opposite, above
Registration of Jews for deportation at Skopje.

opposite, below
Boarding the trains at Skopje: destination, Auschwitz.

In 1943 Mussolini's fascist regime was overthrown. To prevent the Allies advancing through Italy to the Austrian Alps, German troops entered Rome. On 16 October 1943 there was a round-up of Jews in Rome. Two days later, 1,015 Italian Jewish men, women and children – 244 under the age of fourteen – were deported to Auschwitz. Within eight months, 6,746 Italian Jews had been deported. Only 830 survived the war.

The range of Himmler's use of trains was formidable. Jews were deported to Auschwitz even from the tiny principality of Luxembourg; from as far north as the Finnish capital Helsinki, and the Estonian town of Narva; from as far south as Athens, and – through Athens – from the Italian-ruled islands of Kos and Rhodes, which

were occupied by Germany when Italy surrendered. Jews were also deported from the island of Corfu, in the Ionian Sea.

Remote locations did not escape the search and round-up. From Kastoria in Greece, and from Nea Orastea on the Greek-Turkish border, Jews were deported to Auschwitz: both deportations took place in March 1943. That March – as Himmler's request for trains was being answered with great efficiency – 1,814 Jews were deported from the camp at Gurs, within sight of the Pyrenees, the border with neutral Spain. The deportees were mostly German Jews who had been driven from their homes and deported to Gurs two and a half years earlier.

AUSCHWITZ-BIRKENAU

Was present for the first time at a special action at 3 a.m. By comparison, Dante's *Inferno* seems almost a comedy. Auschwitz is justly called an extermination camp!

Diary entry of 2 September 1942, by an SS doctor, **Johann Kremer**, newly arrived at Birkenau. Among those whom Dr Kremer watched being gassed that night were seventy boys and seventy-eight girls under the age of sixteen, who had just been deported from France, many of them without their parents.

'On the side, you dirty Jew!': words forever seared in my brain by SS Sergeant Heinrich Kuhnemann, as he tore my father from me with the crook of his cane in a 'selection' of those to be immediately gassed and burned. When I last saw him – beside the dark and fetid freight car that had transported us into a surreal world of searchlights, high-voltage fences, snarling German wolfhounds, and their black-shirted masters – Chaim Mielnicki was but forty-seven years of age. And I have never recovered from his loss. Nor have I ever been able to reconcile myself to the obscene and mocking death inflicted on him by the forces of Hitlerian malevolence. Such a vital, decent, intelligent devoted, hardworking man, my father – that he'd always seemed to me, his youngest child, the very essence of Chaim, his given name – as in *L'Chaim*, the traditional Jewish toast 'To life'.

Michel Mielnicki, born at Wasilkow, near Bialystok, in 1927. Deported to Auschwitz in December 1942, living in Vancouver since 1966

The largest single centre of the mass murder of Jews was at Auschwitz-Birkenau. Built across the railway from Auschwitz Main Camp, and known as Auschwitz II, the camp at Birkenau had four gas chambers, where more than a million Jews were murdered. It was also a centre of slave labour. In its huts, men and women, their identification numbers tattooed on their forearms, toiled and suffered, were murdered when they became too weak to toil, and watched the crematorium chimneys working night and day to consume the bodies of the murdered Jews – including in almost every case close family members, even parents and children, of those toiling as slave labourers.

At four other death camps – Chelmno, Belzec, Sobibor, Treblinka – as many as a third of the six million murdered Jews were killed. Hundreds of thousands more were murdered in gas vans at Maly Trostinets near Minsk, and in the gas chambers at Majdanek, on the outskirts of Lublin. As many as two million Jews were killed in the pits and ravines of German-occupied eastern Poland, the Baltic States and western Russia. But it was to Auschwitz-Birkenau that the largest number of Jews were deported, and where the largest number were murdered.

The killings at Auschwitz-Birkenau took place between the summer of 1942 and the last months of 1944. The four gas chambers, and the chimneys of the crematoria attached to them, have become the symbols of the Holocaust, as has the entrance gate through which, after March 1944, trains ran directly into the camp, photographed below, in 1993, from underneath a railway wagon.

opposite

David Olère's painting, done in 1945, of a scene outside one of the four crematoria at Birkenau, as a group of Jews enter the outer gate. The truck with the Red Cross markings was intended to give them a sense of reassurance. It was not in fact a Red Cross truck at all, but an SS vehicle used to bring the canisters of poison gas from one of the camp storerooms to the gas chambers. The truck on the far right would take the clothes of the victims to the storehouses of 'Canada' (*see pages 122–3*). Olère was born in Warsaw in 1902. He studied art in Berlin, Munich, Heidelberg and Paris, where he settled, working for the Gaumont Film Company. Interned at Drancy, he was deported to Auschwitz. From Auschwitz he was

transferred to Mauthausen, then to Ebensee, where he was liberated. After liberation he learned that his whole family had been murdered in Treblinka. He continued to paint, at Noisy-le-Grand in France, using as his theme what he called the Eleventh Commandment: 'Don't ever forget the victims of the Holocaust.'

above

Alfred Kantor's painting, drawn immediately after the war, of the barracks and watchtowers at Birkenau, and one of the crematoria chimneys. His caption reads: 'March 1944. Crematories going on full blast – a batch of Dutch Jews has to be disposed of before dawn.'

Memories of Auschwitz

The next day I watched a long column of trucks driving down the main road toward a red brick building about a thousand feet away. They were carrying Jews from Holland, someone told me. Young and old were standing up in canvas-covered trucks. I particularly remember a girl with long blond hair who was wearing a green loden coat. 'Soon you will see the smoke; they are done for' said the man next to me. And sure enough, the chimney started up as if for a command performance.

It was chilling moments like these, in the very first days of Auschwitz, that prompted me to find a way to sketch again. Only now I felt obsessed, driven in fact by the overwhelming desire to put down every detail of this unfathomable place. I began to observe everything with an eye towards capturing it on paper: the shapes of the buildings, the insulators on the barbed-wire poles, the battalions of workers at labour sites, the searching for lice, the women carrying soup in heavy barrels, the incredibly eerie feeling of Auschwitz at night with its strange lights and with the glow of flames from the crematorium. At first I began to memorize scenes of the day's activity and then drawing them at night in the barracks when no one was looking.

Alfred Kantor, born in Czechoslovakia, deported from Theresienstadt to Auschwitz, recollections

'CANADA' IN AUSCHWITZ

above right
Auschwitz, the shoes of the victims.

opposite
Auschwitz, the clothes of the victims.

Loot was a central element in the Nazi persecution of the Jews. The murder of six million people provided a source of rich booty for the SS, for the German war machine and for Germans generally. In 1942, the clothes taken from Jews wherever they had been murdered were sent to Germany to be distributed (naturally without acknowledging their origins) as part of the Winter Aid Campaign. On at least one occasion the recipients complained that the clothes sent to help them out over the winter were bloodstained.

Every Jewish family deported between 1940 and 1944 owned something, had some possessions, even if it was only the simple furniture to be found in a few rooms, or even in a single room: tables and chairs, a chest of drawers, beds, kitchen utensils, pots and pans, cups and saucers, knives and forks, pens, a pram, eyeglasses, a few small items of jewellery, a wedding ring. The Germans also took over the livelihood of every Jewish family that was deported, however poor it might be, however hard the breadwinners had worked to create a livelihood. It might be the contents of a small shop, the tools of some workaday trade, a bicycle, some modest savings, a few American dollars, even an American twenty-dollar gold coin, kept as a souvenir.

Other families inevitably had more: an apartment or a house, a few antiques, carpets and rugs, more substantial furniture, books, a camera, possibly a radio, a few paintings, a stamp collection (which many schoolchildren had, as did adults who had been collecting for years), a coin collection, jewellery – a modest inheritance passed on through the generations – some scientific instruments or a doctor's or dentist's cabinet.

Wealthier Jews had larger homes, a thriving business or a flourishing factory, a truck or even a car, possibly a fine painting or two, or some valuable family heirloom, jewels or a healthy bank account – the accumulated savings of many years of hard work.

Every Jew – rich and poor, worker and employer, city-dweller or farmer – had his or her possessions seized and taken away. In the first days of the German occupation, shops and businesses were looted. All

funds, however small, that had been deposited in a bank, were immediately seized. Further looting took place when the Jews were forced out of their homes and into the ghettos, or immediately after deportation – especially during 1942 and 1943 – when homes were completely ransacked.

The last of the looting was done in the death camps themselves, when the final vestiges of wealth, the last few precious coins, the last pair of spectacles, the last dollar bill, as well as the most personal possessions – family photographs, letters and documents – were taken away together with coats and hats, some small cooking utensil, pots, pans, the food brought for the journey, handbags, a sheet or blanket, a small suitcase or rucksack, a headscarf, dress, pullover, shirt, trousers, underwear, socks and shoes.

The victims who were driven naked into the gas chambers had been forced to hand over the last of their possessions before they were led to their deaths. Even women's hair was put to use and given a commercial value, as insulation material for German army vehicles, aircraft and submarines.

At Auschwitz-Birkenau, to which Jews were brought without interruption from the summer of 1942 to the summer of 1944, a special section of the camp, consisting of several dozen huts and storehouses, was set aside to house the belongings of those who had just arrived, many of whom were about to be murdered, or were being murdered even as their belongings were reaching the sorting area. That area was known by the Jews who worked there as 'Canada' – the land of plenty and prosperity.

A DEPORTATION FROM FRANCE TO KOVNO AND REVAL

On 15 May 1944 a train (Convoy 73) left Paris with 878 Jews locked into its fifteen cattle trucks. Unlike previous deportations from Paris, in which men, women and children were deported together, this deportation consisted almost entirely of men. There were also thirty-seven boys between the ages of thirteen and eighteen.

One boy, David Gelbart, who was deported with his sixteen-year-old brother Maurice, was two weeks short of his thirteenth birthday – the day of his barmitzvah, a Jewish boy's coming of adulthood. The youngest deportee, Maurice Gattegno, born in Nice, was twelve years old. There were no women, no children under twelve, and no old people.

Almost all the deportees had been born far from France. Two had been born in London, one in Cuba, two in Jerusalem and one in Baghdad.

All but four of the previous deportation train 'convoys' from Paris had gone to Auschwitz. Those four trains had gone to the death camp at Sobibor. Convoy 73 went much further east, to the former Lithuanian capital, Kovno, more than a thousand miles from Paris.

The children of Izieu

Among those deported eastward on Convoy 73 were a Jewish educator, Miron Zlatin – who had hidden forty-four Jewish children in a Jewish children's home in the French village of Izieu – and two of the youngsters whom he had protected there, Théodor Reis (aged sixteen) and Arnold Hirsch (aged seventeen). All three perished. The other children from Izieu and their teachers had already been deported from Paris to Auschwitz in earlier convoys. Only one of these forty-four children, Léa Feldblum, survived the war.

It was believed by the deportees that a call had gone out for a labour battalion in the area towards which Soviet troops were steadily advancing.

Some of those on the train had made special efforts to be included, regarding such labour as a chance of work, shelter, food and survival. One of them, sixteen-year-old Guy Sarner, lied about his age, claiming to be older, in order to be taken (and was among the few who survived the war). He recalled that several deportees died of thirst during the journey eastward.

Reaching Kovno after three days and three nights, as many as 400 deportees – from five of the wagons – were taken to the Ninth Fort on the outskirts of the city, the scene of the massacre of tens of thousands of Kovno Jews two and a half years earlier. Inside the fort, they were kept in prison cells. Dozens of them carved their names into the walls. One of them, determined to record their strange plight, wrote: *Nous sommes 900 Français* (We are 900 Frenchmen). One of these deportees to Kovno, Israel Kopelov, had been born in Kovno thirty-eight years earlier.

Most of the Ninth Fort prisoners from Paris were taken to a slave labour camp at Pravieniskes, twenty miles from the Ninth Fort and twelve miles from Kovno, on the Kovno-Vilna railway line. Many were executed there by Lithuanian auxiliaries, on SS orders.

The ten remaining wagons of Convoy 73 – with more than 450 men still locked inside – were taken on by rail north-eastward from Kovno, another five hundred miles to the former Estonian capital, Reval. During the journey there were more deaths from thirst. Six days after their arrival in Reval, sixty of the deportees were taken away, allegedly for work, but were never seen again. The rest were made to work on airfield repairs.

On July 14 – France's national holiday – sixty of the Paris deportees then in Reval were taken to a nearby forest and shot. A month later, on August 14, a further hundred, whom their German guards judged too sick to work, were sent southward to an 'unknown destination' and killed. The rest were sent to Stutthof concentration camp, near Danzig, where many died.

From Convoy 73, only twenty-three of the 878 deportees survived the war.

Also among those deported on Convoy 73, and killed, was Abraham Cherchevsky, who had been born in Jerusalem in 1901. His daughter Eve Line, born in France in 1932, survived the war. Fifty-five years after the deportation, having tracked down a mass of biographical detail of the deportees of 15 May 1944, she published a 443-page book telling their story.

NOUS SOMMES 900 FRANÇAIS

À la mémoire des déportés du convoi n°73
ayant quitté Drancy le 15 mai 1944

above left
Eve Line and her father in 1936 (and above, the cover of her book).

above right
Abraham Cherchevsky's identity card, stamped *JUIF* (Jew). He had to put his fingerprint as well as his signature.

left
Birthplaces of some of the deportees of 15 May 1944, showing the route of Convoy 73, and the frontline reached by Soviet forces at the time of the convoy.

opposite
Words carved by a prisoner on the wall of one of the cells in the Ninth Fort in Kovno: 'We are 900 Frenchmen'.

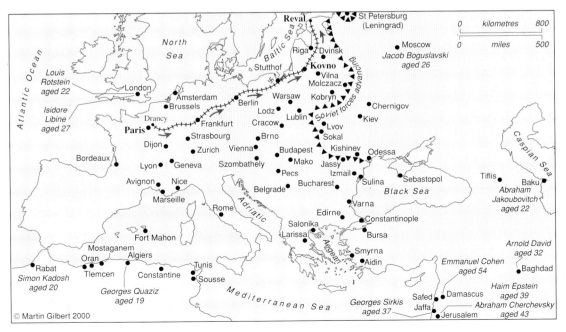

© Martin Gilbert 2000

DEATH CAMP REVOLTS

On reaching a death camp, small groups of Jews were taken out of the trains and made to work in the camp, taking bodies out of gas chambers, and sorting the clothing of those who had just been murdered. Others had to cut off the hair of the murdered women. All of those in these *Sonderkommando* (Special Commandos or Death Commandos) were marked out for death, to be replaced with new arrivals. In every death camp there were attempts by these slave labourers to revolt.

TREBLINKA

On 2 August 1943 the Jewish slave labourers at Treblinka managed to break into the arsenal. Petrol was then put into the camp disinfector, used for the daily disinfecting procedure, and operated by the Jewish slave labourers. Petrol instead of disinfectant was then sprayed on the camp buildings. The next afternoon, the 'disinfected' buildings were ignited, and many of the camp buildings set on fire. The chief of the SS guards was shot dead, and fifteen other German and Ukrainian guards were killed. Of the seven hundred Jewish workers in the camp, 150 escaped. Half of them were hunted down by German and Ukrainian units and shot.

SOBIBOR

To make revolt possible at Sobibor, several Jewish girls who worked in the SS quarters polishing shoes and cleaning floors managed to steal a few hand grenades, pistols, a rifle and a submachine gun. On the night of 13 October 1943, Alexander Pechersky, a Soviet prisoner of war who had been brought into the camp three weeks earlier, and Leon Feldhendler, a Polish Jew, distributed knives and hatchets, as well as warm clothing.

On the afternoon of October 14, as individual German and Ukrainian guards entered the huts on their regular tours of inspection, they were attacked. Nine SS men and two Ukrainians were killed. Then, as another of the conspirators, Yaakov Biskowitz, recalled, the signal was given for the revolt to begin: the password 'Hurrah'. In the ensuing struggle, the Jews killed eleven or twelve SS men.

There had been six hundred prisoners in the slave labour section of the camp at Sobibor. Three hundred of them broke out. The rest were killed inside the camp with the arrival of military and police reinforcements from nearby Chelm. Most of the hundred prisoners who succeeded in evading the German army searches joined partisan units. Some were later killed in action against the Germans, others by anti-Semitic Poles. Only thirty survived the war.

Four girls among the Sobibor escapees, Eda Lichtman from Poland, Ula Stern from Germany, and Kaethe and Ruth (their surnames are unknown) from Holland, joined Jewish partisans in the Parczew forest, thirty miles to the east of Sobibor. Another of the escapees, Semyon Rozenfeld, from Baranowicze in eastern Poland, later joined the Soviet army. In Berlin on the day of victory, he chalked on the Reichstag wall the words: 'Baranowicze-Sobibor-Berlin'.

AUSCHWITZ-BIRKENAU

At Crematorium II – one of the four at Birkenau – three hundred Greek Jews were among the *Sonderkommando* preparing for revolt in early October 1944. Across the railway line, in the Union explosives factory, a group of Jewish girls had collected small amounts of explosives and smuggled them to the plotters. Among the girls were Giza Weissblum and Raizl Kibel, both of whom survived the war.

Three other girls in the Union factory, Ella Garnter, and two girls known only by their first names, Toszka

and Regina, also managed to smuggle explosives to Roza Robota, who was working inside Birkenau. She passed them to a member of the *Sonderkommando*.

The revolt broke out at Crematorium IV on 7 October 1944. That morning a member of the *Sonderkommando* was ordered to draw up lists for 'evacuation' at noon of three hundred men. Fearing this was a prelude to destruction, he refused. The SS ordered a roll-call, insisting that the *Sonderkommando* be sent to work in another camp. As the SS Staff Sergeant called out their numbers, only a few men answered. Then, after repeated SS calls and threats, Chaim Neuhof, a Jew from Sosnowiec, approached the Staff Sergeant, who reached for his gun. Neuhof called out the password, 'Hurrah', and struck the SS man on the head with his hammer. The SS man fell to the ground. The other prisoners then echoed Neuhof's 'Hurrah' and threw stones at the SS.

Reporting these events, Salmen Lewental noted of his fellow *Sonderkommando* (in notes which he managed to hide near the crematorium): 'They showed an immense courage refusing to budge.' After the Jews had stoned the SS guards, they set fire to the wooden roof of Crematorium IV. Lewental commented in his notes: 'Few moments had passed when a whole detachment of SS men drove in, armed with machine guns and grenades. There were so many of them that each had two machine guns for one prisoner. Even such an army was mobilized against them.'

At Crematorium II the Jews hoped to escape through the nearby barracks of the 'Cleaning Installations' Commando. They were joined there by Sol Schindel, a Polish Jew from Rzeszow, who was working in the Cleaning Installations Commando. Schindel, who survived the revolt, later recalled: 'As we ran past the watchtower, I saw the SS men shooting with machine guns. I saw many dead already lying on the ground. I threw myself to the ground and crept through a hole in the barbed-wire fence into the women's camp.' Other *Sonderkommando* continued to flee beyond the wire, in search of hiding places in nearby fields and farmsteads.

Within minutes of the break-out at Crematorium II, the alarm sounded, whereupon SS men with dogs

arrived in trucks and surrounded the whole area. Most of the escapees were shot. The rest found brief sanctuary in a barn. The SS set fire to the barn, then shot the surviving escapees as they ran out.

About two hundred and fifty escapees were killed outside the wire, among them a leader of the revolt at Crematorium II, Jozef Dorebus. Later that day, a further two hundred men of the *Sonderkommando* were shot inside Birkenau.

At Crematorium III the revolt was led by Greek Jews, former officers in the Greek army. Having blown up the crematorium, they were killed by the SS guards. They died singing the Greek national anthem.

CHELMNO

On the night of 17 January 1945, the SS entered the barracks at Chelmno. One of them, waving his flashlight, demanded, 'Five men follow me!' Five people were taken out, recalled one of the prisoners, Mordechai Zurawski, 'and we heard five shots'. Then someone else came in and shouted, 'Five more – out!' There were more shots. Then a third group of five were taken out. After further shots, a fourth group was called, among them Zurawski. 'The SS man came in,' he recalled. 'I hid behind the door – I had a knife in my hand; I jumped on the SS man and stabbed him. I broke his flashlight and stabbed right and left, and I escaped.'

Running from the camp, Zurawski was shot in the foot. He managed to reach the safety of the dense woods. A second Jew of the forty-one had also survived. This was Shimon Srebnik, who later recalled: 'I was the youngest. I also ran. I didn't even put on my trousers. I just had my pants and singlet.' As he fled, Srebnik was hit by a bullet, which entered through the nape of his neck and came out through his mouth. At the Eichmann Trial in Jerusalem in 1961, the court was shown the scar. Srebnik's account of the shooting continued: 'There was one soldier who was just guarding the groups of dead people and finishing off those who still showed signs of life…. I ran away when his gaze was not fixed on me, and I was hiding in the hut of a Gentile up to the liberation.' Srebnik was one of only two survivors of the Chelmno revolt.

At Auschwitz

I have wanted to live through it, to take a revenge for the death of my father, my mother, my beloved sister Nella.

A **Greek Jew** – his name is not known – working at Crematorium II. He was killed in the revolt

Chapter Seven

The Last Year of the War

Last words

I had a dream,
A dream so terrible;
My people were no more!

I wake up with a cry.
What I dreamed was true:
It had happened indeed
It had happened to me.

Yitzhak Katzenelson, a stanza from his *Song of the Murdered Jewish People*, written in Warsaw

You common, cruel murderers of mankind, do not think you will succeed in extinguishing our nation. The Jewish nation will live forever and will not disappear from the world's arena.

Rabbi Mosze Friedman, his words to an SS Lieutenant at the entrance to the gas chamber on the night of 8 April 1944

right

The railway spur inside Birkenau, looking from the crematoria area back towards the main gate, showing the whole length of the 'ramp'. The huts of the women's camp are on the right. The wooden towers on both sides of the line were for armed SS guards, and also for searchlights used when trains arrived at night – as many of them did. This photograph was taken in 1980.

As the pattern of deportations widened, no area of Europe under German influence was overlooked. On 4 April 1944 a train reached Auschwitz from the Adriatic port of Trieste. Its 132 deportees were mainly Jews who had found refuge in Trieste from central Europe five years earlier. Twenty-nine of them were tattooed and sent to the barracks at Birkenau. The remaining 103 were gassed.

Sixty miles from the Swiss border, in the French town of Vittel, 238 Polish Jews had been brought from Warsaw on what they believed was the first part of a journey to freedom. They held passports acquired in Warsaw from neutral Latin American embassies. At the beginning of April, however, they were sent, not to safety across the Atlantic, but 700 miles back to Poland, to Auschwitz. Among them was the Polish Jewish scholar Rabbi Mosze Friedman, and the poet and playwright Yitzhak Katzenelson. Before the First World War, Katzenelson had founded a network of Hebrew schools in Lodz, from kindergarten to high school. He was in Vittel with his eighteen-year-old son. His wife and two younger sons had been deported from Warsaw and murdered at Treblinka more than a year and a half earlier. All but fifty of the Vittel deportees were gassed when their deportation train reached Auschwitz on the night of 8 April 1944.

In September 1943 German troops had taken over the Italian-occupied areas of Greece, and the formerly Italian Dodecanese Islands. In March 1944 they occupied Hungary. To receive Jews from these newly controlled regions, a railway spur was built at Auschwitz, linking the station – from which deportees had hitherto been brought on foot and by truck – direct to a 'ramp' in the centre of Birkenau, only a few yards from two of the four gas chambers.

JEWS IN THE WARSAW UPRISING OF 1944

A high point of Polish heroism during the Second World War came on 1 August 1944. That day, Polish forces, headed by General Tadeusz Bor-Komorowski, raised the flag of revolt over Warsaw, and challenged the German military machine that had held Poland captive for almost five years. Only a few thousand Jews had survived the Warsaw ghetto revolt a year and a half earlier, and the constant searches since then, but the Jewish will to resist was strong, and hundreds of Jews participated in the Polish uprising. Others found the uprising raging in the buildings and cellars of 'Aryan' Warsaw where they were trying to survive in hiding. They too were caught up in the fighting.

In 1943 the Germans had set up a concentration camp at Gesia Street, in Warsaw. By August 1944 there were more than four hundred Jewish prisoners there. Some of them were Greek and Hungarian Jews who had originally been deported to Auschwitz. There were also Jews from France and Belgium, who had likewise been brought from Auschwitz as slave labourers. A small group of them were working outside the camp when the August uprising began. The Polish insurgents secured their freedom, and the Jews joined in the struggle, helping to build barricades for the insurgents, and doing so under heavy German machine-gun and artillery fire. The first to be killed in battle was David Edelman, originally from France.

As the insurgents captured more and more of the city, they reached the Gesia Street camp and released 348 Jews, including twenty-four women. All the released prisoners joined the insurgents. A hundred and fifty of them were organized by the Poles into an entirely Jewish fighting force, which was given the name Auxiliary International Jewish Brigade. Almost all of them were killed in the fighting. Another group of those released from the Gesia Street camp were technicians by training. They formed a platoon for the repair of tanks captured by the Poles from the Germans. Other former Gesia prisoners worked in the weapon repair workshops the insurgents had set up.

Before the Polish uprising, Feliks Cywinski had given refuge to twenty-six Jews (for which he was later honoured by Israel as a Righteous Gentile). When the uprising began, one of those whom he had protected, Shmuel Kenigswein, became the commander of a platoon made up entirely of Jews who had been in hiding. This platoon fought in the fiercest action, suffering heavy losses. So too did a platoon established by the remnants of the Jewish Fighting Organization (ZOB), which had been at the centre of the Warsaw ghetto uprising more than a year earlier. This unit was led by a veteran of the ghetto revolt, Yitzhak Zuckerman, who survived the war, and emigrated to Israel, where he was one of the founders of the Ghetto Fighters' kibbutz, Lohamei Haghettaot.

Jews fought in all the different political groupings that made up the Warsaw uprising of August 1944. A Jewish officer in the Socialist Fighting Organization, Lieutenant Marian Merenholc, was killed in the first day's fighting. A Jewish doctor, Roman Born-Bornstein, served as head of the health service in the centre of the city during the uprising.

Jewish women also made a notable contribution to the Polish struggle. Among those killed in action were several whose surnames are unknown; they are known – to this day – only by their nicknames: 'Maria', 'Janka', 'Stefa' and 'Emilia'. They were buried in mass graves on the streets where they fell. Shoshana Kosower, who led Polish units through the sewer system, was awarded the Polish Cross of Valour.

Even as Jews participated alongside Poles in the Polish struggle, there were serious anti-Jewish incidents perpetrated by Poles. Dozens of Jews who emerged from their hiding places, in which they had found a precarious sanctuary since the ghetto uprising, were set upon and killed. A group of former Jewish prisoners from the Gesia Street camp, who were still wearing their striped concentration camp uniforms, were attacked by Poles who called out: 'We do not need Jews. Shoot every one!' Two of the Jews were killed. Other Poles then intervened, and the rest of the Jews were saved. On one occasion, eight armed Polish soldiers came across fourteen unarmed Jews in hiding. The Jews were killed. The Polish-born historian Shmuel Krakowski, himself a survivor of the Holocaust, has written of those Jews who were killed by Poles: 'It is as impossible to determine the exact number of those murdered as it is to establish the exact number of Jews who fell in battles with the Germans, or as a result of the German bombing and shelling. The Warsaw revolt, which was a tragedy for the population of Poland's capital, was an additional catastrophe to the surviving Jews who were hiding in the city.'

The Warsaw uprising ended on 2 October 1944. Among those shot by the Germans that day were several dozen Jews, former prisoners at the Gesia Street concentration camp, who had taken part in the revolt. An estimated 500 Jews – of a pre-war Jewish population

of 500,000 – remained in Warsaw, hiding, as they had done before the uprising, in cellars and ruins. In one cellar, twenty-nine Jews were hiding, including two who had taken part a year earlier in the revolt in the Treblinka death camp. In another cellar, ten Jews were hiding. When they were discovered – in both cellars – by German soldiers, they fought, but were all killed.

Three Hungarian Jews who had been brought from Auschwitz to the Gesia Street camp that summer were among seven Jews killed when their hiding place was discovered in late October. In all, 300 of the 500 Jews in hiding after the Polish uprising were killed as a result of the repeated and relentless German searches. Only two hundred Jews were still alive in Warsaw when the city was liberated on 17 January 1945.

above, left medal
The Polish Cross of Valour.

above, right medal
The Silver Cross of the Order of Virtuti Militari, the highest Polish award for bravery in action.

left
Yitzhak Zuckerman, leader of the Warsaw ghetto revolt of April 1943 and participant in the Polish uprising in Warsaw in August 1944. This photograph was taken in Soviet-occupied Lvov in December 1939. Shortly afterwards, Zuckerman and several of his friends made their way back across the German border into Warsaw, where they helped organize resistance. He survived the war, and emigrated to Israel.

opposite
The ruins of the Warsaw ghetto. Jews who were brought from Auschwitz in the summer of 1944 as slave labourers to clear these ruins participated in the Warsaw uprising in August 1944. This photograph shows the ruins of a building on Nalewki Street, once at the centre of Jewish Warsaw. Two enterprises are still advertised: Orbach, 1st floor, room 66, making weather-proof garments, and Frydman, a furrier, also on the first floor. In the distance, across the ruins of the ghetto, at its eastern edge, is the spire of St Augustine's Church.

ACTS OF INDIVIDUAL DEFIANCE

above
Emanuel Ringelblum's systematic collection of material relating to the fate of Polish Jews after 1939 was itself an act of defiance. He and his fellow historians in Warsaw were determined that the story would be recorded. They encouraged the writing of diaries, and were themselves active in the search for material. One of Ringelblum's colleagues recalled: 'For weeks and months he spent the nights poring over the manuscripts, adding comments and instructions.' In April 1943, Ringelblum took part in the Warsaw ghetto uprising. On 7 March 1944, while in hiding in 'Aryan' Warsaw, the hideout was discovered and he was taken with those with him, including his wife and son, to the ruins of the ghetto, where they were shot.

opposite
'... the quiet passive heroism of the common Jew.' A group of Jews in the Warsaw ghetto, photographed by a German army sergeant, Willy Georg, in the summer 1941. They are standing in front of a funeral parlour (*Zaklad Pogrzebowy*).

Despite the savagery of the German reprisals, Jewish resistance was never completely crushed, even in the death camps. Acts of individual defiance were recorded in every ghetto and every camp. This was defiance by people scattered in many thousands of different localities, divided by distance, ghetto walls and concentration camp watchtowers. It was defiance by unarmed and isolated individuals, surrounded by captive populations who frequently collaborated with what should have been the common enemy. It was defiance by those who were often betrayed by non-Jewish neighbours, who were in essence fellow victims.

Defiance by individual Jews, like collective acts of resistance, was that of people for whom the possession of even a single, inadequate weapon was punishable by death; even their own 'illegal' existence was punishable by death. It was resistance by an army without arms, by an army of the old, the sick, the frail and the young, of men, women and children. It was resistance by those who were not allowed the right to surrender, who did not possess the basic right of the soldier who is able to save his life by showing the white flag, and by becoming a prisoner of war. A Jew who surrendered after an act of defiance was invariably shot. A Jew who sought safety in surrender was killed without mercy.

For the Jews, resistance almost always ended in death. Resistance was carried out, wrote Rudolf Reder, one of only two survivors of Belzec death camp, by 'the defenceless remnants of life and youth': by Jews who had little strength and few, if any, resources left, only the desire to remain human beings.

The Nazi plan for every Jewish individual under German rule or control was death. That was the Nazi aim, and had become increasingly the Nazi purpose as the war went on. Yet there were many Jews who, sensing the plan and possessing the ability to run away, to find at least a temporary haven in swamp or forest, chose not to try to escape. Instead, explained Zivia Lubetkin, they decided 'to share the same fate' as those who had no means of escape. 'It is our duty,' she wrote amid the horrors of the Warsaw ghetto, 'to stay with our people until the very end.'

A twenty-four-year-old Jewish girl in Cracow, Matilda Bandet, was approached one morning by her friends with news that an 'action' was imminent. A German raid into the ghetto would be a prelude to yet another deportation. The time had come, they said, to try to escape from the ghetto and make for the woods east of the city, where a small Jewish partisan group was hiding. Matilda Bandet hesitated. 'My place is with my parents,' she said. 'They need me. They are old. They have no means of defending themselves. If I leave them, they will be alone. I will stay here, with them.'

Matilda Bandet's friends hurried off to the cellars, the tunnels and the woods. She remained in the ghetto, soon to be deported with her parents to Belzec, and to be murdered with them – like the majority of those who had to decide between surviving elsewhere, or being with their parents at their time of greatest need and trial. In Matilda Bandet's decision not to leave the ghetto, not to try to save herself, but to stay with her parents, she showed that exact human dignity, which it was the German wish totally to destroy.

In every ghetto, in every deportation train, in every labour camp, even in the death camps, the will to resist was strong. It took many forms: fighting with those few weapons that could be found, fighting with sticks and knives, obtaining food under the threat of death – innumerable individual acts of defiance and protest that reflected the nobility of refusing to allow the Germans their final wish to gloat over panic and despair.

Passivity in itself was a form of courage. 'Not to act,' Emanuel Ringelblum wrote in the aftermath of one particularly savage reprisal in Warsaw, 'not to lift a hand against the Germans, has become the quiet passive heroism of the common Jew.'

To die with dignity was in itself courageous. To resist the dehumanizing, brutalizing force of evil, to refuse to be abased to the level of animals, to live through the torment, to outlive the tormenters, these too were courageous aims. Merely to give witness by one's own testimony, painfully recorded during the war, or set down afterwards, was, in the end, to contribute to a moral victory. Simply to survive was a victory of the human spirit.

ANNE FRANK: IN HIDING AND BETRAYED

Anne Frank was born in Germany on 12 June 1929. Her father, Otto Frank, had trained at Macy's Department Store in New York. During the First World War he was a reserve officer in the German army. His daughter Margot was born in 1926, Anne three years later.

Shortly after Hitler came to power in Germany, Otto Frank and his family left for Holland. Anne was four years old. Holland became her home, and Dutch her language. Her father set up a company that made and distributed pectin, for use in homemade jams and jellies. In 1938 he and a German Jewish refugee from Osnabrück, Hermann van Pels, set up a second company, Pectacon, which prepared spices for sausage making. After seven years in Holland the Franks could forget they were refugees. Then, in May 1940, the German army invaded Holland, and they, and thousands of other German Jewish refugees for whom Holland had seemed a safe sanctuary, were once more under Nazi rule.

On 12 June 1942 Anne Frank received a diary as a thirteenth birthday gift from her father. She wrote it in the form of letters to an imaginary friend, Kitty. 'I hope I shall be able to confide in you completely, as I have never been able to do in anyone before,' she wrote on the first day, 'and I hope that you will be a great support and comfort to me.'

As German anti-Jewish measures intensified, Otto Frank prepared a hiding place in an empty annex next to his office, in the attic of Prinsengracht 263. On 5 July 1942 his elder daughter Margot, who was sixteen,

received a letter ordering her to register for 'labour expansion measures', meaning forced labour. The next day the Frank family went into hiding. A week later Hermann van Pels, his wife and their son Peter joined them. That November the seven took in an eighth *onderduiker* (literally, one who dives under). He was Fritz Pfeffer, a Jewish dentist who had fled from Berlin in 1938. Anne Frank gave them other names in her diary: the van Pels became the van Daans, and Fritz Pfeffer became Albert Dussel.

For two years, Otto Frank's four Dutch business helpers smuggled food and clothing into the attic. Then, on 4 August 1944, the German Security Service (SD) in Amsterdam was informed that eight Jews were in hiding at Prinsengracht 263. All eight were arrested, by a German (Austrian-born) Police Sergeant, Karl Josef Silberbauer, and three Dutch members of the security police. Anne Frank's diary was among the papers that Miep Gies, one of her father's Dutch helpers, managed to save from seizure by the Gestapo.

Imprisoned in Amsterdam for four days, the eight Jews from the attic at Prinsengracht 263 were sent on August 8 to Westerbork, the transit camp in north-east Holland. Four weeks later, as the Allied armies were advancing through northern Europe – the nearest Allied troops being only 120 miles away, in Brussels – the Germans despatched the last train from Westerbork to Auschwitz.

This last deportation train from Holland left Westerbork on 3 September 1944. Among the 1,019 Jews on board were Anne Frank and the seven others – including her parents and her sister Margot – who had been in hiding with her. Three days later the train arrived in Auschwitz, where 549 of the deportees, including all seventy-nine children under the age of fifteen, were immediately gassed. The others were tattooed and sent to the barracks.

Anne and Margot Frank, and their mother, found themselves among 39,000 women in the women's barracks at Birkenau. At the end of October 1944, probably on the 28th, Anne and Margot were sent with a transport of prisoners from Auschwitz to Belsen. Their mother had to remain in Auschwitz, where she died

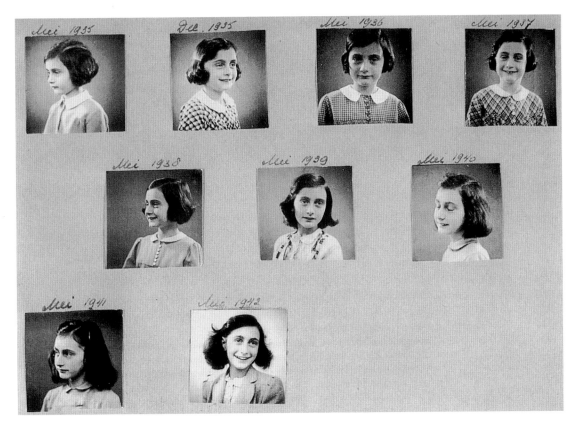

from hunger and exhaustion on 6 January 1945, three weeks before the camp was liberated.

Margot Frank died of typhus at Belsen at the end of February or beginning of March 1945. Anne died a few days later.

With the exception of Otto Frank, none of the others who had been together in the Amsterdam hiding place survived. Hermann van Pels was gassed at Auschwitz in October or November 1944, shortly before the gas chambers ceased operation. His wife died after a death march to Theresienstadt, less than a month before the end of the war. Fritz Pfeffer was sent from Auschwitz to either Buchenwald or Sachsenhausen, and then to Neuengamme concentration camp, where he died. Hermann van Pels's son Peter survived the death march from Auschwitz to Mauthausen that began on 16 January 1945, but died in Mauthausen three days before liberation.

Of the 1,019 Jews deported from Westerbork in the same train as Otto Frank and his family, only forty-five men and eighty-two women survived the war. Otto Frank was among them. He was still in the barracks at Auschwitz when Soviet forces liberated the camp on 27 January 1945 – two months before his daughters' deaths at Belsen.

above
Anne Frank: a panel of photographs that she prepared while in hiding, giving the dates on which they were taken.

opposite
Page seven of the German list of deportees sent from Westerbork to Auschwitz on 3 September 1944, giving their names and dates of birth. Anne Frank's name appears in its original German form, Anneliese.

right, top stamp
A stamp issued by the Dutch Post Office on what would have been Anne Frank's fiftieth birthday, 12 June 1979.

right, bottom stamp
An Israeli stamp honours Anne Frank, and shows a picture of the house in Amsterdam where she and her family were in hiding. It was issued in 1988. Her signature is reproduced on the lower part of the stamp.

Anne Frank's diary

6 June 1944 (two months before the discovery of the annex)
'This is D-day', came the announcement over the British Radio....

The invasion had begun!... According to the German news, British parachute troops have landed on the French coast. British landing craft are in battle with the German Navy, says the BBC....

Great commotion in the 'Secret Annexe'! Would the long-awaited liberation that has been talked of so much, but which still seems too wonderful, too much like a fairy-tale, ever come true? Could we be granted victory this year, 1944? We don't know yet, but hope is revived within us; it gives us fresh courage, and makes us strong again. Since we must put up bravely with all the fears, privations, and sufferings, the great thing now is to remain calm and steadfast. Now more than ever we must clench our teeth and not cry out. France, Russia, Italy and Germany, too, can all cry out and give vent to their misery, but we haven't the right to do that yet!

Oh, Kitty, the best part of the invasion is that I have the feeling that friends are approaching. We have been oppressed by those terrible Germans for so long, they have had their knives so at our throats, that the thought of friends and delivery fills us with confidence!

Now it doesn't concern the Jews anymore; no, it concerns Holland and all occupied Europe. Perhaps, Margot says, I may yet be able to go back to school in September or October.

OSKAR SCHINDLER AND OTHER GERMAN RESCUERS

OSKAR SCHINDLER: CRACOW AND BRUNNLITZ

Just outside the edge of the Cracow ghetto was a factory that manufactured kitchen utensils. It was run by a German Catholic, Oskar Schindler, who, like all German factory managers in the neighbourhood, was allowed to employ Jewish workers.

Schindler, whose relations with the Gestapo were outwardly cordial, had always sought to protect the Jews who worked in his factory. When the Gestapo tried to transfer some of his workers to the nearby slave labour camp at Plaszow, he was able, by bribery and persuasion, to keep them. Thousands of Jews were murdered in Plaszow.

By the summer of 1944 more than five hundred Jews were under Schindler's protection at his factory. With the evacuation of the Cracow and Auschwitz region, as Soviet forces approached in January 1945, Schindler transferred his factory to Brünnlitz, taking his Jewish workforce with him.

On 29 January 1945, while at Brünnlitz, Schindler was told of a locked goods wagon at Brünnlitz station. The wagon was marked on the outside: 'Property of the SS'. It had been travelling on the railways for ten days, covered in ice. Inside were more than a hundred Jews, starving and freezing: they were Jews from Birkenau who had been at the labour camp at Golleschau, Jews who had once lived in Poland, Czechoslovakia, France, Holland and Hungary.

Schindler had no authority to take the wagon. But he was determined to try to save those Jews and asked a railway official to show him the Bill of Lading – the document authorizing the wagon's trans-shipment. When the railway official was momentarily distracted, Schindler wrote on the Bill of Lading: 'Final destination, Brünnlitz.' Schindler then pointed out to the official that the wagon was intended for his factory, and ordered the railway authorities to transfer the wagon to his factory siding. There he broke open the locks. Sixteen of the Jews had frozen to death. Not one of the survivors weighed more than thirty-five kilogrammes. Schindler fed and guarded them. He was helped by his wife Emilie, who provided beds on which they could be nursed back to life. 'She took care of these Golleschau Jews,' a

survivor of Schindler's factories, Moshe Bejski, later recalled. 'She prepared food for them every day.'

Between 1943 and 1945, Schindler saved more than fifteen hundred Jews by employing them in his factory, and by treating them humanely. He died in Germany in October 1974. At his funeral, which was held in the Latin cemetery in Jerusalem, on the slope of Mount Zion, more than four hundred of the Jews whom he had saved paid him their last respects.

JULIUS MADRITSCH: TARNOW

On 25 and 26 March 1943, at the time of the liquidation of the Cracow ghetto, a factory owner in Tarnow, Julius Madritsch, an Austrian from Vienna, had taken 232 Jews – men, women and children – from the Cracow ghetto into his clothing factory at Tarnow. He did not ill-treat them there. Instead, as Oscar Schindler was doing in Cracow, he protected them from deportation. Five months later, on August 31, the commandant of Plaszow, Amnon Goeth, went specially to Tarnow to prepare for the destruction of the Tarnow ghetto. That night he ordered Madritsch to pay a large sum of money to protect 'his' Jews. Madritsch did so. The Jews were saved.

OTTO WEIDT: BERLIN

In Berlin itself, a German brush manufacturer, Otto Weidt, had a small factory. To protect Jews from deportation, he employed several hundred in his factory, insisting in his discussions with the Gestapo that the work they did was essential for the German war economy. Those whom he employed were blind and deaf mutes. He also helped fifty-six men who were in hiding, with food and false documents. He was always under suspicion, and Gestapo searches were frequent. A plaque at his factory records his persistence and his courage. Its last line reads: 'Many men thank him for their survival.' Tragically, of the several hundred whom Otto Weidt helped, only twenty-seven survived the repeated Gestapo round-ups.

GERMANS AND AUSTRIANS: BIALYSTOK

The number of Germans and Austrians who helped the Jews in the Polish city of Bialystok was exceptional. One

of them, a German Social Democrat named Schade, was the manager of a textile mill. Through a group of Jewish girls, led by Maryla Rozycka, he maintained contact with the Jewish resistance organization inside the ghetto and with the partisans in the forests, whom he supplied with arms, clothing and information.

After the liquidation of the Bialystok ghetto, Schade hid twelve Jews in his factory. They survived until the arrival of the Soviet army. On several occasions, guided by Jewish partisans, he travelled into forests to meet, and help, the Soviet partisan commander in the region.

Another German in Bialystok, Beneschek, from the Sudetenland, was a Communist in hiding from the Gestapo under a false identity. He was also the manager of a textile mill, located on the border of the ghetto. He employed both Jews and Poles, and made it possible for Jews to smuggle arms into the ghetto. He also provided Jews with false documents and money.

Beneschek introduced another Sudeten German, Kudlatschek, to the Jewish resistance organization. Kudlatschek, who was in charge of the motor pool of the textile mills, put his own car at the disposal of the local Jewish Anti-Fascist Committee. A number of Jews left Bialystok in his car and travelled to partisan territory. Kudlatschek also transported arms and munitions to the Jewish resistance organization in the Grodno ghetto. Another German, Stefan Blume, rescued twenty Jews from Bialystok prison.

Jews were also helped in Bialystok by a number of German soldiers stationed there. From them the Jews obtained a few weapons and several wireless sets. Another German in Bialystok, Otto Busse, was in charge of a painting shop attached to the SS units. A practising Christian, he had joined the Nazi Party in 1933, left it in disgust in 1935 and rejoined under pressure in 1939. He helped the Jews employed in his shop to smuggle pistols and several rifles inside old stove pipes into the ghetto.

In 1961 Busse visited Israel. On his return to Germany it became known locally that he had helped Jews, 'I was denounced as a traitor to the fatherland and Jew-lover.' Things got so bad, especially from former Wehrmacht soldiers, that he had to leave his home at Bendsheim near Darmstadt and his job.

A 'Schindler Jew' recalls

Every day from 18 October 1944 to 8 May 1945 at midnight, Schindler helped. 'I will not leave you until the last SS-man has left the camp,' he told us. If a Jew lost his glasses, Schindler went and bought glasses. Above the ration of a hundred grammes of bread, a bowl of so-called soup and two cups of erszatz coffee each day, he provided extra rations. When a Jewess became pregnant, an 'offence' punishable by death, Schindler went into Brno and bought the necessary surgical equipment, and the doctor in the camp made an abortion.

Moshe Bejski, a Jew from Dzialoszyce in southern Poland, recalling the factory at Brünnlitz, 1944–45. Bejski was later a Supreme Court judge in Israel

above left
Jewish slave labourers at Plaszow slave labour camp, in the suburbs of Cracow. In 1944 more than 22,000 Jews worked there, including at least 6,000 who had been brought from Hungary. An estimated 8,000 Jews were murdered there. The last commandant, Amnon Goeth, was a sadist who delighted in personally killing Jews – shooting them dead at random – and in showing off his shooting prowess in front of his young son.

left
Julius Eisenstein, one of those saved by Schindler, photographed at Theresienstadt immediately after liberation, still in his concentration camp jacket. Born in 1921, in Miechow, southern Poland, Eisenstein emigrated after the war to the United States, becoming a restaurateur in New York.

THE DEPORTATIONS FROM HUNGARY

The journey to Auschwitz

... we travelled across Slovakia, past the Tatra Mountains. In the clear sunshine the hills looked majestic and strangely indifferent. What did those hills care about us? They stood there for thousands of years, saw generations and generations suffer and die, yet they never moved but stood still. They saw us passing and the rocks did not tumble down on the line. They let us pass. Cruel things those mountains! I felt everything was conspiring against us.

By noon, inside the wagon it was unbearably hot and the bucket in the box stunk to high heavens. There was plenty of food (hardly anyone ate), but the water barrel was nearly exhausted and the little water that was still left in it was warm and full of dirt.

The mountains were left behind and gradually the whole scenery changed. Meadows and cows grazing made a sharp contrast to the high mountains. On the plain I had the feeling that the picture confronting me was a very humble one and suggested peace. The names of the stations were spelt in a different way and German soldiers were more frequent. We were in Poland!

I sat down. There was not room for everyone, so we had to sit between each others' legs. In front of me Gaby, and Dad behind. We were not talking. The train raced with time itself and I was beginning to go mad. The heat, the thirst, the dirt – everything seemed to conspire against me.

Hugo Gryn, then thirteen, recalling the deportation from Berehovo. His brother, Gabi, aged eleven, was murdered on arrival **at** Auschwitz

In April 1943 the Hungarian Regent, Admiral Horthy, was summoned by Hitler to Salzburg. Hitler pressed him to deport Hungary's 750,000 Jews to Auschwitz. Horthy refused. Almost a year later, to prevent Horthy turning his back on Germany and pulling out of the war, German troops marched into Hungary. By a grim turn of events, the fate of Hungary's Jews at last lay with Germany.

With the German troops entering Hungary in March 1944 came an SS unit headed by Adolf Eichmann. He brought a comprehensive deportation plan, devised a few weeks earlier when the SS unit met at Mauthausen concentration camp. Each of the five men devising it were experts on the 'Final Solution': Eichmann himself, SS Major Dieter Wisliceny, a thirty-three-year-old former theology student who had been responsible for the deportation of tens of thousands of Slovak Jews to Auschwitz in 1942, SS Major Alois Brunner, who had deported the Jews from Paris, SS Major Krumey from Vienna, and SS Captain Siegfried Seidl from Belsen.

Among their first orders was the uprooting of Jews throughout Hungary into ghettos.

The first deportations from Hungary to Auschwitz began on 15 May 1944. SS units supervised the round-ups. When Jews, having been taken from the ghettos to the train stations, tried to resist boarding the trains, as they did at Munkacs and Satoraljaujhely, the SS shot them down. Hungarian railway workers drove the trains, and armed Hungarian police guarded them, to the Slovak border.

When the Hungarian Jewish leader Rudolf Kastner asked Eichmann for six to eight hundred exemptions to the deportations, Eichmann told him: 'You must understand me. I have to clean up the provincial towns of their Jewish garbage. I must take this Jewish muck out of the provinces. I cannot play the role of the saviour of the Jews.'

On May 25, SS General Edmund Veesenmayer, Reich Plenipotentiary and Hitler's deputy in Hungary (he was thirty-nine years old), reported to Berlin that

138,870 Jews had been deported to their 'destination' in the previous ten days. On the day of his report, a group who were being led around Birkenau's electrified perimeter fence to one of the two gas chambers situated at the far edge of the camp, sensed that something was wrong. Calling out to each other to run, they scattered into the birch wood along which, at that moment, they were being led to the gas chamber. The SS immediately switched on the searchlights installed around the gas chambers, and opened fire with machine guns on those who were trying to flee. There were no survivors. A similar act of revolt took place on May 28, and was likewise ruthlessly suppressed.

On May 29 more than a thousand Jews reached the German border from the southern Hungarian city of Baja, on route to Birkenau. They had been sealed in the wagons for three and a half days. At the border the

wagons were opened for the first time. Fifty-five Jews were dead. Two hundred had gone mad.

As many as three deportation trains left Hungary every day for more than fifty days. As the weeks passed, fewer and fewer of these deportees were taken as slave labourers when they reached Auschwitz. Of more than a thousand Jews from the town of Bonyhad who were deported in one of the last trains, on 6 July 1944, just over a thousand were murdered. Only seventy survived the war. From Bonyhad, Edith Low wrote a postcard to a relative in Budapest, which she threw into the street just before the deportation. The card was sent on by the local post office. 'We are about to start our journey to an unknown destination,' she wrote. 'God bless you all and may He help us to be able to endure it.' Edith Low survived. Her parents, deported to Auschwitz with her, did not.

above
Auschwitz-Birkenau: children and adults in the birch grove before being taken to the gas chambers and murdered. This is one of more than two hundred photographs taken by SS Sergeant Ernst Hoffman on a single day in June or early July 1944, of Jews brought from the Berehovo ghetto, in Ruthenia, then part of Hungarian-occupied Czechoslovakia.

opposite
One of SS Sergeant Hoffman's photographs at the 'ramp' at Birkenau. These women and children have already been selected to be sent to the gas chambers. The figure on the right, in striped uniform, is one of the Jewish prisoners who had to take away the baggage of all new arrivals to be sorted.

ESCAPE FROM AUSCHWITZ: RUDOLF VRBA'S STORY

On 7 March 1944 more than 4,000 Czech, Austrian and German Jews, who had been deported the previous September from Theresienstadt to Auschwitz and kept alive at Birkenau as a group – known as the Czech Family Camp – were sent to the gas chambers. A second group was then brought from Theresienstadt, and likewise kept together. Seeing this, a young Slovak Jew, Rudolf Vrba, then nineteen-and-a-half years old, who worked first in the 'Canada Commando' (*see pages 122–3*) and then as a registrar, was determined to alert the world to the imminent fate of the second Family Camp. He was convinced that if there were an international outcry, the second Family Camp would not be destroyed.

Vrba made plans to escape, together with a fellow-Slovak Jew, Alfred Wetzler, twenty-six years old, who had personally witnessed the destruction of the Czech Family Camp. Watching the plans that were being made

to prepare Birkenau for a considerable number of new arrivals, the two men also wanted to alert Hungarian Jews to their impending fate. The office in which Vrba worked was only a hundred yards from the rail spur being built into Birkenau from the Auschwitz railway line. 'The purpose of this ramp was no secret in Birkenau,' he later recalled. 'The SS were talking about "Hungarian salami" and "a million units".' In addition, several dozen new barracks were being constructed just outside the perimeter fence.

On 7 April 1944 Vrba and Wetzler hid in a pile of wooden planks being used for the construction of the new barracks. Two days later they escaped from Auschwitz, making their way southward into Slovakia. There they told the story of the deportations and the gas chambers to the surviving leaders of Slovak Jewry. Vrba had memorized precise details about the incoming deportations and the tattoo numbers allocated to those sent to the barracks. His information made it clear that the place to which so many hundreds of thousands of French, Dutch, Belgian and Italian Jews had been deported, hitherto known in the West (and in those countries themselves) only as 'somewhere in the east' or 'the unknown destination', was Auschwitz and its gas chambers.

Shortly after Vrba and Wetzler made their report in Slovakia, they were joined by two more escapees, a Czech Jew, Arnost Rosin, and a Polish Jew, Czeslaw Mordowicz. Rosin and Mordowicz had witnessed the first few days of the arrival and destruction of Hungarian Jewry. The Vrba-Wetzler Report was combined with the details brought by Rosin and Mordowicz into what later became known as the 'Auschwitz Report'.

On 24 June 1944 the Auschwitz Report, having been smuggled by courier from the Slovak capital, Bratislava, to the Hungarian capital, Budapest, and then by rail through Vienna to Geneva, in Switzerland, was taken from Geneva to the Swiss capital, Berne, from where it was telegraphed to London and Washington. It was then broadcast by the Allies and widely reported in the Allied newspapers. Pressure on the Hungarian Regent, Admiral Horthy, to stop the deportations was intense. Three neutral States – Sweden, Spain and Turkey – protested immediately. They were joined in their protests by the International Red Cross, with its headquarters in Geneva, and by the Vatican representative in Budapest, Angelo Rotta.

On June 26, Clifford Norton, a British diplomat in the Swiss capital, Berne, sent a three-part telegram to London. Prepared by one of the Jewish Agency representatives in Geneva, Richard Lichtheim, the first and second parts set out the full details of the Auschwitz Report, and the mass murder of the Hungarian deportees. The third part called for the 'widest publicity', and also for bombing, in an attempt to halt the deportations. The bombing request had been turned down two days earlier in Washington, by the Assistant Secretary for War, John J. McCloy, who subsequently turned it down three more times. But as soon as this same bombing request reached Churchill, he wrote to the Foreign Secretary: 'Get anything out of the Air Force you can, and invoke me if necessary.'

Lichtheim suggested three possible bombing objectives: the railway lines from Hungary to Auschwitz, the death camp installations at Auschwitz and 'all government buildings in Budapest'. On July 2 – as part of the Allied air campaign against German railway marshalling yards – American bombs fell on Budapest. Several Hungarian government buildings were hit – in error. Horthy, who had been shown intercepted copies of the three-part telegram from Berne, was convinced that the American bombers had hit these government targets deliberately, and had done so in direct response to the Auschwitz Report.

On June 28, as soon as President Roosevelt was shown the Auschwitz Report, he had issued a public warning to Horthy to halt the deportation of Hungarian Jews. Horthy did not want his capital destroyed. On July 7, five days after the American bombing raid on Budapest, he ordered the deportations from Hungary to stop. The German authorities, who did not have the power to carry them out without Hungarian help, had no alternative but to accept.

Between May 15 and July 7 more than 437,000 Hungarian Jews had been deported to Auschwitz. Of them, 365,000 had been murdered there. The rest had been tattooed and sent to the barracks. There, many

died of starvation and the brutality of the SS guards. Others had been sent as slave labourers to Buna-Monowitz, less than four miles from the gas chambers. Just over 170,000 remained alive in Budapest. Eichmann was ready to begin their deportation, when Horthy's ruling, issued on July 7, made further deportations impossible. Eichmann left Hungary and returned to Germany. The Jews of Budapest would not be sent to Auschwitz. The four escapees from Auschwitz had saved more than 170,000 lives.

The Vrba-Wetzler Report

The crematorium contains a large hall, a gas chamber and a furnace. People are assembled in the hall, which holds 2,000.... They have to undress and are given a piece of soap and a towel as if they were going to the baths. Then they are crowded into the gas chamber which is hermetically sealed. Several SS men in gas masks then pour into the gas chamber through three openings in the ceiling a preparation of the poison gas maga-cyclon.... At the end of three minutes all the persons are dead. The dead bodies are then taken away in carts to the furnace to be burnt.

A section of the summary of the **Vrba-Wetzler Report**, as telegraphed to London on 26 June 1944

There is no doubt that this is probably the greatest and most horrible crime ever committed in the whole history of the world, and it has been done by scientific machinery by nominally civilized men in the name of a great State and one of the leading races of Europe. It is quite clear that all concerned in the crime who may fall into our hands, including the people who only obeyed orders by carrying out the butcheries, should be put to death after their association with the murders has been proved.

Winston Churchill, writing on 11 July 1944, after reading the Auschwitz Report

top left map
The escape route of Rudolf Vrba and Alfred Wetzler.

above left map
The Auschwitz Report reaches the Allies.

RAOUL WALLENBERG AND OTHER DIPLOMATS: BUDAPEST

With the ending of the deportations from Hungary to Auschwitz in the first week of July 1944, more than 170,000 Jews living in and around Budapest, who had not been deported, appealed for protective documents that might enable them to survive attacks by the Hungarian Arrow Cross fascists, and any future deportations. The United States and Britain both responded immediately, and positively, to this appeal.

In Washington, the War Refugee Board – set up by President Roosevelt at the beginning of 1944 to help European Jewry – appealed to neutral States to grant protection to the Jews in Budapest. The War Refugee Board would provide whatever money was needed. A group of Swedish officials who were then in Washington were asked by the Board to recommend someone to carry out this difficult, even dangerous task on behalf of Sweden. The group recommended Raoul

Wallenberg, a thirty-two-year-old Swedish banker from a prominent Swedish family. He reached Budapest, with diplomatic credentials, on 9 July 1944. The last of the trains from Hungary to Auschwitz had left two days earlier. But Wallenberg's presence in the capital gave heart to the Jews, whose future was uncertain. His first task was to issue Swedish visas to 630 Hungarian Jews. At the same time, his Swiss diplomatic colleague, Charles Lutz, issued 700 Swiss visas to Hungarian Jews who had British permission to enter Palestine.

On 15 October 1944 the Arrow Cross seized power in Budapest. There was an upsurge of anti-Jewish violence. Using money from the War Refugee Board, Wallenberg rented thirty-two buildings, in which 15,000 Jews were sheltered, under the Swedish flag. The passes that he issued to them said that they were in transit to Sweden, under Swedish government

above, top
A stamp commemorating Wallenberg's work in Budapest, issued by Israel in 1983. The quotation in Hebrew and English under the stamp is from the Book of Proverbs, 'But the path of the just is as the shining light'.

above, middle
Wallenberg honoured by his native land, Sweden, on a stamp issued in 1988.

above, bottom
A Swiss stamp, issued in 1999, honouring Charles Lutz.

right
Wallenberg at work in Budapest, 26 November 1944.

protection. Legally, Wallenberg was authorized by the Swedish government to issue 4,500 passes. To protect the growing number of Jews in danger of attack, he ignored his instructions and issued three times that number. Two hundred Hungarian Jewish volunteers helped distribute the passes.

Other diplomats accredited to Hungary also made extraordinary efforts that October to save the Jews of Budapest from being murdered in the streets. An 'International Ghetto' was set up, within which the Jews were protected from attack by diplomats who extended their national flags to help them. One of these diplomats was Giorgio Perlasca, an Italian citizen, who was serving as the senior diplomat in charge of the Spanish embassy in Budapest. Perlasca issued Spanish government protective passes to as many as three thousand Jews. He also established a number of 'safe houses' for Jews under Spanish government protection.

Two other foreign diplomats who extended protection to the Jews of Budapest within the confines of the International Ghetto were Friedrich Born, the Director of the Budapest office of the Geneva-based International Committee of the Red Cross, and Charles Lutz, the Swiss Consul in the Hungarian capital. Lutz issued 7,800 protective documents under his own signature.

The protective documents and safe houses provided by Wallenberg, Perlasca, Lutz and Born saved tens of thousands of Budapest's Jews from Eichmann, who returned to Budapest in October 1944. The deportations to Auschwitz had stopped three months earlier, and were not renewed. But Eichmann was able, with the help of Hungarian fascist militiamen, to round up 80,000 Jews in Budapest, and send them on foot towards Austria. Conditions on the march were terrible. German guards shot without compunction those who could not keep up. More than 30,000 died on the march.

Determined to bring back as many of the deportees as possible, Wallenberg went to the route of the march, and on the spot issued protective documents. Several hundred Jews were able to return to Budapest.

On 24 December 1944 Soviet forces besieged Budapest. Eichmann, who had once more left the city, this time to avoid capture, ordered the execution of the

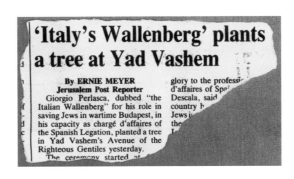

top
Part of a report in the *Jerusalem Post* of 26 September 1989. The previous day, Giorgio Perlasca had planted a tree in the 'Avenue of the Righteous Gentiles' at the Holocaust memorial and museum, Yad Vashem, in Jerusalem. Perlasca was also given honorary citizenship of Israel.

above
Friedrich Born, the Director of the Budapest office of the Geneva-based International Committee of the Red Cross.

70,000 Jews in the Budapest ghetto who had no protective passes. Wallenberg immediately sent a message to the SS General who was to carry out the order (and who had assembled 500 machine gunners for the task) that if the planned slaughter was not cancelled, he would ensure that the general was hanged as a war criminal. The general cancelled the order.

Perlasca's work recalled

The gate-keeper at the embassy tried to keep me out, but I got in by a miracle. Using what little German I knew, I presented the letter to a secretary. As I was speaking to her, a man came out of an adjoining room and looked over her shoulder at the letter. I presented my passport pictures of my father, my mother, my older sister and myself. The man nodded and went back to his room. A short while later, he came back and handed me a *Schutzpass* (protective pass) made out to all four of us. Later I learned that the man had been Mr Perlasca. I personally saw Mr Perlasca come to our house almost every day, bringing powdered milk and food.

Avraham Ronai, born in Budapest in 1932, recalling reaching the Spanish Embassy doors

Wallenberg's fate

On 13 January 1945 Soviet troops entered Budapest. Wallenberg drove, under Soviet military escort, to the headquarters of the Soviet commander, to present a plan he had drawn up for the relief of the surviving Jewish population. He was never seen again: the Soviets had arrested him and taken him to the Lubyanka prison in Moscow. They seem to have suspected that he was an American spy. Ten years later, the Soviet Foreign Minister announced that Wallenberg had been executed in the Lubyanka in 1947. But rumours persisted that he was still alive, and individuals claimed to have seen him in Soviet labour camps. In the year 2000 Wallenberg would have been 88 years old.

THE DEATH MARCHES

Recalling a death march

When the Russians approached Auschwitz the whole camp was evacuated. The date was January 18, 1945. We were lined up in rows of five and told that we will have to walk, and that anybody trying to escape will be shot. It was very cold and snowing.

We went westward walking in our wooden shoes on icy snow-covered roads. We were still in our striped thin clothes. Many collapsed and they were immediately shot on the spot. We had to take the corpses and throw them into a ditch next to the road. The SS surrounded each of our columns and were ready with their guns.

After walking the whole day and part of the night, we reached a brick factory where we were allowed to rest and sleep under cover. Only half of us were still alive when we reached the factory. One in our group, a French political prisoner, did not wake up. He was dead, frozen stiff. I took his red triangle from his tunic, put it in my pocket, hoping to exchange it later for the Star of David insignia. Finally we were taken to a railway station and squeezed into an open cattle wagon, standing room only. We thus travelled through Austria and Germany seven days and seven nights until we reached our destination. Nine in our wagon died during the journey.

Freddie Knoller, born in Vienna, deported to Auschwitz from France

As the Soviet army moved closer to the slave labour camps that the Germans had set up on Polish soil, the slave labourers were evacuated westward, to factories and concentration camps on German soil. The largest slave labour camp region to be evacuated was the factory zone that German industrialists had created around Auschwitz. More than 30,000 Jewish men and women were being employed there at the time of the evacuation.

The evacuations started in mid-1944 and accelerated in January 1945. Many began on foot. After several days, most of the evacuees were put on trains – open trucks. Some marches continued on foot for many days, even weeks. An estimated 100,000 Jews died during these 'death marches'.

Thousands who were too weak to march away were shot on the eve of evacuation. On the marches, those who were too weak to continue were also shot. 'Anybody who was weak,' Israel Gutman – a survivor of Majdanek and Auschwitz – recalled, 'anybody who had to sit down for a few minutes, was shot at.'

On the marches in the region of Blechhammer, fifteen hundred Jews were shot. 'We heard shooting all the time,' Alfred Oppenheimer recalled, of his own march to Blechhammer from Gleiwitz. 'We were not allowed to turn our heads, but we knew what the shooting meant. All those lagging behind were shot dead.'

As the death marches continued from the Auschwitz region, the bodies of the murdered Jews were thrown into the nearest roadside ditches. At the village of Leszczyny a memorial records the murder of 250 prisoners who had been taken from the march to an evacuation train. They had been shot as they jumped from the train and tried to flee to the neighbouring forests.

Among the Jews on the death marches was Polish-born Moses Finkelstein. Under the name of Michael Fink, he had fought with the French resistance in the Vosges. Captured during an armed clash with the Germans, he had been deported to Birkenau. Within sound of the guns of the Soviet forces – and liberation – he was killed by the German guards.

By the end of February 1945 the factories to which the Jews from Birkenau had been evacuated two months earlier were themselves within a few days of being overrun by the Soviet forces. On February 23 the Jews in Schwarzheide, on the Dresden to Berlin autobahn, were evacuated. The three hundred weakest were sent in open goods wagons to Belsen. There, all but one of them perished.

A month earlier, from a camp at Neusalz, on the Oder, a thousand Jewish women, many of them survivors of Auschwitz, had been marched away from the advancing Soviet forces. As with so many of the death marches, they passed through many German towns and villages. One of those on the march, Gisela Teumann, later recalled: 'We passed through some German town. We asked for food. At first they thought that we were German refugees. The SS man who accompanied us shouted: "Don't give them anything to eat, it's Jews they are." And so I got no food. German children began to throw stones at us.'

Of the thousand women who set off from Neusalz, only two hundred reached Flossenburg alive, forty-two days after they had been sent on their tragic way. From Flossenbürg, they too were sent on by train to Belsen.

Those who survived the death marches were already survivors – of ghettos, deportations and slave labour camps. Their final torment came in the camps to which they were sent. In some camps, slave labour continued. In others, the marchers were left, often without food or

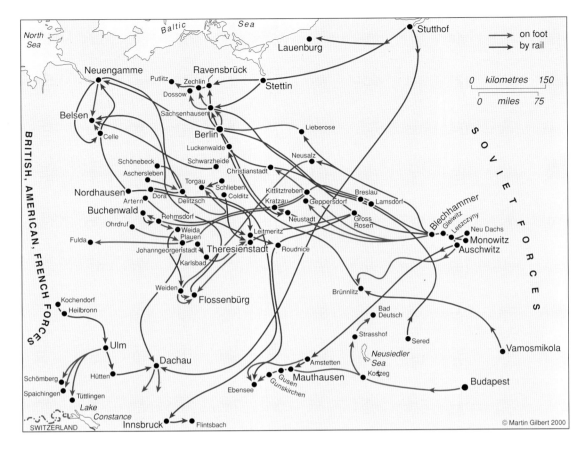

medical attention, to die in the thousands and tens of thousands. These last camps included Belsen, Dachau and Mauthausen, and their many sub-camps.

Many of the death marches were to slave labour camps on German soil. One of the largest was Dora-Nordhausen, where Jews were among tens of thousands of slave labourers forced to work in factories built underground, assisting Germany's flying-bomb and rocket production.

Belsen and Dachau, Buchenwald and Mauthausen, Sachsenhausen and Ravensbrück, and their many sub-camps, became the destinations of hundreds of evacuation trains and marches. Throughout February and March columns of men and women, and crowded railway trucks, converged on the long-existing concentration camps, which had a new task. These camps had been transformed into holding camps for the remnant of a destroyed people, whose labour was still of some last-minute utility for a dying Reich, or whose emaciated bodies were to be left to languish unattended, and in agony.

For the death marchers, there was no respite. On 30 April 1945, Hitler committed suicide in Berlin. That day 2,775 Jews from Rehmsdorf, near Buchenwald, were

above

This map shows some of the main routes that were recorded by Allied intelligence officers immediately after liberation, when they questioned survivors. The routes shown in red are those of the death marches that took place on foot, often over great distances. Those in blue were by rail, frequently in open goods wagons, in the depth of winter.

opposite

Photograph of a gravestone at the side of a road at Bad Deutsch-Altenburg, Austria. On it, under the Star of David, is written, in German: 'War grave, 1939–1945. 11 unknown Jews, 1945.' They had died during a death march.

being marched towards Theresienstadt. A thousand of them, fleeing from the march during an Allied air raid, were caught by their guards and shot. The remaining fifteen hundred continued on the march. Only five hundred reached Theresienstadt alive.

Hugo Gryn, a survivor of several death marches, later reflected: 'For the Nazis, the destruction of the Jews had an unchanging function until the very end of the war; it was the only thing about which they have never changed their policies. I have never ceased to be amazed by the priority they gave it, even when everything was collapsing.'

Recalling a death march

When the SS marched us out of Dresden they made us halt in an area like a small market place. We were made to sit down on the cobblestones. Germans from nearby houses came to look at us. The SS wanted to entertain these German onlookers. So they began throwing bits of carrots and bits of turnip in amongst us hoping that we will fight and claw for them. But we didn't. Hungry that we were, we passed the word around 'to sit passively' and 'behave with dignity'. This angered the SS so much that they began kicking us into action.

Roman Halter, aged sixteen during the death march

My father recalled that during the death marches, when the prisoners were marched through German areas, women and children would smash bottles at their feet so that these prisoners, whose footwear consisted, at most, of rags tied around their feet, would rip their feet on the broken glass. By contrast, while walking through Czech territory, Czech people were throwing bread to the prisoners, and my father remembered that a woman risked her life to run out and hand him a piece of bread, ensuring that he got his piece of bread amidst the scramble, and she was hit on her head by a guard with the butt of a machine gun for her troubles.

Marilyn Herman, second generation. Her father, Abraham Herman, had been born in Mukacevo, Czechoslovakia (in 1944 part of Hungary), in 1931, and was deported to Auschwitz in 1944. After liberation he went to Britain

THE FATE OF NON-JEWS

below right
A Gypsy family in Volhynia, part of eastern Poland between the two world wars.

below
A Gypsy child photographed at Auschwitz. The letter 'Z' on his tattoo stands for *Zigeuner* (Gypsy).

From the first days of the German invasion of Poland, Polish civilians were executed in every city and town: at least 16,000 in the first two months. Civilian hostages were shot in retaliation whenever a German was attacked. Religious, political and communal leaders were tortured and killed. By the end of the war, in addition to three million Polish Jews, as many as two million non-Jewish Poles, most of them Roman Catholics, had also been murdered. Throughout Poland there are memorials to individual Poles murdered in towns and villages, and to mass executions.

After the German invasion of the Soviet Union in June 1941, Communist political commissars were shot on sight. Throughout German-occupied Russia, villagers were murdered in the hundreds of thousands, and hundreds of villages burned to the ground. More than three million Soviet soldiers, taken prisoner on the battlefield, were murdered in captivity.

The killing of prisoners of war was not confined to captive Soviet prisoners. In May 1940, at two villages near Dunkirk (one of them named Paradis), SS troops shot dead 170 British soldiers after they had been captured and disarmed. In June 1944, at three villages near Caen, seventy disarmed Canadian soldiers were also shot dead by SS troops.

Hundreds of thousands of civilians in Greece and Yugoslavia were rounded up, held hostage and killed, their bodies often left hanging in the streets as a deterrent to resistance and protest. As many as a million Serbs were murdered by the Germans. At Kragujevac, 7,253 Serbs were shot down in cold blood in a single massacre.

Gypsies were everywhere singled out for detention and death. By 1939 many German and Austrian Gypsies had been sent to Buchenwald and Dachau. In 1940 all surviving German Gypsies were deported to Poland and forced to live in sections set aside for them within Jewish ghettos. In January 1942, some Gypsies were included in almost every deportation of Jews to the death camp at Chelmno, where 4,300 Gypsies were killed. On 16 December 1942 an SS decree ordered Gypsies from all over Europe to be deported to Auschwitz: 16,000 were murdered there on arrival.

In Auschwitz, where more than a million Jews were murdered, there were many non-Jewish victims. These included a quarter of a million Poles, 20,000 Gypsies, and 12,000 Soviet prisoners of war.

Hundreds of thousands of civilians were also the victims of the wartime bombing of cities and towns

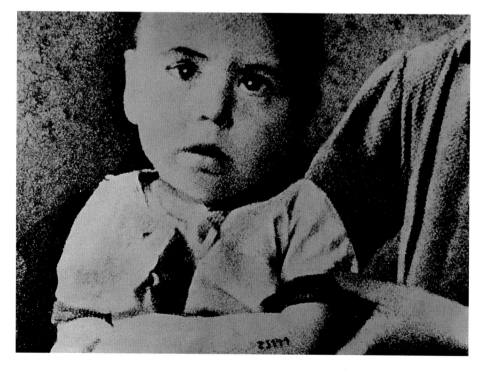

throughout Europe. In Warsaw, Rotterdam, Coventry and Belgrade, many thousands of Polish, Dutch, British and Yugoslav civilians were among the victims of German aerial attack between 1939 and 1941. Later in the war it was German civilians who suffered most from bombing. In Hamburg, on the night of 28 July 1943, more than 42,000 German civilians were killed in a single British bombing attack. Tens of thousands of civilians in Berlin and Dresden were also killed – in Berlin over a three-year period, in Dresden during a single raid less than three months before the war ended.

Young children were frequently the victims of bombing. Even those in Britain who had been evacuated for safety from the main cities were not always safe. On 17 August 1942 a German bomber flew over the Cornish fishing village of Coverack. Four people were killed. One of them, John Herbert White, was a three-year-old local boy; another, Leslie Albert Chambers, was a four-year-old evacuee from Enfield, near London. He had been sent to Cornwall for safety. On the day of the death of these two children in Britain, twenty-seven children under the age of four, who had been deported three days earlier from Paris, were among more than five hundred Jewish deportees murdered at Auschwitz.

There were also occasions, when the Germans acted against a local population, where the victims were predominantly Christian, but where Jews were caught up – in some cases by accident – in the killings. On 24 March 1944, seventy-three Jews were among the 335 Italians seized at random in Rome and executed by the SS in the Ardeatine caves outside the city, as a reprisal against Italian partisan activity. On 10 June 1944, four days after the Allied landings in Normandy, the Germans killed 642 French villagers at Oradour-sur-Glâne, as a reprisal for the killing by a French partisan, in another village, of a German SS army commander. The women and children of Oradour were ordered into the church, which was then locked and set on fire. The men were killed by machine-gun fire. Among the dead were seven Jews. Two years earlier they had found a refuge in Oradour and had no reason to believe that they would not be safe until liberation. One had been born in Warsaw, and another in Budapest.

Following the assassination of Reinhard Heydrich in Prague in June 1942, two Czech villages, Lidice and Lezaky, were burned to the ground, and more than three hundred of their inhabitants killed. Eighty-two children from Lidice were sent to Chelmno, and murdered there. In Prague, 860 Czechs were shot in reprisals; in Brno, 395 were shot. Reprisals in German-occupied Greece were also savage. The death of a single German soldier, shot by a Greek partisan, could lead to the destruction of a whole village. At Klissura, where 233 villagers were killed, fifty of the dead were children under ten years of age. At Mikulino, in Russia, all 275 women patients in the town's mental hospital were killed.

An estimated 32,000 German civilians were executed by the Nazis between 1933 and 1945 for so-called 'political offences'. They included Communists, Socialists, Catholics and Protestants, writers, journalists and teachers. An additional 100,000 Germans, many of them children, whom the Nazi regime judged to be too mentally weak or physically disabled to 'merit' life, were murdered by gas at Grafeneck and six other special institutions in Germany, starting more than two years before the setting up of the gas vans and gas chambers for Jews. This euthanasia 'action' was authorized by Hitler in September 1939. It was brought to an end two years later when it was condemned by the German churches. German homosexuals were singled out for brutaliy and execution in the concentration camps. So too were Jehovah's Witnesses who refused to acknowledge the supremacy of the nation over God or to sign a statement repudiating their religion.

Gypsies murdered 1939–1945	
Western Russia	42,000
Roumania	36,000
Poland	35,000
Croatia	28,000
Hungary	28,000
Germany	15,000
France	15,000
Serbia	12,000
Austria	6,500
Bohemia	6,500
Latvia	2,500
Lithuania	1,000
Estonia	1,000
Slovakia	1,000
Italy	1,000
Belgium	600
Holland	500
Luxembourg	200
Total	**231,800**

above left
The graves of 215 Poles murdered in the village of Skloby, in central Poland, on 11 September 1940. The inscription reads: 'Resting place. 215 inhabitants of the village of Skloby and its surroundings. Bestially murdered by the Hitlerite occupiers on 11 April 1940. Honour their memory.'

above
Map showing towns mentioned in the text where non-Jews were killed.

Chapter Eight

Liberation: Bearing Witness

right

Inside a barrack at Buchenwald on the day of liberation, 11 April 1945. Survivors look at a camera held by one of their liberators. These men were to be among the hundred thousand eye-witnesses of the Holocaust, through whom some of its darkest moments would be recounted. One of them, Elie Wiesel (circled in this photograph), later wrote several accounts (novels and memoirs) of the Holocaust, and of Auschwitz.

In Buchenwald alone, 56,549 inmates – Jews and non-Jews – had died since the camp was opened on 15 July 1937. The causes of their death: executions, the deliberate sadism of their guards, starvation and disease.

A survivor reflects

I am sending you a photo of my adopted daughter. Look well at her and remember that such children were flung into the burning ovens. Just imagine that my little Tulcia is one of the few who was saved, and that hundreds of thousands of children like her were lost in the gas chambers when they were torn away from their parents.

If you have a pathological imagination you may be able to picture this yourself, but if you are a normal person you will never be able to bring this chapter of horrors to life in spite of all your imaginings.

A Jewish lawyer who had survived the war in Poland, writing to a friend, from Warsaw, on 2 December 1945

From the day the war in Europe ended on 8 May 1945, the need to record the events of the Holocaust was uppermost in the minds of survivors. Even during the war itself, Jews were convinced that they must preserve knowledge of their story. Moshe Posner, a twenty-five-year-old dental assistant from Wloclawek, in western Poland, was hiding with a friend in a wood near Lublin in 1943. Knowing that he would soon be killed, he said to his friend:

'For some time now this idea has obsessed me: does there still exist an eye which sees all this, and which hears all this, for future generations?

I am tired. I cannot go on. One thing I demand of you; you have to make every effort to survive, to live.

Guard yourself, as one has to guard every document, every piece of evidence, from this time of our universal destruction.'

Guarding every document became an imperative during the war in many ghettos, Warsaw, Lodz, Kovno and Lvov among them.

With the coming of liberation, those people outside Europe who knew about the death camps only from reading the Allied newspapers or from harrowing snatches of film showing the liberation of the concentration camps, found it hard to comprehend the scale of the horror. The savagery perpetrated on the Jews of Europe between 1939 and 1945 – the murder of six million people amid unprecedented savagery – was such that, even as the twenty-first century begins, ordinary people, going about their daily lives, living in civilized societies, find it extremely difficult to grasp it in all its enormity.

THE LIBERATION OF THE CONCENTRATION CAMPS

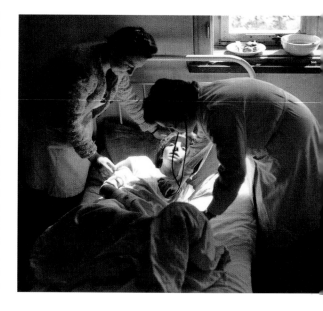

The Allied soldiers who entered the concentration camps did so as liberators. But in every camp that they reached in April and May 1945 they found as many dead prisoners as living ones. Sometimes they reached a camp while killings were still taking place.

Even on the death marches, the moment of liberation could come suddenly and unexpectedly. On 22 January 1945, Leilah Svirsky was with a group that was led into the forest to spend the night in an abandoned barracks. She later recalled: 'We did not sleep that night. The following morning we noticed that our guards were gone. A strange sensation: no one is watching us any more.' Then the Russians arrived. 'The first Russian soldier we saw was a captain, a Jew named Weisbrot. He belonged to the first military Intelligence group of the army and rode a white horse. Our Messiah, we called him, and kissed the horse's feet.' It was 23 January 1945. Leilah Svirsky was free. 'I am no longer one of a driven herd. I can decide my fate alone.'

On 27 January 1945, Soviet forces entered Auschwitz. The gassing there had ceased more than two months earlier. Most surviving inmates had been sent westward on death marches. Those whom the Soviet army liberated were the fortunate few. Among them was Anne Frank's father, Otto Frank. Before they fled, the SS had burned down twenty-nine of the thirty-five stores filled with the clothing of the victims. In the six stores that remained intact, the Soviet troops found 836,255 women's dresses, 348,000 men's suits and 38,000 pairs of men's shoes.

In April 1945, during their advance into Germany, British and American troops, among them many Jewish soldiers, reached the camps to which more than a hundred thousand Jews had earlier been sent, on a series of death marches that had often crossed and re-crossed Germany. On April 4, United States forces reached the village of Ohrdruf. Just outside the village they found a deserted labour camp: a camp in which four thousand inmates had died or been murdered in the previous three months. Hundreds had been shot on the eve of the American arrival. Some of the victims were Jews, others were Polish and Russian prisoners of war. They had been forced to build a vast underground radio and telephone centre, intended for the German army in the event of a retreat from Berlin.

Among the Jews who had been sent to Ohrdruf was Leo Laufer. With the American army approaching, he had managed, with three other prisoners, to escape before the camp was evacuated. He left his wooden camp shoes behind in order 'to run faster and not make any noise'. For four days he and his three fellow prisoners hid in the hills above Ohrdruf. When the American soldiers arrived, Laufer accompanied them into the camp. Many of the corpses they found were of prisoners who had been in the camp infirmary at the time of the evacuation of the camp four days earlier. They had been killed because they were too sick to get up and walk.

The sight of the emaciated corpses at Ohrdruf created a wave of revulsion that spread back to Britain and the United States. General Eisenhower, who visited the camp, was so shocked that he at once telephoned Churchill to describe what he had seen. He then sent photographs of the scene to Churchill, who circulated them to each member of the British Cabinet, and arranged for an all-Party delegation of British Members of Parliament to be flown to Germany to witness the sight at first hand.

above right
A former inmate at Belsen being examined by two former internees who had joined the Allied medical staff: Dr Nysenhauz (left) and nursing Sister Renée Erman.

Allied troops reached several dozen other camps in rapid succession. In each of them were hundreds of starving and emaciated prisoners, Jews and non-Jews, many of them far too weak and sick to survive more than a day or two beyond their liberation.

Most of the Jews in Buchenwald had been evacuated on April 8, before the American troops could reach the camp. But a few remained. One of them, Israel Lau, originally from the Polish city of Piotrkow, was only eight years old. He had survived because of the devotion and ingenuity of his elder brother, Naftali, then aged nineteen. On April 11, American forces arrived. One of the American officers was a Jew and a rabbi, Herschel Schechter. He later recalled pulling a small, frightened boy from a pile of corpses. The rabbi burst into tears. Then, hoping to reassure the child, he began to laugh. 'How old are you?' he asked the eight year old, in Yiddish. 'Older than you,' was the reply. 'How can you say that?' asked the rabbi, fearing the child was deranged.

'You cry and laugh like a little boy,' Lau explained, 'but I haven't laughed for years and I don't even cry any more. So tell me, who is older?'

The little boy later became a Chief Rabbi of Israel.

On 29 April 1945, American troops entered Dachau. Amid the corpses of those who had died during the previous week they found 33,000 survivors. On the roads south of Dachau, many hundreds of Jewish prisoners had been marched during the previous days towards the mountains, under guard, and repeatedly victimized. On April 29 those same Jews wandered, free but bewildered. They did not know what they would encounter in liberated Europe, or whether any of their relatives were still alive.

In most cases, each survivor of the concentration camps liberated at the end of the war was the sole member of his or her immediate family to have lived to see the day of liberation. In many cases, fathers who had managed to stay with their sons almost to the end, died a few days before liberation, or were among those tens of thousands of camp inmates who were not able to regain sufficient strength to live more than a few days after the arrival of the Allies.

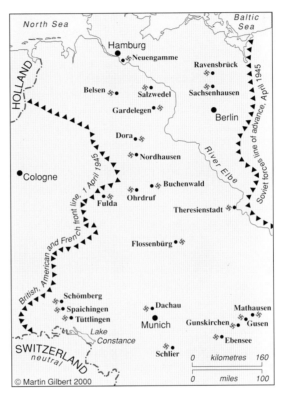

An eye-witness to liberation

On a railway siding there is a train of fifty wagons – all full of terribly emaciated dead bodies, piled up like the twisted branches of cut-down trees. Near the crematorium – for the disposal of the dead – another huge pile of dead bodies, like a heap of crooked logs ready for some infernal fire. The stench is like that of Belsen; it follows you even when you are back in the Press camp.

There were 2,539 Jews among the 33,000 survivors, almost all of them Lithuanian Jews, the remnants of the ghetto Slobodka. I found some old friends, among them, people who went to school with me and others who used to be fellow members of the Maccabi. And there was my doctor and friend of the Kovno days. He solemnly shook hands with me and enquired after my health.

Recollections of **Sam Goldsmith**, a Lithuanian Jew who had emigrated to Britain before the war. He was among the Allied journalists who entered Dachau with the American troops

top left
Map showing some of the concentration camps liberated by the Allies between 4 April and 8 May 1945.

centre left
A Belgian stamp, issued on 22 April 1995, commemorating the liberation of the concentration camps.

bottom left
A Slovak stamp, issued on 5 May 1995, commemorating the fiftieth anniversary of the liberation of the concentration camps.

THE DAY OF LIBERATION

top
Idel Levitan, the son of Micha and Mira Levitan. After liberation he was taken to a home at Ulm for Jewish children. Those who questioned the children there noted: 'He was with his parents in the Kovno ghetto. His parents gave him to Christians. Parents were killed. An aunt took him from the Christians to Lodz.'

above
Renja From, born in Stryj, in Eastern Galicia. After liberation she too was taken to the Jewish children's home at Ulm. 'She thinks that at the outbreak of the war her mother gave her to Poles. She knew then that she is Jewish, but the Christians with whom she was living forbad her to speak about it. She learned that her mother was murdered by the Germans and thrown into a ditch. She does not remember her father.'

For every survivor the day of liberation was engraved in his or her memory. Shocking though the sight of the camps was for the liberators – even for the battle-hardened soldiers of the Allied armies – the sight of those liberators affected every survivor. Yet every survivor also felt an undercurrent of pain: so many loved ones – family and friends – had been killed, homes and possessions had been lost, livelihoods, and Jewish life itself, had been destroyed over much of Europe.

Zivia Lubetkin, a former Warsaw ghetto fighter, liberated in Grodzisk, near Warsaw, on 17 January 1945:

> 'The people rejoiced and embraced their liberators. We stood by crushed and dejected, lone remnants of our people.'

Yitzhak Zuckerman, a leader of the Warsaw ghetto revolt, recalling 17 January 1945 in Warsaw:

> 'The day the Red Army entered Warsaw, we felt like orphans; we had a sense that there was no Jewish people any more. We had no estimate, we didn't know how many were left.'

Bronka Klibanski, a courier for the Jewish Fighting Organization in Bialystok, liberated in Poland in January 1945:

> 'The first to come were the Soviet sappers, searching for mines. When we heard Russian being spoken, we cautiously stepped forward to meet them, but only after satisfying ourselves beyond doubt that they were indeed Soviet soldiers. Then came the tanks. We ran to kiss their grimy crew members and thank them for having liberated us from the Germans at long last.
>
> Our joy was boundless, our smiles unlimited. We organized a small parade the next day, clutching red flags and marching to the outskirts of the city, where we welcomed the general who led the troops into the town. He was moved to receive this kind of welcome

on Polish soil. We were drunk with happiness that day, having witnessed our people's murderers in flight.

> But what then? How were we to go on? What followed were days of mourning and bereavement. There were no homes left, no families. I wandered through the streets looking for familiar faces. Once a Russian soldier whispered to me: *"Nye platch, dyevushka; lubimiy tvoy vernyetsa."* ("Don't cry, my girl; your lover will come back.") I did not even feel the tears streaming down my face.'

Maria Rebhun, liberated by Soviet troops at Lauenburg camp in Pomerania. Her parents had perished in the Warsaw ghetto uprising. Her brothers and sisters had been killed:

> 'We were in a daze. Barely moving, supporting the ones who were not able to make a step, and pushing the ones that were already written off in a wheelbarrow, we went to face new reality. Our minds were like a vacuum, our hearts empty of any desires.
>
> On the streets, ecstatic Russian soldiers offered us sweets and cigarettes amidst laughter and songs, but we were mute. Who are we? Where are we to go? Whom to turn to?'

Benjamin Bender, born in Czestochowa, Poland, liberated at Buchenwald on 11 April 1945, at the age of seventeen:

> 'I stood up, feeling weak. I stared at the beds around me. Motionless people, wax masks, totally unaware that finally they were free. I wanted to scream, to share with them the moment of joy, but I couldn't. There was no joy in my heart, but a gaping emptiness....
>
> I was afraid to walk out to face the new alien world. Would I ever be able to regain my lost human dignity all alone?
>
> Wounds never turned to scars. The tormented soul had never a chance to recover. A day in Buchenwald was a lifetime in Hell.'

Agnes Sassoon, liberated in Belsen, 15 April 1945:

... 'many were too sick in mind and body to realise just what was happening and were unaware that their day of liberation had arrived.

I was drifting through a dense fog. My eyes flickered open and shut as I tried to think where I was. Was I dead? I did not think so. I moved my head and tried to look around me. I heard voices in many languages speaking softly close by. I wondered whether I was dreaming. As my eyes focused properly I saw nurses and doctors and beds with clean white sheets.'

Mania Salinger, born in Radom, Poland, liberated at Belsen on 17 April 1945, at the age of twenty-one:

'Hundreds and then thousands of skeleton-like figures were running to the front gates screaming hysterically. I was up front and saw the first English tank enter the camp. We almost tore these poor soldiers apart. Other tanks followed. Through the loudspeakers and with tear-filled voices they repeated over and over again in several languages: "You are free. We are the English army. Be calm. Be calm. Food and medical help is on the way."'

Hugo Gryn, liberated at Gunskirchen, May 1945:

'It was sunny. Around mid-morning we could hear distant gunfire coming closer, the rumbling of tanks. Suddenly our guards, the most sadistic bunch of Ukrainian teenagers who had volunteered for the SS and were still too small for the standard uniforms, and some elderly but no less vicious Austrians who were too large for them – literally the dregs of the SS – dropped their guns, stripped off their death's-head insignia, and started to run.

Suddenly there appeared an American tank and that was, as far as I was concerned, the end of the war. On the tanks, the five pointed star of the United States, and crouching behind them, soldiers who took one look at us and began to throw their food rations in our direction before

moving on. Behind them followed infantry soldiers, and both fired at the retreating Germans. By the time this blessed and bloody procession had passed beyond our camp – we sat there, silent, unbelieving, and free.'

Levi Shalit, a survivor of the Siauliai ghetto in Lithuania, liberated in the Austrian Alps in May 1945 after a death march:

'There were many streets in that little town at the foot of the Tyrolean Alps. How lovely everything was. How quietly dreamed the little red-tiled houses with their little green gardens. There were the outlying houses.

Four days before, the inhabitants had rushed out at us with axes and blades. Now they were invisible. Now and again one of them slunk past with a band on his arm and wearing the short, greasy leather Tyrolean pants – slunk along with stealthy steps to take his turn at guard duty at the town entrance.

How quickly they had organized themselves! Not a sign of their defeat, of their world-destroying end. In only one building, in the schoolhouse, there was hubbub. Food was being distributed to refugees, Germans who had fled from their homes and had been overtaken by the Americans. I pushed my head into the open doorway. The smell of bread and milk met my nostrils. "Please, sir, do you want something to eat?" One of them tried this approach carefully, fawning like a dog.

The main street of the town was quiet. No one was to be seen – as if they all had died out. They kept within their houses, which bore not the lightest trace of war damage.

Here and there American solders were on patrol. One came up to me, a short fellow with a cheeky face, little more than a child.

"A Jew?"

"A Jew!" I stuttered.

Our arms intertwined and we burbled crazily, "A Jew, a Jew."'

above

A United States soldier at Dachau, on the day of liberation. Behind him are the bodies of those who had died in the days before liberation.

LIBERATION AT THERESIENSTADT

By the last day of April 1945 more than fifteen thousand survivors of the death marches had been brought to Theresienstadt, some on foot, others in open railway trucks. As the German commandant and guards had fled, they were met by Czech doctors and nurses. Food was being provided by the Red Cross.

Even as the railway trucks reached the safety of Theresienstadt there were those who were not to see liberation. Aron Zylberszac, a seventeen-year-old Polish Jew who had survived the Lodz ghetto and Auschwitz, was with his older brother Iser as the train they were on neared Theresienstadt. Aron later recalled:

'My brother died in my arms from dysentery. He faded away to nothing. A man who was a giant died a skeleton. I held him in my arms when he died. There was just nothing I could do. When I think about it, I sometimes blame myself. He did so much to keep me alive. I feel that had he saved some of that energy for himself he would have had a better chance to survive. I was so low physically and mentally I felt there was just nothing to live for, and I put myself on one of the carts with the dead bodies. I must have become unconscious. It was only when they were removing the dead bodies that they discovered there was still some life left in my body. They transferred me to this hospital, and that is where I found myself when I eventually regained consciousness.'

Arek Hersh, born in the small Polish town of Sieradz, was just sixteen when the war ended. A survivor of the Lodz Ghetto and of Auschwitz, he later recalled:

'We came to a railway station in a place called Roudnice, a few miles from Theresienstadt. After about ten minutes we were ordered to get off the train ....

I saw that on the other side of the transport a Czech policeman was giving boys some bread and meat. One of the Ukrainian SS guards

also saw this, and he turned his rifle round to get hold of the barrel to hit one of the starving boys over the head. A Czech policeman saw what was happening and drew his revolver. He pointed it at the SS guard and said, "If you touch this child, I will shoot you." I saw the SS guard immediately put his rifle down and walk away. We realized that something we had never seen before was happening: an SS guard had taken orders from someone else.

Soon after that the Czech policemen rounded up all the SS guards and took them away. It was said later that they had shot them. Our train was slowly taken into Theresienstadt.'

Pinkus Kurnedz, from Piotrkow, had reached Theresienstadt after a death march from a slave labour camp at Colditz. Of the six hundred slave labourers who set out from Colditz, only sixty were alive when they reached Theresienstadt. 'I remember well my day of liberation,' he wrote half a century later. 'I think I was one of the first people who saw the Russian tanks, and I remember my first bowl of Russian soup, which I was given by a member of a tank crew, and then I remember falling asleep, and missing the opportunity of looting, because on that day we could do anything with the Germans....' Among those who had been on the same death march from Colditz as Pinkus Kurnedz was Jack Aizenberg, born in the small Polish town of Staszow, a

former slave labourer at a German-owned factory in Kielce. He too recalled the first days of May 1945 in Theresienstadt. 'One heard rumours that the war was coming to an end. At this time I was so weak and getting weaker – that I am sure I was dying. Miraculously, on May 8, as I was lying on the boards which were my bed, I heard a lot of noise, and Russian music coming from accordions. Luckily I still had the faculties to realize that I might be free. With my last bit of energy I managed to get downstairs.'

Many of those liberated at Theresienstadt – as those at all the concentration camps liberated in April and May 1945 – were at the very end of their strength and physical ability to survive. For thousands, survival for another two or three days would have been impossible. Abraham Goldstein, a Polish-born survivor of Majdanek and Buchenwald, as well as the slave labour camps at Skarszysko-Kamienna and Schlieben, reflected fifty years after liberation: 'Were it not for the fact that I was liberated by the Russians just in time, I would have shared the fate of all those millions of Jews who perished in the Holocaust.'

above left
Survivors wave at their liberators from the open German railway trucks in which they had been shunted across Germany to Theresienstadt.

above
The survivor on the left is still wearing his striped concentration camp jacket.

'THE BOYS' LIBERATED, REACH A NEW WORLD

Survivors reflect

Most of us can be proud that soon after our liberation and our arrival in England, we harnessed all our energies and concentrated all our efforts on rebuilding and revitalizing our lifeline and spiritual revival. We did not allow Hitler to enjoy a posthumous triumph over us. In our early upbringing our parents inculcated in us a deep sense of purpose, compassion and responsibility to our fellow citizens and this has stood us in good stead. No matter how much we were degraded and deprived of all vestiges of human dignity, we did not succumb to corruption. The idea of revenge hardly entered our minds nor were we consumed with hatred and venom.

Ben Helfgott, from the Polish town of Piotrkow, aged fifteen when the war ended

After arriving in Windermere, I was given a room to myself with a single bed, and blankets, and other bits and pieces that we had been deprived of for so long. The three months I spent in Windermere I was given food and some basic education in English. I used to go a lot to the cinema, walking, sightseeing and boating on Lake Windermere. It was sheer heaven; never in my life until then had I known such luxuries. I only have beautiful memories of this place.

Krulik Wilder, also from Piotrkow, aged sixteen when the war ended. Of Piotrkow's 24,500 Jews in 1939, fewer than one thousand survived the war

Among those liberated in Theresienstadt when the war ended were several thousand teenage survivors, mostly Polish born, who had been brought there from slave labour camps in Germany. The British government offered to take in a thousand of them, and a Jewish refugee organization, the Central British Fund, made plans to provide them with a new life.

Known among themselves as 'The Boys' (although there were also a dozen girls), the first group, several hundred in all, made the journey from Prague to Britain by air, in British Lancaster bombers sent out specially to Prague to bring them back, at the end of 1945. They were taken to a hostel on the shore of Lake Windermere, in the Lake District, where the long, hard process of rehabilitation and renewal began.

Joseph Finklestone, later Foreign and Diplomatic Editor of the *Jewish Chronicle*, and Chairman of the Guild of Jewish Journalists, recalled how he found himself at a small airport near the Lake District on 14 August 1945, as the first Lancaster bomber landed:

'As a teenage junior reporter of the *Carlisle Journal* I had been ordered to "cover the arrival of some young people from Europe". It was not explained to me who they were. Only when I saw the boys and girls, in their ill-fitting clothes, tense as they entered a new world, did I suddenly realize with a pang that they had experienced the greatest human-made hell in history. They had seen their parents, sisters and brothers shot, starved and gassed by the Nazis.'

From the Lake District, The Boys were sent to hostels throughout Britain, where they perfected their English. Half of them then moved on to new lands: to the United States and Canada, to Australia, South America and Israel. In 1948, many of those who had stayed in Britain or gone across the Atlantic – by then in their late teens or early twenties – volunteered to fight alongside the Israeli forces during the Israeli War of Independence. Since then, through their '45-Aid Society, they help those who have fallen on hard times and, at their annual reunion in Britain, celebrate their survival.

An eye-witness

Seeing these youngsters, brought out from the horrors of Nazi Europe, had a profound effect on me. By that time, I already knew that most of my own close relatives, including cousins of the same age as the youngsters at the airport, had been murdered. As I sat down in front of the typewriter in the office to write the report for the paper, I was suddenly overwhelmed by emotion. Putting my head down on the typewriter, I wept.

Joseph Finklestone, who had been born in Chelm, Poland, but had come to Britain with his parents shortly before the Second World War

opposite, top
The first group of teenage survivors to reach British soil from Prague leave the Lancaster bomber.

opposite, centre
A group of the new arrivals, still uncertain of their future in their new surroundings, look at the camera.

opposite, bottom
Three of 'The Boys' enjoy the pleasures of boating on Lake Windermere.

left
At an airfield in the British Lake District, one of the youngest of the survivors brought from Theresienstadt is helped down from the plane as others wait their turn.

THE SEARCH FOR HAVENS

above right
Idel (Jack) Kagan's identity card, issued on 28 April 1947 at the Displaced Persons camp in Landsberg, Germany. The language of the card is Yiddish. Aged eighteen when the card was issued, Kagan was a survivor of the Nowogrodek ghetto, and had fought with the partisans in the forests. His mother, father, sister and grandmother had all been murdered in the ghetto.
From Germany, he made his way to Britain, arriving on 23 June 1947, and making Britain his home.

Many concentration camp survivors, liberated in Germany or at Theresienstadt, made their way back eastward to their homes, for the most part in Poland. Some found those homes destroyed. Most found them inhabited by others – by Poles who had moved in either during the war or immediately after it.

Survivors who returned to Poland in the immediate aftermath of the Second World War were astounded by the violence against them. Within a year, more than a thousand Jews had been murdered on Polish soil – by Poles. The killings took place in a hundred towns to which Jews had returned after liberation. Ten Jews were killed when they went back to their village, Kosow-Lacki – a mere six miles from Treblinka. Four Jews were killed when they went back to Parczew, whose forests had seen so much Jewish heroism and suffering.

One of the leaders of the Sobibor revolt, Leon Feldhendler, was killed by Poles after liberation. Yaakov Waldman, one of the very few people who had managed to escape from a deportation of Chelmno, was killed by Poles immediately after the war in the nearby town of Turek. One of only two survivors of Belzec, Chaim Hirszman, was killed in Lublin on the day he gave evidence to a Polish war crimes tribunal about what he had witnessed at Belzec (the other survivor of Belzec, Rudolf Reder, emigrated to Canada).

When a husband and wife returned to Skarzysko in January 1946 they received an anonymous letter promising that soon 'the Jews here will be slaughtered' and 'advising' them to leave. They did. A few other survivors of Skarzysko returned and decided to stay. Two of them, Icchak Warszauer and Eliezer Lewin, began to look into the possibility of regaining their property, which was being held by Poles. Warszauer succeeded in being given back one apartment in his former house. Four Jews moved in with him. One night in February 1946 they were attacked, and all five were killed. There were 2,200 Jews living in Skarzysko in 1939. In October 1942, more than 2,000 of them were deported by train to Treblinka and killed. No Jews were living in Skarzysko a decade after the Second World War. Such was true of 90% of the localities in which Jews lived in Poland, Lithuania and western Russia before 1939.

The climax of the post-war killings in Poland came on 4 July 1946, when a group of Jews, all of them survivors, who had gathered in the town of Kielce, most of them on their way to Palestine, were set upon by a local mob. Other survivors in Kielce were attacked in their homes. Forty-two Jews were killed that day. One of them had no identity papers or anything that might reveal his name. The only indication of his past was a tattoo number on his arm, B 2969. The numbers B 2903 to B 3449 had been given to Jews deported from the Radom ghetto to Auschwitz on 2 August 1944. No more precise identification was possible. Radom and Kielce were only fifty miles apart.

As a result of the killings in Kielce, within twenty-four hours more than five thousand survivors had left Poland in search of a haven elsewhere. Those who reached the Slovak capital of Bratislava, on the Danube, were confronted by anti-Jewish demonstrations. They continued westward.

In search of new homes, the Displaced Persons were helped by many international aid agencies, in particular by the United Nations Relief and Rehabilitation Agency (UNRRA). In the years following the war, the Displaced Persons camps were slowly emptied, and those who had been forced to make them their home – some for as long as five years and more – were found havens in Western Europe and beyond, often far beyond. Survivors groups can be found in several cities on the Pacific coast of the United States and Canada, in Mexico, Latin America, South Africa and Australia.

The majority of survivors tried to make their way to Palestine. On their way there – before the establishment of the State of Israel in 1948 – several thousand were intercepted by the British and interned in Cyprus. Some were even sent back to detention camps in Germany. By 1950, more than half the survivors, as many as 100,000 in all, were living in Israel. In 1968, after an upsurge of anti-Semitism in Poland, most of the survivors who had stayed in Poland after the war also made their way to Israel. After 1988, with the relaxation of Communist controls in the Soviet Union, several thousand Soviet Jewish survivors of the Holocaust emigrated to Israel, the United States and even to Germany.

above, left and right
Two teenagers, survivors of death marches and concentration camps in Bessarabia, reach Palestine in the autumn of 1944. During 1943 the British government suspended its restrictions on entry to Palestine to enable any survivors who reached neutral Turkey – like these boys and more than 4,000 other survivors – to proceed immediately to Palestine, which they were able to do by train.

left
Jewish refugees from Europe approach the shore of Palestine after the end of the war. The British government allowed in only 13,000 survivors; most ships were intercepted by the Royal Navy, and the refugees interned in camps on the island of Cyprus, guarded behind barbed wire by British soldiers. In 1948, after Israel became independent, they were allowed to make Israel their home.

'We don't want you here!'

I arrived in Cracow around noon. The station was full of returnees, most of whom were not Jewish. All were interested in their train schedule. I saw a man who was still wearing the stripes from the concentration camp. As I tried to approach him, two Polish people started to question him. 'Hey Jew, where are you going? Why aren't you going to Palestine? We don't want you here!' I was dumbfounded. I saw tears come down the man's face and nobody came to his defence. I was scared too, and angry. How dare they? Yes, I am a Jew, but I am also a Pole. How dare they? I felt that the multitude of people were looking at me. I met their glare of hate with my own hate.

I felt like shouting at them: 'You didn't help us; you turned us in; you are worse than the Germans. I watched you in the ghetto through the barbed wire and saw how your stores were full of meats, fruits, dairy products and other commodities, while we were starving. You could have helped us, but you didn't. My father fought for Polish independence in World War One and was wounded. He received a medal for valour. He died in the ghetto at the age of 41, a broken man, from the wound he got following General Anders to Roumania. He returned to be with his family, only to die in the ghetto. He loved Poland and so did I. I don't need you! I have a choice. I am going back to Theresienstadt. From there I will go to Palestine or to England. I swear I will never go back to Poland.

Victor Breitburg, a survivor of the Lodz ghetto, who emigrated to Britain after the war

WAR CRIMES TRIALS

Even before the defeat of Germany, war criminals were being brought to trial. Starting on 27 November 1944, and lasting for six days, the Polish authorities put on trial six SS guards from Majdanek. They were found guilty of torturing and killing prisoners, and raping women, and were executed.

Hundreds of those who had acted during the war as if they would never be held to account were brought to trial when the war ended. Joseph Darnand, founder of the French Milice, whose men had arrested several thousand Jews for deportation, was himself arrested when the war ended and brought to trial in France. He was condemned to death on 3 October 1945 and executed. A month later Josef Kramer, who had been Deputy Commandant at Auschwitz before being appointed Commandant at Belsen, was likewise executed, after being tried by a British military tribunal.

The twelve leading Nazis convicted of war crimes at the Nuremberg Tribunal were hanged on 16 October 1946. Among them was Julius Streicher, whose pre-war newspaper *Der Stürmer* had been at the forefront of the Nazi Party's anti-Semitic campaign. In the American zone of occupation in Germany, which included Dachau, 462 war criminals were sentenced to death; in the British zone, 240; and in the French zone, 104. Leniency, which the war criminals themselves had never shown, was, however, granted to them. Of the 806 Allied death sentences imposed, only slightly more than half were carried out.

In 1946 the Czechoslovak government brought Kurt Daluege to trial. An SS General, he had succeeded Heydrich as Protector of Bohemia and Moravia, and had ordered savage reprisals. He was executed. Amnon Goeth, the sadistic Commandant of Plaszow concentration camp, was also brought to trial and executed in 1946, in Cracow. That year a British military tribunal in Germany sentenced and hanged both the owner and the manager of the company that had manufactured the poison gas Zyklon B, used by the SS in Auschwitz and other death camps.

In 1947 the former President of the Slovak Republic, Father Yosef Tiso, a Roman Catholic priest, was tried by a court in Bratislava, condemned to death and hanged.

JÜRGEN STROOP GENERAL

He had been the first Head of State allied to Germany who sent his Jewish population to slave labour and to the death camps in German-occupied Poland. Also in 1947, Jürgen Stroop, who had brutally suppressed the Warsaw ghetto uprising in 1943, was sentenced to death by an American military court in Dachau for the execution of American airmen shot down over Poland. He was then extradited to Poland, where he was sentenced to death again, for his crimes in Warsaw, and hanged.

In 1948 SS Major Dieter Wisliceny was executed in Bratislava. He had been responsible for the deportation of Jews from Slovakia, Greece and Hungary. SS-General Oswald Pohl, chief of the SS Economic-Administrative Main Office, was tried by an American military tribunal in 1951. He had organized the despatch to Germany of the personal possessions of Jews murdered in the death camps – including clothing, gold tooth fillings, wedding rings, jewellery and women's hair. At his trial he told the court: 'Everyone down to the lowest clerk knew what went on in the concentration camps.' He was sentenced to death, and hanged.

Adolf Eichmann, who had escaped to Argentina after the war, was captured in 1960 by Israeli agents, flown to Israel, tried, found guilty and hanged. Two years later the Deputy Commander of the Gestapo in Lithuania, Heinrich Schmitz, was brought to trial in Wiesbaden, West Germany. He committed suicide in his cell before sentence was passed.

From 1963 to 1965, twenty-one leading SS officers

More trials were held during the 1970s and 1980s. Helmut Rauca, who had selected more than ten thousand Kovno Jews for execution on 28 October 1941, and had gone to Canada after the war, was charged in 1984 by a Toronto court with entering Canada under a false declaration, found guilty and stripped of his Canadian citizenship. Extradited to West Germany, he was charged by a court in Frankfurt with the murder of 11,500 Jews. He died in the prison hospital while awaiting trial.

In the forty years following 1945 as many as 5,000 convicted war criminals were executed; ten thousand were imprisoned. A further ten thousand – a minimum estimate – escaped being brought to trial. The search for them continued. War crimes trials took place in the 1990s in Israel, France and Britain. In 1992 the Canadian Supreme Court upheld a lower Canadian court's acquittal of Imre Finta, who had been accused of confining and deporting thousands of Hungarian Jews in 1944. In his defence Finta argued that he had believed wartime newspaper articles that the Jews must be deported because they were 'dangerous to the State'.

In the last year of the twentieth century – in May 1999 – the British government tried, convicted and imprisoned Anthony Sawoniuk, who had participated in the execution of Jews in the former Polish town of Domachevo in 1942. After the war, hiding the facts of his past, he had emigrated to Britain. At the time of his trial he was eighty-eight years old. He was sentenced to two terms of life imprisonment for the killing of eighteen Jews. As with each war crimes trial since 1945, this British trial produced detailed historical evidence – some of it collected at the site of the killings, in what had become Belarus – which added to public knowledge of the events of more than half a century earlier.

As war crimes trials continued, German youth were taught that the behaviour of their parents' generation towards the Jews was criminal. Young people worldwide learned of the barbarities practised against the Jewish people. In the last two decades of the twentieth century, war crimes trials relating to Nazi crimes overlapped with trials relating to more recent atrocities, emphasizing the need for justice, and intensifying the cry 'Never Again'.

The accused

I only knew one mode of conduct: to carry out the orders of superiors without reservations.

Wilhelm Boger, Gestapo, Auschwitz, at his trial

I believed in the Führer. I wanted to serve my people.

Hans Stark, Gestapo, Auschwitz, at his trial

I had no feelings in carrying out these things, because I received an order. That, incidentally, is the way I was trained.

Josef Kramer, Commandant of Belsen, speaking at his trial of his feelings when taking part in the gassing of eighty Jewish women at Auschwitz in 1943

opposite, left
Rudolf Höss, Commandant at Auschwitz, during his trial.

opposite, right
Jürgen Stroop in prison.

above left
Adolf Eichmann on trial in Jerusalem.

who had worked at Auschwitz were tried at Frankfurt-on-Main. It was the longest legal case in German records. Three of the accused were acquitted. Twelve were sentenced to 3 to 14 years in prison. Six were sentenced to life imprisonment with hard labour, among them Wilhelm Boger, who was found guilty of 144 murders, ten murders committed with others, and complicity in the deaths of 1,000 inmates. Another Gestapo officer, Hans Stark, who was found guilty of taking part in murders on 41 separate occasions – one of them involving 200 camp inmates – was sentenced to ten years in prison.

CEMETERIES, GRAVES AND TOMBSTONES

Travellers in Eastern Europe are often surprised at how many pre-war Jewish cemeteries survived the Second World War. While hundreds, perhaps thousands, of cemeteries – such as the Grosse Hamburger Strasse cemetery in Berlin – were desecrated by the Germans, and their often venerable tombstones taken away for trench supports or pavements, hundreds of other cemeteries survived, many of them virtually intact. The two largest pre-war Jewish cemeteries in Europe, the Weissensee cemetery in Berlin, with 115,000 graves, and the Gesia Street cemetery in Warsaw, with more than 100,000 graves, remain – at the dawn of the twenty-first century – vast expanses of tombstones, the last resting place of the Jews of two once large and vibrant communities.

Elsewhere the traveller is similarly surprised by the size of the surviving Jewish cemeteries, even where they are overgrown with trees, bushes and ivy. In the old Jewish cemetery in Prague, the huddled stones of ten generations of Jews survived the destruction of Czech Jewry, and the murder of the descendants of many of those buried there. In Poland, at Czestochowa, Cracow and Lodz, Jewish cemeteries with magnificent tombstones attest to the prosperity in the late nineteenth and early twentieth centuries of the leading Jewish citizens. In Lublin, most of the cemetery was destroyed. Some stones remain, however, including those of leading rabbis, which recall the great days of Jewish learning.

In thousands of surviving cemeteries, individual Jews are memorialized. Abrasza Blum was a leader of the Bund (Jewish Socialist Workers' Party) in Poland. He managed to hide in 'Aryan' Warsaw after the ghetto uprising of 1943, but was betrayed, tortured and then shot. His gravestone (opposite page, bottom left), with wording in Yiddish and Polish, is in the Warsaw Jewish cemetery.

Memorial pyramids, with a Star of David at the top, have been erected on the outskirts of a number of Polish towns. To prevent the Jewish cemetery disintegrating through neglect – there being no Jews left in the town to look after it – local Polish authorities used the gravestones to create a monument. The pyramid opposite is in Lubartow, which had a pre-war Jewish population of 5,000. Most were deported in 1942 to Sobibor and murdered.

In front of the surviving gravestones in the Jewish cemetery in Radomsko, Poland (opposite page, bottom right), is a memorial stone to the mass executions of Jews and Poles in the cemetery during the war. When I took this photograph in 1980 the cemetery was a grassy meadow, awash with flowers. It has since been fenced, and is maintained as a cemetery. Of Radomsko's 16,000 Jews (in 1939), more than 14,000 were deported to Treblinka and murdered there between 10–12 October 1942. Several hundred were shot in the cemetery.

The photograph by Arunas Baltenas (top left) of fragments of gravestones in the Jewish cemetery in Vilna (now Vilnius), was issued in 1997 in Vilnius as a postcard for tourists to Lithuania by the R. Paknys Publishing House.

Tombstones (left), in the former Jewish cemetery outside the Polish town of Jaroslaw. From 1939 to 1941 Jaroslaw was on the border between Nazi Germany and Soviet Russia: Hitler went there to watch his troops march into Russia on 22 June 1941. Most of the 10,000 Jews of Jaroslaw had been expelled into the Soviet Union in September 1939. In 1942, the few hundred who remained were brought from the town to the cemetery and killed. When I photographed the cemetery in 1997 it was in ruins and overgrown: one of the tombstones had recently been painted green.

In Warsaw, after liberation

We made our way to the entrance of the cemetery. It had not escaped the bombardment. The surrounding wall stood broken in several places; there was no gate, nor was there anyone in sight. Only silence....

Wherever I turned, there was nothing but overturned tombstones, desecrated graves and scattered skulls – skulls, their dark sockets burning deep into me, their shattered jaws demanding, 'Why? Why has this befallen us?'

Although I knew that these atrocities were the handiwork of the so-called 'dentists' – Polish ghouls who searched the mouths of the Jewish corpses to extract their gold-capped teeth – I nevertheless felt strangely guilty and ashamed. Yes, Jews were persecuted even in their graves. Deliberately, in order not to trample the skulls and not to slip into an open grave, we made our way through this place of rest to the spot where my father's bones had lain. Though the location was well-known to me, I could not find his grave. The spot was desolate, destroyed, the soil pitted and strewn with broken skulls and markers.

We stood there forlorn. Around our feet lay skull after skull. Was not one of them my own father? How would I ever recognize it?

Nothing. Nothing was left me of my past, of my life in the ghetto, not even the grave of my father....

Vladka Meed, recollection

MONUMENTS AND MEMORIALS

below left

Sobibor: the two memorials on the road to the gas chamber.

below right

The children's house in the Theresienstadt ghetto, now a museum. Over the door is the Hebrew word *yizkor* (memorial).

above right

The dedication page of *Shattered Faith: A Holocaust Legacy*, by Leon Weliczker Wells.

opposite, top left

Belzec death camp: the memorial gates; beyond them, the road to the gas chamber.

opposite, bottom left

Belzec, the memorial on the site of the former gas chamber. The Polish inscription reads: 'In memory of the victims of the Hitlerite terror, murdered in the years 1942–1943.'

Since the Second World War many thousands of monuments have been erected at the sites of the mass murder of Jews, and of the killing of individual Jews. In the last two decades of the twentieth century the number of such monuments grew considerably. Survivors of a particular town, who had emigrated after the war, or even before it, often sought – as they approached their own old age – to create a permanent memorial to their family and fellow-townsmen. At Treblinka, large stones have been placed around the gas chamber area, each one inscribed with the name of a town whose Jews were murdered there. There is one memorial at Treblinka to an individual – Janusz Korczak, who insisted on accompanying the children of his orphanage on their last road.

The Warsaw ghetto, reduced to rubble after the ghetto uprising, was built on after the war for the housing needs of Polish citizens. Monuments and plaques to the ghetto uprising, and to a few individuals – including Korczak – have been set up at several points in the former ghetto. There is also a memorial at the Umschlagplatz, the railway deportation point. During the Communist period in Poland, Jewish visitors to Warsaw were surprised at how few plaques there were, given the scale of the killing. More were put up in the 1990s, when the Warsaw ghetto uprising was added to the list of battle honours on the Polish Unknown Soldier's memorial in the centre of Warsaw.

During the Communist period in the Soviet Union, memorials to Jewish victims – even at Babi Yar, where 33,000 Jews were killed in three days – seldom made reference to the fact that the victims were Jews. They were called 'Soviet citizens'. Since the fall of Communism in 1991, new memorials in the former Soviet Union mention when the victims were Jews, or display a Jewish symbol.

Many countries have issued postage stamps as memorials to the Holocaust. In Israel, a new stamp is issued each year on Holocaust memorial day – known as Heroes and Martyrs Day. The date chosen is the first day of the Warsaw ghetto revolt, the 18th of April in the Christian calendar, the 27th of the month of Nissan in the Hebrew calendar.

Several thousand books on the Holocaust have been dedicated by their authors to those who were murdered. Thus the names of loved ones live on.

The lamentation for the Jews in Europe has not subsided for fifty years. I want to dedicate this book to my immediate family who were killed during the Holocaust:

My father, *Abraham,* who was killed at the age of forty-eight
My mother, *Chana,* at the age of forty-six
My sister *Elka* at the age of nineteen
My brother *Aaron* at the age of seventeen
My brother *Jakob* at the age of fourteen
My sister *Rachel* at the age of twelve
My sister *Judith* at the age of ten
My sister *Bina* at the age of seven

above
Three stamps issued in 1968 by the Czechoslovak government to commemorate the children of Theresienstadt who had been murdered at Auschwitz. Each stamp reproduces a drawing by a child who was later murdered. The three young artists were Jiri Beutler, Jiri Schlesinger and Kitty Brunnerova.

below
A stamp issued in Uruguay, in 1995, showing the Holocaust memorial in the capital, Montevideo. Several thousand survivors went to Uruguay after the war.

MASS GRAVES

In the summer of 1943, as the tide of war turned slowly but steadily against the Germans, Hitler had given orders to destroy the evidence of mass murder, to prevent the Soviet army uncovering the bodies of millions of murdered Jews in the death pits and ravines of the East. On Himmler's instructions, a special unit was set up, called Commando 1005 (the Blobel *Kommando*), to dig up the mass murder sites and to burn the bodies. The bones were to be ground to powder.

The work of the Commando 1005 units took more than a year to complete. More than two million bodies were dug up. Jewish slave labourers were made to carry out this horrific task. At large mass murder sites, such as Babi Yar near Kiev, and the sands of Janowska on the outskirts of Lvov, it took many months before all the bodies were reduced to ashes.

The Germans did not want the workers of the Commando 1005 units to survive, and to tell the world what they had witnessed. After each mass murder site was cleared, the Jews who had been forced to clear it were killed. A few, however, managed to escape. The unit at Janowska, which began its task in July 1943, revolted four months later. In the mass murder site at Borki, outside Chelm, where there were an equal number of armed guards and prisoners, the prisoners revolted. All but three were killed as they tried to escape.

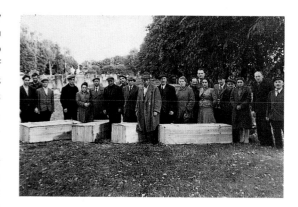

top right
The exhumed bodies of 560 Jewish men, women and children, murdered in the Rakow forest on 20 December 1942, were brought in collective coffins to the Piotrkow cemetery in 1946 by a few returning survivors.

centre right
A memorial stone in the Piotrkow Jewish cemetery to the Jews killed in the Rakow forest on 20 December 1942. Memorial candles, flowers and an Israeli flag have been placed on the memorial by recent visitors. On the left, paying his respects (in 1993), is Ben Helfgott, a survivor, whose mother Sara and little sister Lucia, aged eight, were among those who were killed.

At Ponar, seventy Jews, and ten Soviet prisoners of war whom the Germans suspected of being Jewish, were made to dig up the corpses. The eighty men were chained while working. At night they were kept in a deep pit, the only access to which was a ladder that was pulled up once they were in it. After digging an escape tunnel with their hands, forty escaped on the night of 15 April 1944. Twenty-five were caught and killed. Fifteen eluded their pursuers and survived.

After the war many of these fields of ash were marked out by low concrete borders, and grassed over. At Sobibor, one mound of ash was itself turned into a memorial, rather than levelled to the ground. At Belzec some of the ash was put into memorial urns. In many of the mass murder sites that were dug up by Commando 1005, trees were planted over the ashes, so that the

fields, pits and ravines have become woodland. At Ponar, near Vilna, local villagers pick mushrooms where once the ashes were scattered.

Other, smaller mass murder sites were not exhumed during the war: there were too many of them. Some were exhumed by survivors immediately after the war, and the remains reburied in local Jewish cemeteries.

Visitors to mass murder sites are often confronted by pits and mounds of human ash. Some are marked by memorials and memorial plaques, as at 'the sands' in Lvov-Janowska, where tens of thousands of Jews were murdered, and by the ponds at Auschwitz-Birkenau, where the ashes of those gassed and cremated were thrown. Other sites across eastern Europe have no memorial: they are known locally to some of the older people, and found only with difficulty.

above
The pyramid of human ash at Sobibor.

opposite, bottom
A monument two miles outside the town of Nowogrodek. It commemorates the mass murder of more than five thousand Jews of the town, killed on 8 December 1941, the first and main slaughter of that community. Eighty-five per cent of the Jews of the town were killed on that one day. The monument, on which are Hebrew, Belorussian and English inscriptions, was erected in 1993, after the fall of Communism, by Jack Kagan, one of only 400 survivors of a Jewish community of six thousand.

SYNAGOGUES THAT SURVIVE

Many hundreds of synagogues were burned down during the Holocaust. The first to be set on fire were in Germany and Austria on the night of 9–10 November 1938: the Kristallnacht. Hundreds more were burned down in German-occupied Poland in 1939, and when the German armies moved eastward into Russia in 1941. Their sites became wasteland.

Among the synagogues totally destroyed were the Great Synagogues in Warsaw and Vilna. The synagogue in Luxembourg, centre of worship for the 3,500 Jews in the principality, was demolished brick by brick in 1943.

Many hundreds of synagogues survived, some intact, some damaged. Today's visitors to any European country occupied by Germany during the Second World War are often surprised at how many synagogues are still standing from the pre-1933 era.

In recent years many damaged synagogues have been restored, including the magnificent Oranienburger Strasse synagogue in Berlin, the Dohanyi Street synagogue in Budapest and the Nozyk synagogue in Warsaw. In Poland many towns have restored the interiors of synagogues whose painted walls and decorations are often one of the finest sights in the town. Other synagogues are now museums of Jewish life, or used for modern cultural purposes, such as libraries and theatres.

In 1999 the Auschwitz Jewish Centre Foundation was set up. Its aim was to restore the synagogue in Auschwitz/Oswiecim town (in Yiddish, Oshpitzin) where 7,000 Jews lived before the Second World War, and to create a study centre next to the synagogue, which had been in use from 1900 to 1939. Fred Schwartz, President of the foundation, explained: 'We want to represent Jewish life here before the Shoah, not the anonymity of mass death.' Michael Lewan, Chairman of the United States Congress Commission for the Preservation of America's Heritage Abroad, which helped finance the project, added: 'The synagogue is a testament to those vibrant souls who prayed, studied, sang and danced within its walls.'

Abandoned synagogues can also be found, stark in their desolation. The great synagogue in Brody – where a hundred years ago Jews fleeing from Tsarist oppression first worshipped in the freer air of Austria-Hungary – is a ruin. The main synagogue in Dzialoszyce has gradually collapsed. When I first saw it in 1980 it had a roof and a women's gallery. Twenty years later it was roofless and the women's gallery had gone.

In the centuries before the Holocaust, the synagogues of Europe were the centre of Jewish communal life. Where that life was not totally destroyed, or was renewed after 1945, the synagogue has returned to its former use as a place of worship, prayer and communal activity. Where no Jewish community could be reconstituted after the war, the synagogue building is often all that remains – usually the most impressive physical structure that remains – of what had once been the life and beliefs of millions of people.

opposite, above
The 17th-century synagogue in Pinczow, whose Jewish community made up 70 per cent of the town's population at the end of the nineteenth century. The building survived the war; but the community, of 3,500, was destroyed.

opposite, below
The Nozyk synagogue in Warsaw, founded in 1900. It survived the Second World War because the Germans used it as a stables, and as a store for food. Badly damaged during the fighting in the Warsaw uprising of 1944, it was restored sufficiently in 1945 to be used as a place of worship for the survivors who returned to Warsaw after the war. Detailed restoration began in 1977. In April 1983, the 50th anniversary of the Warsaw ghetto uprising, it was re-opened for services. This photograph was taken in 1996.

above left
The Tall Synagogue in Cracow, photographed by Jacek Weislo in 1996 for a tourist postcard. All but one of the seven synagogues in the Kazimierz quarter of Cracow survived the war and have been restored.

above right
Entrance to the Orthodox synagogue at 40 Tucholsky Street, in the former old Jewish quarter of Berlin. It was opened in 1904, set back from the street, beyond a courtyard. The Gestapo closed it down in 1940, but did no damage to it. It was re-established for worship in 1989.

left
A former Jewish street in the town of Auschwitz, part of the Austro-Hungarian Empire before 1914, then, as Oswiecim, within Poland. The synagogue is the tall building on the right with three arched windows.

SURVIVORS' REFLECTIONS, AND REPARATIONS

Survivors' reflections

There is one thing that I understood very precisely: what happened to us was not because of what God did, but what people did after rejecting him. I witnessed the destruction that follows when men try to turn themselves into gods.

If you take the Ten Commandments, from the very first that starts: 'I am the Lord your God who brought you out of the land of Egypt'; here you had people who set themselves up to be gods, to be masters of life and death, and who took you into Egypt: into an Egypt of the most bizarre and most obnoxious kind, and all the way creating their own set of idols, to taking God's name in vain, to setting generations against each other so that children dishonoured parents.

Certainly they murdered. Certainly they committed robbery. Certainly there was a great deal of coveting, of envy, involved in it. In other words, you had here an outbreak of the very opposite of everything that civilization was building towards.

It was a denial of God, it was a denial of man. It was the destruction of the world in miniature form.

Hugo Gryn was thirteen when he was deported to Auschwitz. His younger brother Gabi was murdered there. Thirty-five years after the war, while serving as a rabbi in London, he voiced these reflections on how the ethical code that was a part of his own Jewish heritage, and also of the Judaeo-Christian tradition, had been 'denied and reversed'

Most survivors of the Holocaust are the sole survivors of large families. As they look back across more than half a century, they recall those whom they lost – who were so savagely taken away from them. Having survived, often for three or four years in concentration and slave labour camps, and then on death marches, many did not have even a single photograph to recall the images of loves ones. Each survivor bears the burden of his or her last, lost contact, with parents, brothers and sisters, grandparents, uncles and aunts, cousins, friends – the lost world of European Jewry – Jewish lives, and Jewish life.

In the last decade of the twentieth century, many survivors pondered the question of reparations and recompense. At the start of the twenty-first century, former slave labourers still struggled to have their claims met. Many German industrial enterprises – which remain active and profitable more than fifty years after the war – made considerable profits exploiting Jewish and other slave labour. The names of the enterprises are the same at the beginning of the twenty-first century as they were in the Second World War, but their acceptance of responsibility is hard to obtain.

Many national and private banks, including several in neutral Switzerland, profited by transferring or guarding money made by the German war machine, often from the seizure of Jewish property, and even from the results of the melting down of hundreds of thousands of wedding rings, and small pieces of dental gold torn from corpses taken out of the gas chambers. Jewish pre-war bank accounts, safety deposit boxes, insurance policies, works of art, businesses, shops and homes were all confiscated during the Holocaust. Their return remained an acrimonious issue half a century after the Holocaust.

In April 1946, Soviet troops in Prague had confiscated 396 kilogrammes of gold belonging to Jewish victims of Nazism; during the war the gold had been held in the Czech National Bank. As well as gold there were precious metals, share certificates, savings, property deeds and insurance policies. The Russian government, as of November 1999, was refusing to return these assets to Prague, to be used for the heirs of those from whom it was taken, for the Jewish community in Prague, or for other victims of the Holocaust, such as the Czech Romany (Gypsy) community.

Some countries – Hungary, Czechoslovakia and Poland among them – have made gestures, at times substantial ones, to survivors with claims. Jewish communities that were set up again after the war have also benefited from the restitution of Jewish communal property. But much of this remains on a small scale.

A significant start in reparations for Jewish victims of Nazism was made as early as 1952, when the Federal Republic of Germany (West Germany), headed by Konrad Adenauer, signed the Luxembourg Accords with Israel. These accords granted a considerable sum of money by contemporary standards ($867 million) as 'reparation for the material damage to the Jews at the hands of the Nazis'. Only 15 per cent of this sum was for victims outside Israel – the home of up to half the survivors. Some survivors living elsewhere than Israel did receive compensation directly from the Federal Republic, but many did not.

On 22 January 1999 agreement was reached between lawyers for Holocaust survivors and several Swiss banks, including the Swiss National Bank, ending a dispute that had festered for a decade. The banks agreed to a $1.25 billion settlement as compensation for Holocaust-era assets that had not been returned after the war. Those eligible for a share of the settlement were defined as 'targets and victims of Nazi persecution'. If this sum were to be divided equally among the 80,000 Holocaust survivors still alive, each would eligible to $15,000.

Impossible to quantify in monetary terms was the destruction of the peace of mind of the survivors, their ability to live in a world that had inflicted such suffering on them. Survivors often reflect on how there can be no compensation for their recurring nightmares – indeed, there is no full understanding, except among fellow-survivors, of how intense and terrible those nightmares can be. The scale of their suffering defies adequate recompense. Those whom they have lost – family and friends whose barbaric murder, arrest or deportation many of them witnessed – can never be brought back. Nor can the pain of the unknown fate of so many be assuaged.

Dov Levin, a survivor of the Kovno ghetto, who escaped from the ghetto and joined the partisans, wrote in his diary immediately after liberation, recalling the Nazi regime (which had killed his parents and his sister):

'We have been freed from the regime and all its terrors. But who will ever release us from the pain in our hearts, from the loneliness, from our memories of orphans gazing out from every street corner, from the echoes of cries that call out to us from every piece of earth?'

Moniek Goldberg was born in Glowaczow, a small Polish town, in 1928. After being deported to Auschwitz when he was sixteen, he became a slave labourer at Buna. Later sent to Buchenwald, he was finally liberated at Theresienstadt in May 1945. Half a century after his liberation he wrote, from his home in the United States:

'Fifty years on, I reflect that I could tell my father that I have not forgotten what I learned as a boy. I helped my fellow man when I could. I am proud to be a Jew, for I have seen man behave worse than beasts, but the Jews remembered Rabbi Hillel who taught us, "If you find yourself in a place where there are no men, you must strive to be a man." We were amongst beasts and I am proud to declare that we upheld the dignity of man.'

left
Dov Levin as a teenager. This photograph was saved from the ruins of the Kovno ghetto.

above
Moniek Goldberg (holding a flag) among a group of young survivors who had been liberated at Theresienstadt in May 1945.

opposite, left
Hugo Gryn, a survivor of Auschwitz, photographed shortly after his liberation in 1945.

opposite, right
Hugo Gryn in London in 1993, when he was senior rabbi of the North-West London Reform Synagogue (a photograph taken by Mark Gerson).

Reparations

The profits from confiscated assets should not remain with the organizations who have been holding them until now. It is a matter of justice. Fifty years on, the situation of the orphans of the deportation – who experienced the pain of losing their parents and the difficulty of being Jews under threat of round-ups and deportation – demands a gesture worthy of the Republic.

Lionel Jospin, Prime Minister of France, speaking in November 1999 about the three to five thousand surviving children of Jews deported to Auschwitz. The sum to be paid was $500 (£300) a month

SECOND GENERATION

Name   Who are you named after   Who do you resemble Who do you replace   Whose life   Whose body   Whose skin Do you ever want to ask   Do you ever not want to hear   Do you ever wish they would stop telling   Wish they would start   Are you protective of your parents   Are you allowed to ask questions about their experiences   Are some things prohibited   Do you ever tell others   Do you wish you hadn't   Do you feel relief   Is so much information missing that it's impossible to piece together   Is information withheld or unknown   Which stories hurt most   Which details   Which silences   Do you ever go numb or try to   Do you ever find yourself crying uncontrollably   Do you feel guilty when you are sad or happy or misbehave   Do you have to remind yourself it was not your fault   Do you experience feelings that seem to belong to someone else   Do you know whose memories inhabit you   Whose conscience   Whose nightmares play over and over   The ones that end with barbs in your skin   The ones that last all night   What feelings trouble you most   Are you prone to negativity and distrust   What feelings serve you well   Whose perseverance Whose spirit Do you empathize easily   Do you have bull's eye intuition   Do you have an irksome sense that you are on loan from the past, or borrowed from the future   For whom do you live   According to whose dreams   Whose desires   Whose prayers   Do you make excuses for your existence   Do you have feelings of inadequacy, resentment or remorse   Do you dislike questionnaires like this and feel none of this applies to you   Does the holocaust manifest as a steel chain rusting in your gut   Do you worry more than is comfortable   Do you ever wish you could just turn it off   Do you double check the front door lock   Do you panic when the phone rings at an odd hour   Do you ride the brakes   Do you make endless back up plans   If *this* happens, then do *that*   If *that* happens, then do *this*   Do you always keep an eye on the lookout for trouble   Do you make note of exits and possible escape routes   What one recurring thought or image do you wish you could stop forever   What event do you fear above all else   What do you do to prevent it How will you know when it's too dangerous   Do you anticipate when you would flee   Do you worry about where you would go and what you would take   Who you would leave behind   Do you think you could survive ?

The children of survivors have become known as the 'Second Generation'. They have lived in the shadow of the pain inflicted upon one or both of their parents. They have also seen the determination of the survivors to try to build a normal life, to put the horrors behind them, and to raise a family in a new world, free from the terrifying uncertainties that plagued their own early years. But the past can seldom, if ever, be ignored, and Second Generation children often bear a heavy burden. Many of them also worry that this burden will not end with them, but will be transmitted to their children, and to succeeding generations.

In 1979, Helen Epstein, herself a second generation child living in the United States, wrote a book about the second generation, *Children of the Holocaust*, that gave examples of many second generation individuals and their problems. In doing so, it defined similarities that gave the second generation its separate identity.

In her book Helen Epstein drew attention to the work, begun more than a decade earlier, of Dr Bernard Trossman, of the Student Mental Health Clinic at McGill University, Montreal. Starting in the 1960s, he had begun to see children of survivors. Their problems ranged from difficulties at school and college to stuttering. Dr Trossman identified several common features among those of the second generation whom he saw:

'The first and perhaps most innocuous is that these parents are excessively over-protective, constantly warning their children of impending danger…. Consequently, many of the children have become moderately phobic, others locked in combat with their parents as they try to throw off the smothering yoke.

Another feature consists of the child being used as the audience in the relentless recounting of their terrifying memories. It is hard to assess the effect of this since the student often treats it with bored disdain. It is likely to contribute to pathology of a depressive nature – the student feeling guilty about his better fortune.

A third frequently-met family outlook consists

in two bitter, hardened Jewish parents presenting a suspiciously hostile attitude to the Gentile world around them and expecting their children to follow suit. We see the children in the phase of active rebellion, where they may insist on dating non-Jewish partners to their parents' mounting rage or, as in one humorous yet pathetic situation, an angry young girl failed all her subjects but one – German!

Perhaps the most deleterious parental attitude is the spoken or unspoken communication that this child must provide meaning for the parents' empty lives…. Thus the expectations on the child are enormous. He is treated not as an individual but as a heavily invested symbol of the New World.'

In her book, *Children of the Holocaust*, Helen Epstein reflected, in 1979, on her personal experience:

'I am thirty now and, like my two brothers, almost as tall as my father. Both my brothers are skiers, as avid for the mountains and the winter snow as my father was for the water. My brother Tom lives in a small town in Vermont and spends his days on the slopes teaching people how to ski. My brother David, who has just graduated from high school, spends a great deal of time watching television and studies electronics.

They do not give much thought to history and neither of them cares much for books. But when we are together with my mother at home, we feel a bond so strong that our differences melt away. None of us is frightened anymore when our mother succumbs to exhaustion or depression. Instead, we have learned to tell her that she is one of the strongest persons we have ever known, that she has survived far worse, and that she most

probably needs a rest. My mother, in turn, has learned that her children cannot always be happy, healthy and free of pain. She worries less....

In 1978, when a series of nationally televised programs was aired on the Holocaust, my youngest brother arrived at school surprised to find his classmates discussing the subject he had never heard them talk about before. "It was just weird," he said, laconic as always. Then he added, "I told them that my parents were there."'

Ruth Mandel, of the second generation, was born in Canada in 1963. Her father Ray, born in Poland in 1935, survived the war as a young boy in hiding in the Cracow ghetto, where he witnessed terrifying brutality. As a grown woman, a poet and writer, Ruth Mandel visited the scenes of her father's youth. She also visited the grave of her uncle Henryk, whom she had never known – he had been murdered, as a child, twenty years before she was born. Among the poems she wrote on that visit was one about her father in hiding.

A poem by Ruth Mandel
Occupied Cracow

He was a small child
my father,
in 1942,
7 years old.

Hiding, still.
Motionless for 2 years.
Two
Years

No heart beats allowed.

above and below left
Ruth Mandel's poem, written in 1994, and a photograph of her with a bag of seeds, preparing the ground in front of the memorial (in the Cracow Jewish cemetery) to her father's brother Henryk, and his mother Henia.

below
Ray Mandel saying *Kaddish* (the Jewish memorial prayer for the dead) at the grave of his mother Henia, who died while giving birth immediately after the war, and his brother Henryk, who was murdered in the Cracow ghetto at the age of ten. The area in front of the grave had been planted with seeds by Ray's daughter a year before his visit.

BEARING WITNESS

Heard how the rabbi from Wegrow was killed on Yom Kippur. He was ordered to sweep the street. Then he was ordered to collect the refuge into his fur hat; while he was bending over, they bayonetted him three times. He continued working, and died at work.

Emanuel Ringelblum, notes, Warsaw ghetto, 26 April 1941

Comprehensiveness was the main principle of our work. Objectivity was the second. We endeavoured to convey the whole truth, no matter how bitter, and we presented faithful, unadorned pictures.

Emanuel Ringelblum, from an essay written in December 1942

Dear finder, search everywhere, in every inch of soil. Dozens of documents are buried under it, mine and those of other persons, which will throw light on everything that was happening here. Great quantities of teeth are also buried here. It was we, the Kommando workers, who expressly have strewn them all over the terrain, as many as we could, so that the world should find material traces of the millions of murdered people. We ourselves have lost hope of being able to live to see the moment of liberation.

Salmen Gradowski, notes of a Sonderkommando, buried at Auschwitz in 1944, and discovered after the war

As early as 1933, Emanuel Ringelblum, a young Jewish historian in Warsaw, was so distressed by the news of Hitler's anti-Jewish measures in Germany that he decided to begin – as he wrote in his diary on 2 June 1933 – 'the intensive collection of materials relating to the Hitler decrees'. Ringelblum collected photographs, official documents, posters and private letters. He also collected material on what he called 'Jewish counter-measures'.

Seven years later, in 1940, Ringelblum and his *Oneg Shabbos* (Joy of Sabbath) circle in the Warsaw ghetto encouraged keeping diaries and collecting documentary material. In Lvov a group of Jewish historians, among them Philip Friedman, did likewise. In Lodz the diarists included several who kept meticulous records. In Kovno the Secretary to the Jewish Council, Avraham Tory, kept a diary in which he also recorded the texts of the German decrees.

Photographers like Zvi Kadushin, painters like Esther Lurie – both in the Kovno ghetto – sought to bear witness through their respective skills. After photographing his dead neighbour's bloodstained message 'Jews revenge', Kadushin wrote: 'I don't have a gun.... My camera will be my revenge.'

Even inside Auschwitz-Birkenau, efforts were made to record what was happening. On 6 September 1944 a member of the Jewish Sonderkommando, Salmen Gradowski, who had been in Auschwitz since February 1943, collected the notes he had managed to write over the previous nineteen months and buried them. 'I have buried this under the ashes,' he wrote, 'deeming it the safest place, where people will certainly dig to find the traces of millions of men who were exterminated.'

Gradowski dedicated his notes to the members of his family 'burnt alive at Birkenau': his wife Sonia, his mother Sara, his sisters Estera-Rachel and Liba, his father-in-law Rafael and his brother-in-law Wolf.

At the end of the war a vast quantity of documentation emerged, covering every aspect of German actions. The evidence collected by the Allies, and submitted at the Nuremberg Trials, was published in forty-two volumes between 1947 and 1949. Making full use of it, Gerald Reitlinger published *The Final Solution* in 1953; Raul Hilberg published *The Destruction of European Jews* in 1961.

Many survivors and eye-witnesses gave evidence at Nuremberg. Then, as in subsequent war crimes trials, the experiences of the survivors became part of the historical record. The Eichmann Trial transcripts fill five volumes. In the four decades after the war, more than five hundred *yizkor* (memorial) books were compiled for Jewish communities – four hundred of them for towns in pre-war Poland – whose survivors wanted to set down as comprehensive a record as possible while memories were still fresh.

Survivors' magazines have encouraged the publication of recollections. In 1977 the first issue was published of *The Voice of Auschwitz Survivors*, the newsletter of the Public Committee in Israel of Survivors of Auschwitz-Birkenau and other Extermination Camps. Its inspiration was Lilli Kopecky, who had been deported from Slovakia to Auschwitz in 1942. Among other journals that publish regular accounts by survivors are *The Voice of Piotrkow Survivors*, edited by Ben Giladi, and the *'45 Aid Society Journal*, edited by Ben Helfgott. Several thousand individual memoirs have also been published. One of the first was Elie Wiesel's *Night* (1960).

Academic journals, among them *Holocaust and Genocide Studies*, *The Journal of Holocaust Education* and *Dimensions: A Journal of Holocaust Studies*, publish documentary and eye-witness accounts. Conferences of survivors generate the publication of yet more material. The first International Gathering of Holocaust Survivors, held in Jerusalem in 1980, was followed by gatherings of other groups with important stories to tell. Among these were the Kindertransport children who found refuge in Britain in 1938 and 1939, and the Hidden Children who survived the war in hiding, mostly sheltered by non-Jews.

Oral and video testimony programmes, including Steven Spielberg's Shoah Foundation project – which by the end of 1999 had recorded more than 50,000 testimonies – have encouraged survivors to speak out. Many have done so in talks to schools, or in radio and television interviews. Television programmes, including

NBC's fictional *Holocaust* series in 1978, Claude Lanzmann's documentary film *Shoah* in 1985, and Steven Speilberg's feature film *Schindler's List* in 1993, have brought awareness of the Holocaust to millions of people.

Museums also serve to bear witness, and to perpetuate memory. In October 1944, three months after Soviet soldiers reached Majdanek, the whole site was designated a permanent memorial and museum, and its main gas chamber and crematorium preserved. In 1947, Auschwitz-Birkenau was also designated a memorial and museum. A small museum was opened at Treblinka in 1968.

In Israel a kibbutz – the Ghetto Fighters' House – was established near the northern town of Nahariya in 1949. Two of its members, Yitzhak Zuckerman and Zivia Lubetkin, had fought in the Warsaw ghetto revolt. Archives, including a film archive, and a library of more than 50,000 volumes, are available for public study.

In 1953 the Israeli Parliament passed a law establishing the Martyrs' and Heroes' Remembrance Authority. Yad Vashem, a memorial and museum, opened in 1961. The name Yad Vashem ('a place and a name') was from the Book of Isaiah: 'Even unto them will I give in mine house and within my walls a place and a name better than of sons and of daughters: I will give them an everlasting name, that shall not be cut off.'

Yad Vashem's journal, *Yad Vashem Studies on the European Catastrophe and Resistance*, was first published in 1957. Its first scholarly congress took place in 1968, on the theme of 'Jewish Resistance in the Holocaust'. Starting in 1969, Yad Vashem published an *Encyclopedia of Jewish Communities*, region by region. The volume for Bavaria was published in 1972, for the Lodz region in 1976, and for Eastern Galicia in 1980.

In the United States, the home of more than 70,000 survivors, the Simon Wiesenthal Centre was opened in Los Angeles in 1977, named after the Viennese Nazi-hunter whose mother was murdered in Belzec. It was later extended to include a Museum of Tolerance, with a substantial Holocaust section. In Washington, the United States Holocaust Memorial Museum was opened in 1993, on the fiftieth anniversary of the

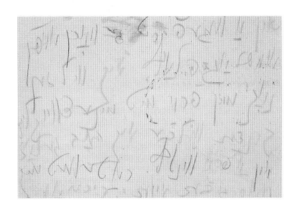

Warsaw ghetto uprising. The museum's architect, James I. Freed, was a pre-war refugee from Nazi Germany. Its library contains more than 100,000 volumes. Many other American cities have Holocaust museums and study centres. Two of the earliest were in San Francisco, and in Orlando, Florida. The first Holocaust memorial centre in Britain, Beth Shalom, was opened in Nottinghamshire in 1994. In the year 2000, the Imperial War Museum in London opened a permanent Holocaust Exhibition.

With the fall of Communism in 1991, Eastern Europe began to deal openly with the fate of the Jews. In the former ghetto of Theresienstadt, a museum was opened on 17 October 1992. Three hundred survivors came from all over the world to attend the opening. In Vilnius the story of the Holocaust in Lithuania is told at the Vilna Gaon Jewish State Museum of Lithuania, in front of which stands a memorial to Chiune Sugihara, the Japanese Consul to Lithuania before the war who saved several thousand Jews by issuing transit visas.

top far left
Yitzhak Katzenelson, whose *Song of the Murdered Jewish People* was written in the Warsaw ghetto, and his son: they were both murdered in Auschwitz.

top left
Emanuel Ringelblum and his son Uri, photographed before the war. They were among a group of Jews in hiding in 'Aryan' Warsaw in 1944, who were betrayed and killed.

left
A letter written to one of the *Oneg Shabbos* members, and preserved in its archive. It was addressed to Yitzhak Gitterman, a Warsaw-based director of the American Jewish Joint Distribution Committee: 'Dear, dear Gitterman, I beg you most dearly, save me if it is still possible. I have been taken off the streets and carried away.... I want to see my wife and two little children again, whom I have left in the province. Save me as soon as possible....'

below
One of the milk churns in which the *Oneg Shabbos* circle buried their archive in the Warsaw ghetto. This churn was discovered in the ruins of the ghetto on 1 December 1950.

'THE PEOPLE OF THE BOOK'

'... pages, copybooks'

One of the most desolate and heartrending scenes imaginable was the sight of the ghettos after an *Aktion* – the empty flats from which people were dragged away, feathers flying from bedding ripped open to disclose hidden treasures, odd articles of clothing lost or abandoned, corpses of those who were not able to keep pace, and papers, single sheets or sheaves of pages, copybooks strewn over staircases or flying in the wind – the writing, choked half-way. What flowering of human thought and feeling, what possible masterpieces ...

Rafael Scharf, born in Cracow in 1914, reflecting in 1993

An incident in Warsaw

In the hotel lobby a crowd of people were milling around, hustling and shoving, transacting business. In that crowd – a heartstopping moment this – I spot a familiar face, a former school-mate of mine! We shake hands, embrace...

As we talk, feverishly, exchanging information about mutual friends, a Polish peasant who, I notice, has been observing us for a while, comes up to us. 'You are Jews?' he asks. 'Indeed we are,' we reply.

He takes out from his breast-pocket a bundle of papers, pages from an exercise-book, covered in Hebrew handwriting, in fading ink. With it a scrap of paper, scrawled in Polish. 'Pious soul,' the message reads, 'this is a man's life work. Give it into good hands.'
(continued on the next page)

The Jewish religion found strength and cohesion from the five books of Moses – Genesis, Exodus, Leviticus, Numbers and Deuteronomy – known to the Jews as the Torah. These books contain the narrative history of the Jewish people from the time of Abraham to the Exodus from Egypt and the forty-year journey through the wilderness to the Promised Land – a journey that included the dramatic handing by God to Moses of the Ten Commandments.

The Hebrew Bible holds within its covers a vast array of wisdom and guidance, centred upon a comprehensive ethical code. Based on it, a great apparatus of commentary grew up, to which generations of sages and rabbis contributed. Jewish teaching through the ages derived from these books, and led to an outpouring of Jewish literature, in which the stories of individuals, their hopes, fears and aspirations, and their humour, often reflected and illuminated the experience of a whole people. Thus, writing, recording, narrating, publishing and reading have been engraved in the Jewish character from biblical times.

After Hitler came to power in 1933, the first Nazi imperative was to burn books. During the Holocaust tens of thousands of writers were among the murdered six million. After the Holocaust, Jewish writing resumed with an added impetus. 'In one respect at least,' wrote Cracow-born Rafael Scharf in 1993, 'the Germans were unlucky in their choice of victim. "The People of the Book" were literate and had faith in the written word. The compulsion to record, to leave a trace in writing, was widespread and overwhelming. The fear that the incredible events of which they were the witness and victim might not become known or would not be believed was greater than concern for their own survival. The last words in one of the most searing documents of that time, the diary of Chaim Kaplan, before his deportation to Treblinka, were: "If I die, what will happen to my diary?"'

Chaim Kaplan's diary, written in the Warsaw ghetto,

survived, as did many other diaries whose authors were murdered. Hundreds more diaries, thousands perhaps, were destroyed. But the outpouring of books since 1945 has ensured that the history of the Holocaust would not only be written, but would cover every region, every town, every aspect of the destructive process. It was the Jewish historian, Philip Friedman, a survivor of the Lvov ghetto, who published two of the first books on the Holocaust, both in 1946, both in Polish: a book on Auschwitz and a book on the fate of the Jews of Lvov. The first was published in Bydgoszcz, the second in Lodz. 'The People of the Book' had begun again to write. Five and a half terrible years – the years of the Second World War – had given them a new theme.

Among the books published after the Holocaust were many that listed the names of the victims. Some of these books, deemed to have no commercial interest, were published in small and private editions. What mattered to their authors was the existence of material in book form, not the size of the market. In 1991 the

municipality of Frankfurt published a book (1) listing all the Jews of Leipzig who were deported between 1942 and 1945. Only thirty copies were printed. Yad Vashem's pioneering list (2) of all the Jewish communities that were destroyed , giving the number of Jews living in them between the wars, has been out of print for more than a quarter of a century. A recent search at Yad Vashem itself found only a single copy.

A Soviet book on the Holocaust on Russian soil, the 'Black Book' (3), edited by Vasilij Grossman and Ilja Erenburg in 1946, was banned by the Soviet authorities a year later, and all copies were destroyed. Only in 1993, after forty-seven years, could it be published, when, with the fall of Communism, the original printer's page proofs were found in Moscow in the archives of the KGB. It was republished in book form on what was former Soviet territory – in the newly proclaimed Republic of Lithuania, the destruction of whose Jewish life the book graphically describes.

The decade following the end of Communist restrictions saw in Eastern Europe an upsurge in books that set out the basic data of Jewish life before 1939, and its destruction in the Holocaust. In 1994 a multi-volume publication project (4) began to appear in Hungary. It consisted of factual details compiled fifty years earlier – in April 1944 – by the Central Council of Hungarian Jews, on the order of the German authorities. In Britain, a former British police officer, Robin O'Neil, compiled a list of every community whose Jews were deported to Belzec and killed. His list (5) was published in London in the journal *East European Jewish Affairs*.

The People of the Book – and those non-Jews, like Robin O'Neil, who have been drawn to research into the Holocaust – will continue to research and to publish. The library shelves devoted to books about the Holocaust will continue to expand. Not only the story of the destruction, but the story of the Jewish life that was destroyed, of Jewish culture and faith, of Jewish achievement and aspirations, the histories of towns, the saga of families, and the biographies of individuals, will continue to illuminate the depths of barbarism that those who created the Holocaust reached in their attempt to destroy Jewish civilization in Europe.

left
The railway line to Belzec, at the point where it leaves Lvov.

opposite
Five of the many thousands of books and journals containing detailed factual information about the fate of the Jews during the Holocucaust.

'NEVER AGAIN'

In the sixth decade since the Holocaust, the dwindling number of survivors reflect on what the terrible events of those years mean not only to them but to mankind. The words 'Never again' are often on their lips. In the final decade of the twentieth century, barbarities around the world caused many survivors to speak with growing concern about what they read in the newspapers or saw on television.

The brutal murder of civilians in parts of Africa, particularly in Rwanda, but also in a dozen other African countries, and the killing of civilians wherever in the world it has been reported, has been a source of anguish for those Jews who experienced the Nazi-era barbarities.

At the height of the ethnic cleansing in Bosnia in 1992, when Serbs and Croats renewed, in horrific bloodshed, their historic enmity, Elie Wiesel, Nobel Prize winner – and Holocaust survivor – spoke out at a Press Conference in London. He was 'eloquent', reported *The Times*, 'in his denunciation of the detention camps; so much so that Radovan Karadzic, the Bosnian Serb leader, promised to empty Serb-controlled camps immediately'.

Seven years later, when armed Serbs massacred several thousand unarmed Kosovar Albanians in the Serb province of Kosovo, one of the first to speak out against the killings was, once again, Elie Wiesel. For him, 'never again' is an urgent global need. As he said during a commemoration ceremony at Auschwitz-Birkenau on 27 January 1995 – the fiftieth anniversary of the liberation of Auschwitz, to which he himself had been deported – 'As we reflect upon the past, we must address ourselves to the present, and the future. In the name of all that is sacred in memory, let us stop the bloodshed where it is still being conducted.... Let us reject, and oppose more effectively, religious fanaticism and racial hate.'

Survivors are not alone in reflecting on the nature of human society and on the fragility of the bonds of civilized behaviour. But they have a first-hand personal understanding of just how powerful the instinct of destruction can be in human beings – so deep that large numbers of people can set aside all religious and ethical imperatives, and ignore their links with humanity.

As the Holocaust recedes into history, many people,

Bad tempers cool over war nobody knows how to stop

By MICHAEL BINYON, DIPLOMATIC EDITOR   28 August 1992

WHAT must have been one of the most bad-tempered conferences in London began with everyone angry about something: the seating, the speaking order, the status of the delegations, the aims of the conference and the wording of documents. So much so that the final breakthrough came as a surprise to all. Despite the breakthrough, however, everyone cautioned that peace would be hard work and prophesied that there would be many pitfalls on the way.

The delegations from former Yugoslavia feared and mistrusted one another and each was convinced the rest of the conference was ganging up to isolate it. The leaders of minority ethnic groups in the republics were furious at being excluded from the plenary sessions and being made to watch proceedings on closed-circuit television. The opposition parties, peace activists and academics from the region were upset at being kept out altogether, and held an

LONDON CONFERENCE

alternative "Conference for a Balkan Peace" nearby.

The Europeans were frustrated by their previous failures; the distant powers, such as Japan and China, were baffled by the complexity of the arguments, and the British organisers were wearily sick of all the bickering. Everybody is disgusted by the war; nobody knows how to stop it.

The Balkans began on the pavement outside the Queen Elizabeth 2 conference centre. Groups of demonstrators, each waving their messages of hate, jeered every time a rival group approached. "EC blackmail is no solution", said the Serbs. "Stop media lies. Tell the truth," their banners proclaimed. The entire crisis, they insisted, was "manufactured in Germany".

Almost within spitting distance, the blazing-eyed Albanians from Kosovo passionately denounced their Serbian oppressors as they chanted "Free Ko-so-vo." One cynic even denounced the British hosts: "Go on Major, threaten them with another conference," his notice read.

At the conference, Lord Carrington delivered a historical lecture on why the Balkans were so ungovernable and followed that with a denunciation of those who did not keep their word. Lawrence Eagleburger, the acting American Secretary of State and former ambassador to Belgrade, was also stung into a sharp defence of his Yugoslav entanglements after George Kenney, head of the department on Yugoslav

affairs, quit with some tart accusations that the conference was a charade.

Perhaps the only note of reconciliation and humanity came from two Jewish outsiders, Elie Wiesel, the American Nobel prize winner, and Israel Singer, the secretary-general of the World Jewish Congress. Mr Wiesel, a concentration-camp survivor, was eloquent in his denunciation of the detention camps; so much so that Radovan Karadzic, the Bosnian Serb leader, promised to empty Serb-controlled camps immediately. But promises, alas, do not necessarily mean action.

Status inevitably caused a fuss on the first day. What exactly was the diplomatic standing of the unrecognised rump Yugoslav delegation? Would a man such as Milan Panic, the new prime minister from California, have official status? "He will sit behind his own nameplate. It will simply say Slobodan Milosevic," said a hapless British official, his faux pas inadvertently summing up the real relationship between the two men, who soon fell to public squabbles about which of them could really speak for Yugoslavia.

By the start of the second and last day, when everyone had got his set speech on the record, the real haggling began.

A draft on the key statement on Bosnia had all the right phrases on a ceasefire, heavy weapons, a possible international peacekeeping force and inhuman expulsions of civilians. But a word here, a phrase there were enough to keep tempers on the boil almost to the end.

Wiesel: denounced the detention camps

Jews and non-Jews, have joined the survivors in seeking means of halting further genocides. International diplomacy has come to adopt a more active stance against regimes that carry out, or attempt to carry out, racial and ethnic killings.

Governments turn to the memory of the Holocaust to stress the dangers of racism. To this end, in 1999 the British government proposed a Holocaust Memorial Day, to be observed nationwide, similar to the annual Remembrance Day that recalls the dead of two world wars.

More and more educational curricula – most notably in the United States, Britain and Sweden – have sought to integrate the study of the Holocaust into the teaching of history and of human rights. The Anne Frank Foundation in Holland, and the Anne

18 News 20 Octobr 1999

Rabbi condemns Czech 'ghetto' wall

By Roger Boyes

MOVES to wall off a Romany community in a Czech town have been condemned by the ... the most delicate phase of its EU entry negotiations. But Pavel Tosovsky, the local ... Czechs. They complained about a wave of thefts and fights erupted on the street. ... Sidon. "We could perhaps boycott goods produced in Usti." But local government cannot ...

Chechens beg the West to 'stop genocide'

BY ALICE LAGNADO IN MOSCOW AND RICHARD BEESTON

CHECHNYA yesterday accused Russia of committing "genocide" against its people ... So far, Russia has all appear for ...

opposite, top right
The Times, 28 August 1992: Elie Wiesel, survivor and Nobel Prize winner, speaks out against ethnic cleansing.

above left
The main foreign news item in *The Times* of 20 October 1999. A Czech town, Usti nad Labem (Usti on the Elbe), had just announced plans to build a wall around its Gypsy quarter. The proposal was at once condemned by the Chief Rabbi of the Czech Republic, Karol Sidon, as the beginning of a ghetto 'for people who suffered with us in Nazi concentration camps'. At the same time, the President of the European Commission, Romano Prodi, commenting on the proposed wall, said: 'Europe will never again accept new walls separating European citizens.' He was referring to the Berlin Wall that separated East and West Berlin between 1964 and 1989, but he could equally well have been referring – as was the Chief Rabbi of the Czech Republic – to the ghetto walls erected in order to confine Jews during the Second World War. As a result of these protests the wall was abandoned.

below left
An appeal to 'stop genocide' in Chechenya, sent from the capital, Grozny, on 6 November 1999, and published in *The Times* on the following day.

Frank Educational Trust in Britain, have been at the forefront of this, linking the suffering of one Jewish girl with the sufferings of millions of girls and boys in the new millennium, wherever they might be in danger. As a result of an initiative by the Trust, the European Parliament's human rights declaration, calling in November 1999 for 'an end to bigotry' in the new millennium, was designated the Anne Frank Human Rights Declaration.

Another public perception influenced by the Holocaust was saying 'never again' to admitting war criminals as immigrants. In 1998 the Canadian government, which had been criticized in previous decades for allowing former collaborators of Nazi Germany to enter Canada after the Second World War, refused entry to 307 individuals suspected of having recently participated in war crimes and expelled 23 who were already in Canada – originally from Uganda, Roumania, Guatemala, Honduras and El Salvador.

Writing in Germany in 1960, in one of the first German books on the Holocaust, later published in English as *The Yellow Star*, Gerhard Schoenberner

reflected: '... we must become aware of our responsibility for what goes on around us. We do not escape the past by thrusting it to the back of our minds. Only if we come to terms with it and understand the lessons of those years, can we free ourselves of the legacy of Hitlerite barbarism. Policies are not pre-ordained by fate. They are made by people and people can change them.'

Pinchas Gutter, living in Canada, was a survivor of the Warsaw ghetto and Majdanek. His parents, grandparents and sister were murdered in the Holocaust. In 1996 he reflected: 'Let us hope that there will be an end to suffering for all the oppressed people of our world.'

A British Member of Parliament, Tony McNulty, commenting on the proposed Holocaust Day in Britain – a day that the European Union had already established as Genocide Remembrance Day – told a Jewish gathering on 15 November 1999: 'This day will be not just an act of remembrance but a universal reflection on humanity and tolerance. "Never again" cannot be simply a glib phrase.'

CHRONOLOGY

Adolf Hitler

Reinhard Heydrich

Adolf Eichmann

Dr Joseph Mengele

Heinrich Himmler

1933

30 January Hitler comes to power in Germany
1 April   Jewish shops in Berlin boycotted
7 April   All Jewish government employees in Germany, including civil servants, professors and schoolteachers, removed from their posts
10 May   Burning of books written by Jews, liberals and opponents of Nazism

1935

15 September The Nuremberg Laws make German Jews second-class citizens

1936

Jewish doctors forbidden to practise in government hospitals in Germany

1938

13 March Germany annexes Austria
25 June   German Jewish doctors forbidden to treat non-Jewish patients
9 November   Kristallnacht, synagogues burned throughout Greater Germany

1939

1 September Germany invades Poland; atrocities against Jews begin in every occupied town
3 September Britain and France declare war on Germany
28 September Poland partitioned between Germany and the Soviet Union
8 October   The first ghetto established by the Germans in Poland, in Piotrkow
23 November Jews in German-occupied Poland forced to wear a Star of David

1940

9 April Germany invades Denmark and Norway
30 April   Lodz ghetto established; 165,000 Jews confined in under two square miles

10 May Germany invades Belgium, France and Holland
15 November Warsaw ghetto set up; more than 500,000 Jews confined there

1941

6 April Germany invades Yugoslavia and Greece
22 June   Germany invades the Soviet Union; the mass execution of Jews begins at once
8 July   Wearing of the Jewish star made compulsory in the former Baltic States
1 September German Jews over the age of six forced to wear the Yellow Star with the word 'Jude' (Jew) printed on it in black
29-30 September 33,000 Jews murdered in two days at Babi Yar, outside Kiev
10 October   Theresienstadt ghetto set up; German and Czech Jews deported there
16 October   Mass deportation begins of Jews from Greater Germany to the East
28 October   10,000 Jews 'selected' in the Kovno ghetto and murdered
7 December Japan attacks the United States at Pearl Harbor
8 December   The first killing of Jews by gas begins, at the death camp at Chelmno
11 December Germany declares war on the United States

1942

20 January   The Wannsee Conference discusses the 'Final Solution'
21 January   United Partisan Organization founded in the Vilna ghetto
17 March   First deportation of Jews from Galicia to Belzec death camp
24 March   First deportation of Jews from Germany to Belzec
26 March   First deportation of Slovak Jews to Auschwitz

27 March   First deportation of Jews from France to Auschwitz

4 May   First mass murder of Jews by gas at Auschwitz-Birkenau

6 May   First deportation to the death camp at Sobibor

6 May   First deportation to the death camp at Maly Trostinets

18 May   Jewish act of defiance in Berlin

15 July   First deportation of Dutch Jews to Auschwitz

22 July   Daily deportation of Jews from Warsaw to Treblinka begins

4 August   First deportation of Jews from Belgium to Auschwitz

October   22,000 Jews deported from Piotrkow to the death camp at Treblinka

2 October   Round-up of 13,000 Jews in Holland

25 October   Norwegian Jews deported to Auschwitz

16 December   Himmler orders Gypsies deported to Auschwitz

22 December   Jewish resistance in Cracow

1943

4 January   Czestochowa ghetto resistance

18 January   Four-day revolt begins in the Warsaw ghetto, against the deportations

20 January   Continuing the deportations, Himmler demands: 'I must have more trains'

3-22 March   Deportation of Jews from Thrace and Macedonia to Treblinka

15 March   Deportation begins of Jews from Salonika to Auschwitz

17 March   Bulgaria refuses to deport Jews

17 April   Hungary refuses to deport Jews

19 April   Warsaw ghetto revolt begins

11 June   Himmler orders the deportation of Jews from all remaining ghettos

2 August   Revolt of the slave labourers at Treblinka

1 October   Most Danish Jews reach the safety of Sweden on the eve of deportation

14 October   Revolt of the slave labourers at Sobibor

3 November   Mass murder of 42,000 Jews at Majdanek and nearby camps

9 November   First deportation of Jews from Italy to Auschwitz

1944

23 March   Ten-day deportation of Jews from Greece to Auschwitz begins

9 April   Two Jews escape from Auschwitz, to get news of the camp to the West

15 May   Mass deportation of Jews from Hungary to Auschwitz begins

June   As Soviet forces move towards Germany, the Germans begin to evacuate hundreds of thousands of Jews on 'Death Marches'

6 June   **Allied troops land in Normandy**

August   Jews take part in Slovak uprising

1 August   Warsaw uprising: Jews participate

2-3 August   Almost all the Gypsies in their 'family camp' at Birkenau murdered

4 August   Anne Frank and her family arrested in Amsterdam

6-7 October   Uprising of Jewish slave labourers at the crematoria in Birkenau

November   Death Marches throughout Eastern Europe

1945

17 January   Final Death Marches from Auschwitz-Birkenau

27 January   Soviet troops reach Auschwitz, liberating a remnant of the inmates

11 April   American troops enter Buchenwald

15 April   British troops enter Belsen

29 April   American troops enter Dachau

30 April   **Hitler commits suicide in Berlin**

5 May   American troops reach Mauthausen

7 May   **Germany surrenders to the Allies**

November   **Nuremberg trials open**

Anne Frank

Emanuel Ringelblum

Dolek Liebeskind

Yitzhak Zuckerman

Renja From

Bibliography

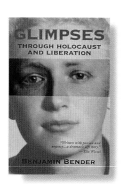

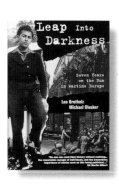

I have taken quotations from eye-witnesses and survivors – as well as documentary material, factual information and illustrations – from the following published works, to whose authors, editors and publishers I am extremely grateful:

ENCYCLOPAEDIAS, DOCUMENTS, REFERENCE BOOKS

Black Book of Localities Whose Jewish Population was Exterminated by the Nazis, Yad Vashem, Jerusalem, 1965.

Encyclopaedia Judaica, sixteen volumes (with supplements), Keter, Jerusalem, 1972.

Israel Gutman (Editor in Chief), *Encyclopedia of the Holocaust*, four volumes, Macmillan, New York, 1990.

State of Israel, Ministry of Justice, *The Trial of Adolf Eichmann: Record of Proceedings in the District Court of Jerusalem*, six volumes, Jerusalem, 1992.

John Mendelsohn (editor), *The Holocaust, Selected Documents in Eighteen Volumes*, Garland Publishing, New York, 1982.

Louis L. Snyder, *Encyclopedia of the Third Reich*, Robert Hale, London,1976.

Trial of the Major War Criminals Before the International Military Tribunal, Nuremberg, 14 November 1945–1 October 1946, Secretariat of the International Military Tribunal, Nuremberg, 42 volumes, 1947–1949.

GENERAL BOOKS

Michel Abitbol, *The Jews of North Africa during the Second World War*, Wayne State University Press, Detroit, 1989.

Alan Adelson and Robert Lapides (editors), *Lodz Ghetto: Inside a Community under Siege*, Viking, New York, 1989.

Reuben Ainsztein, *Jewish Resistance in Nazi-Occupied Eastern Europe: with a historical survey of the Jew as fighter and soldier in the Diaspora*, Paul Elek, London, 1974.

Yitzhak Arad, *Ghetto in Flames: The Struggle and Destruction of the Jews in Vilna in the Holocaust*, Yad Vashem, Jerusalem, 1980.

Dorothy and Pesach Bar-Adon, *Seven Who Fell*, Palestine Pioneer Library, No.11, Tel Aviv, 1947.

Wladyslaw Bartoszewski and Zofia Lewin (editors), *Righteous Among Nations: How Poles Helped the Jews, 1939–1945*, Earlscourt Publications, London, 1969.

Paul R. Bartrop, *Australia and the Holocaust, 1933–1945*, Australian Scholarly Publishing, Melbourne,1994.

Arieh L. Bauminger, *The Fighters of the Cracow Ghetto*, Keter, Jerusalem, 1986.

Morris Beckman, *The Jewish Brigade: An Army with Two Masters*, Spellmount, Staplehurst, Kent, 1998.

Solon Beinfeld, *Hidden History: Songs of the Kovno Ghetto* (compact disc brochure), United States Holocaust Memorial Museum, Washington DC, 1997.

Judith C. E. Belinfante, Christine Fischer-Defoy and Ad Petersen, *Charlotte Salomon, 'Life? or Theatre?'*, Uitgeverij Waanders, Zwolle, Netherlands, 1992.

Arieh Ben-Tov, *Facing the Holocaust in Budapest: The International Committee of the Red Cross and the Jews in Hungary, 1943–1945*, Martinus Nijhoff, Dordrecht, Netherlands, 1988.

Benjamin Bender, *Glimpses: Through Holocaust and Liberation*, North Atlantic Books, Berkeley, California, 1995.

Norman Bentwich, *The Rescue and Achievement of Refugee Scholars: The Story of Displaced Scholars and Scientists, 1933–1952*, Martinus Nijhoff, The Hague, 1953.

Michael Berenbaum (editor), *A Mosaic of Victims: Non-Jews Persecuted and Murdered by the Nazis*, I.B. Tauris, London, 1990.

Michael Berenbaum, *The World Must Know: The History of the Holocaust as Told in the United States Holocaust Memorial Museum*, Little, Brown, Boston, 1993.

Jadwiga Bezwinska and Danuta Czech (editors), *Amidst a Nightmare of Crime: Manuscripts of Members of Sonderkommando*, Publications of State Museum at Oswiecim, Oswiecim, 1973.

Leslie Blau, *Bonyhad: A Destroyed Community: The Jews of Bonyhad, Hungary*, Shengold Publishers, New York, 1994.

Eve Line Blum, *Nous Sommes 900 Français: A la mémoire des déportés du convoi no 73 ayant quitté Drancy le 15 mai 1944*, Besançon, 1999.

Emilia Borecka and Leonard Sempolinski (editors), *Warszawa 1945*, Panstwowe Wydawnictwo Naukowe, Warsaw, 1975.

Randolph L. Braham, *The Destruction of Hungarian Jewry: A Documentary Account*, two volumes, Columbia University Press, New York, 1963.

Randolph L. Braham, *The Politics of Genocide: The Holocaust in Hungary*, Columbia University Press, New York, 1981.

Randolph L. Braham and Scott Miller (editors), *The Nazis' Last Victims: The Holocaust in Hungary*, Wayne State University Press, Detroit, Michigan, 1998.

Elinor J. Brecher, *Schindler's Legacy: True Stories of the List Survivors*, Hodder and Stoughton, London, 1994.

Leo Bretholz (with Michael Olesker), *Leap into Darkness: Seven Years on the Run in Wartime Europe*, Woodholme House, Baltimore, Maryland, 1999.

Stéphanie Bruchfeld and Paul A. Levine, *Tell your children… A book about the Holocaust in Europe 1933–1945*, Regeringkansliet, Stockholm, 1998.

Susan Cohen, Howard M. Epstein and Serge Klarsfeld (editors), *French Children of the Holocaust: A Memorial*, New York University Press, New York, 1996.

Photini Constantopoulou and Thanos Veremis (editors), *Documents on the History of the Greek Jews*, Kastaniotis Editions, Athens, 1999.

Danuta Czech, *Auschwitz Chronicle, 1939–1945*, I.B. Tauris, London, 1990.

Szymon Datner, *Las Sprawiedliwych (The Forest of the Righteous)*, Warsaw, 1968.

Alexander Donat (editor), *The Death Camp Treblinka, A Documentary*, Holocaust Library, New York, 1979.

Gusta Davidson Draenger, *Justyna's Narrative*, University of Massachusetts Press, Amherst, 1996.

Lucjan Dobroszycki (editor), *The Chronicle of the Lodz Ghetto, 1941–1944*, Yale University Press, New Haven, 1984.

Joel Elkes, *Values, Belief and Survival: Dr Elkhanan Elkes and the Kovno Ghetto: A Memoir*, Vale Publishing, London, 1997.

Helen Epstein, *Children of the Holocaust: Conversations with Sons and Daughters of Survivors*, G.P. Putnam's Sons, New York, 1979.

Etty, *A Diary, 1941–43*, Jonathan Cape, London, 1983.

Alfred Etzold, Joachim Fait, Peter Kirchner and Heinz Knobloch (editors), *Die jüdischen Friedhöfe in Berlin*, Henschel Verlag, Berlin, 1991.

Alex Faitelson, *Heroism & Bravery in Lithuania, 1941–1945*, Gefen, Jerusalem, 1996.

Louis Falstein (editor), *The Martyrdom of Jewish Physicians in Poland*, Exposition Press, New York, 1963.

Mary Lowenthal Felstiner, *To Paint Her Life: Charlotte Salomon in the Nazi Era*, HarperCollins, London, 1994.

Benjamin B. Ferencz, *Less than Slaves: Jewish Forced Labor and the Quest for Compensation*, Harvard University Press, Cambridge, Massachusetts, 1979.

Jerzy Ficowski, *A Reading of Ashes* (poems), Menard Press, London, 1981.

Jiri Fiedler, *Jewish Sights of Bohemia and Moravia*, Sefer, Prague, 1991.

The Diary of Anne Frank, Vallentine, Mitchell, London, 1953.

Otto Frank and Mirjam Pressler (editors), *The Diary of a Young Girl, The Definitive Edition, Anne Frank*, Doubleday, New York, 1995.

Saul Friedländer, *When Memory Comes*, Farrar, Straus and Giroux, New York, 1979.

Philip Friedman, *Their Brothers' Keepers: The Christian Heroes and Heroines Who Helped the Oppressed Escape the Nazi Terror*, Crown Publishers, New York, 1957.

Varian Fry, *Surrender on Demand, The Dramatic Story of the Underground Organization Set Up by Americans in France to Rescue Cultural and Political Refugees from the Gestapo*, Johnson Books, Boulder, Colorado, 1997 (originally published by Random House, New York, 1945).

Marian Fuks, Zygmunt Hoffman, Maurycy Horn and Jerzy Tomaszewski, *Polish Jewry: History and Culture*, Interpress, Warsaw, 1982.

Solomon Gaon and M. Mitchell Serels (editors), *Sephardim and the Holocaust*, Yeshiva University, New York, 1987.

G.E.R Gedye, *Fallen Bastions: The Central European Tragedy*, Victor Gollancz, London, 1939.

Leo Goldberger (editor), *The Rescue of Danish Jews: Moral Courage under Stress*, New York University Press, New York, 1987.

Gerald Green, *The Artists of Terezin*, Shocken, New York, 1978.

Hugo Gryn (with Naomi Gryn), *Chasing Shadows*, Viking, London, 2000.

Luba Krugman Gurdus, *The Death Train: A Personal Account of a Holocaust Survivor*, Holocaust Library, New York, 1978.

Israel Gutman, *The Warsaw Ghetto*, Indiana University Press, Bloomington, Indiana, 1982.

Israel Gutman, *Resistance: The Warsaw Ghetto Uprising*, Houghton Mifflin, Boston, 1994.

Israel Gutman and Shmuel Krakowski, *Unequal Victims: Poles and Jews During World War II*, Holocaust Library, New York, 1986.

Philip Hallie, *Lest Innocent Blood Be Shed: The Story of the Village of Le Chambon and How Goodness Happened There*, Harper and Row, New York, 1979.

The Hidden Child, Second International Gathering, Directory of Children Who Survived the Holocaust, Anti-Defamation League, New York, 1993.

David A. Hackett (editor and translator), *The Buchenwald Report*, Westview Press, Boulder, Colorado, 1995.

Cyril Hart, *Cornish Oasis: A Biographical Chronicle of the Fishing Village of Coverack, Cornwall*, Lizard Press, Mullion, Cornwall, 1990.

Joe J. Heydecker, *The Warsaw Ghetto: A Photographic Record, 1941–1944*, I. B. Tauris, London, 1990.

Raul Hilberg, *The Destruction of European Jewry*, Quadrangle Books, Chicago, 1961.

Sandra Joseph (editor), *A Voice for the Child: The Inspirational Words of Janusz Korczak*, Thorsons, London, 1999.

Jack Kagan and Dov Cohen, *Surviving the Holocaust with the Russian Jewish Partisans*, Vallentine, Mitchell, London, 1998.

Alfred Kantor, *The Book of Alfred Kantor*, McGraw Hill, New York, 1971.

Solly Kaplinski, *Lost and Found: A Second Generation Response to the Holocaust*, Creda Press, Cape Town, 1992.

Slawomir Kapralski (editor), *The Jews in Poland, Volume II*, Judaica Foundation, Cracow, 1999.

Felicja Karay, *Death Comes in Yellow: Skarzysko-Kamienna Slave Labour Camp*, Harwood Academic Publishers, Amsterdam, 1996.

Donald Kenrick and Grattan Puxon, *Gypsies under the Swastika*, University of Hertfordshire Press, Hatfield, Hertfordshire, 1995.

Joseph Kermish and Shmuel Krakowski (editors), *Emmanuel Ringelblum: Polish-Jewish Relations During the Second World War*, Yad Vashem, Jerusalem, 1974.

Joseph Kermish (editor), *'To live with honor, and die with honor!': Selected Documents from Warsaw Ghetto Underground Ghetto Underground Archives 'OS' ('Oneg Shabbath')*, Yad Vashem, Jerusalem, 1986.

Serge Klarsfeld (editor), *Le Mémorial de la déportation des juifs de France*, Beate Klarsfeld Foundation, New York, 1978.

Serge Klarsfeld (editor), *The Auschwitz Album: Lili Jacob's Album*, Beate Klarsfeld Foundation, Paris, 1980.

Serge Klarsfeld (editor), *Le Mémorial de la déportation des juifs de Belgique*, Beate Klarsfeld Foundation, New York, 1982.

Serge Klarsfeld (editor), *David Olère, 1902–1985: Un Peintre au Sonnderkommando à Auschwitz*, Catalogue, Beate Klarsfeld Foundation, New York, 1989.

Dennis B. Klein (general editor), *Hidden History of the Kovno Ghetto*, Little, Brown and Company, Boston, 1997.

Eugen Kogan, Hermann Langbein and Adalbert Rückerl (editors), *Nazi Mass Murder: A Documentary History of the Use of Poison Gas*, Yale University Press, New Haven, 1993.

Isaac Kowalski (editor), *Anthology on Armed Jewish Resistance, 1939–1945, volume four*, Jewish Combatants Publishers House, New York, 1991.

Shmuel Krakowski, *The War of the Doomed: Jewish Armed Resistance in Poland, 1942–1944*, Holmes and Meier, New York, 1984.

Robert Krell (editor), *Messages and Memories: Reflections on Child Survivors of the Holocaust*, Memory Press, Vancouver, 1999.

Marie Rut Krizkova, Kurt Jiri Kotouc and Zdenek Ornest (editors), *We Are Children Just the Same: 'Vedem', The Secret Magazine By The Boys of Terezin*, Jewish Publication Society, Philadelphia, 1994.

Zofia S. Kubar, *Double Identity: A Memoir*, Hill and Wang, New York, 1989.

Zdenek Lederer, *Ghetto Theresienstadt*, Edward Goldston and Son, London, 1953.

Wim van Leer, *Time of My Life*, Carta, Jerusalem, 1984.

Isabella Leitner, *Fragments of Isabella: A Memoir of Auschwitz*, Laurel, New York, 1987.

H.D. Leuner, *When Compassion was a Crime: Germany's Silent Heroes*, Oswald Wolff, London, 1966.

Bertha Leverton and Shmuel Lowensohn (editors), *I Came Alone: The Stories of the Kindertransports*, The Book Guild, Lewes, Sussex, 1990.

Hillel Levine, *In Search of Sugihara: The Elusive Japanese Diplomat Who Risked His Life to Rescue 10,000 Jews from the Holocaust*, The Free Press, New York, 1996.

David Low, *Years of Wrath: A Cartoon History, 1932–1945*, Victor Gollancz, London, 1949.

Willy Lindwer, *The Last Seven Months of Anne Frank*, Pantheon Books, New York, 1991.

Zivia Lubetkin, *In the Days of Destruction and Revolt*, Hakibbutz Hameuchad and Am Oved, Israel, 1981.

Esther Lurie, *A Living Witness: Kovno Ghetto, Scenes & Types (30 drawings and water colours)*, Dvir, Tel Aviv, 1958.

Andy Marino, *Quiet American: The Secret War of Varian Fry*, St Martin's Press, New York, 1999.

Jane Mark (editor), *The Hidden Children: The Secret Survivors of the Holocaust*, Ballantine Books, New York, 1993.

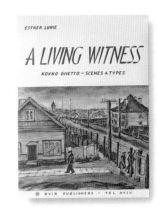

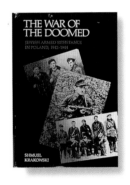

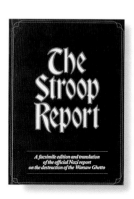

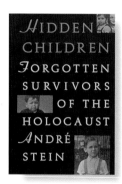

Vladka Meed, *On Both Sides of the Wall: Memoirs from the Warsaw Ghetto*, Ghetto Fighters' House, Israel, 1972.

Benjamin Meirtchak, *Jewish Military Casualties in the Polish Armies in World War II*, four volumes, Association of Jewish War Veterans of Polish Armies in Israel, four volumes, Tel Aviv, 1994–7.

Michel Mielnicki, *From Bialystok to Birkenau: Memories of a Holocaust Survivor*, as told to John Monro, Ronsdale Press, Vancouver, 2000.

Miriam Novitch, *Spiritual Resistance: 120 Drawings from Concentration Camps and Ghettos, 1940–1945*, Comune de Milano, Milan, 1979.

James N. Pellechia, *The Spirit and the Sword: Jehovah's Witnesses Expose the Third Reich*, Watch Tower Bible and Tract Society of Pennsylvania, 1997.

Franciszek Piper and Teresa Swiebocka (editors), *Auschwitz: Nazi Death Camp*, Auschwitz-Birkenau State Museum, Oswiecim, 1996.

Samuel Pisar, *Of Blood and Hope*, Macmillan, New York, 1982.

Prayer Book for Jewish Members of HM Forces, His Majesty's Stationery Office, London, 1940.

Dr J. Presser, *The Destruction of the Dutch Jews*, E.P. Dutton, New York, 1969.

Ralph Georg Reuth, *Goebbels: The Life of Joseph Goebbels, The Mephistophelean Genius of Nazi Propaganda*, Constable, London, 1993.

The Diary of Dawid Rubinowicz, William Blackwood, Edinburgh, 1981.

Yitskhok Rudashevski, *The Diary of the Vilna Ghetto, June 1941–April 1943*, Ghetto Fighters' House, Israel, 1977.

Reinhard Rürup (editor), *Topography of Terror: Gestapo, SS and Reichssicherheitshauptamt on the 'Prinz-Albrecht-Terrain', A Documentation*, Willmuth Arenhövel, Berlin, 1989.

Ctibor Rybár, *Jewish Prague, Notes on History and Culture – A Guidebook*, Akropolis, Prague, 1991.

Rosa M. Sacharin (transcriber and compiler), *Recollections of Child Refugees from 1938 to the Present*, Scottish Annual Reunion of Kinder, Glasgow, May 1999.

Harvey Sarner, *Rescue in Albania: One Hundred Percent of Jews in Albania Rescued from the Holocaust*, Brunswick Press, Cathedral City, California, 1997.

Agnes Sassoon, *Agnes: How my Spirit Survived*, Lawrence Cohen, Barnet, Hertfordshire, 1983.

Rafael F. Scharf (editor), *In the Warsaw Ghetto, Summer 1941: Photographs by Willy Georg with Passages from Warsaw Ghetto Diaries*, Aperture Foundation, London, 1994.

Rafael F. Scharf, *Poland, What Have I To Do With Thee...: Essays without Prejudice*, Fundacja Judaica, Cracow, 1996.

Gertrude Schneider, *Journey into Terror: Story of the Riga Ghetto*, Ark House, New York, 1979.

Gwynne Schrire (editor), *In Sacred Memory: Recollections of the Holocaust by survivors living in Cape Town*, Holocaust Memorial Council, Cape Town, 1995.

Gerhard Schoenberner, *The Yellow Star: The Persecution of the Jews in Europe, 1933–1935*, Transworld, London, 1969.

Henry Schwab, *The Echoes that Remain: A Postal History of the Holocaust*, Cardinal Spellman Philatelic Museum, Weston, Massachusetts, 1992.

Leon Shapiro, *The History of ORT: A Jewish Movement for Social Change*, Schocken Books, New York, 1980.

Lore Shelley, *Auschwitz: The Nazi Civilization*, University Press of America, Lanham, Maryland, 1992.

William J. Shirer, *Berlin Diary: The Journal of a Foreign Correspondent, 1934–1941*, Hamish Hamilton, London, 1941.

Michael Smith, *Foley: The Spy Who Saved 10,000 Jews*, Hodder and Stoughton, London, 1999.

Shmuel Spector, *The Holocaust of Volhynian Jews, 1941–1944*, Yad Vashem, Jerusalem, 1990.

Martin Spitzer, *Storm over Tatra*, Kitchener Press, Adelaide, South Australia, 1989.

André Stein (editor), *Hidden Children: Forgotten Survivors of the Holocaust*, Viking, New York, 1993.

Jonathan Steinberg, *All or Nothing: The Axis and the Holocaust, 1941–1943*, Routledge, London, 1990.

W.C. Stiles, *Out of Kishinev, The Duty of the American People to the Russian Jew*, G.W. Dillingham, New York, 1903.

The Stroop Report: The Jewish Quarter of Warsaw Is No More, Secker and Warburg, London, 1980.

Teresa Swiebocka (editor), *Auschwitz: A History in Photographs*, Indiana University Press, Bloomington, Indiana, 1993.

Alan Symons, *The Jewish Contribution to the 20th Century*, Polo Publishing, London, 1997.

Zvi Szner and Alexander Sened (editors), *Mendel Grossman, With a Camera in the Ghetto*, Ghetto Fighters' House, Israel, 1970.

Roy D. Tanenbaum (as told to him by Sigmund Sobolewski), *Prisoner 88: The Man in Stripes*, University of Calgary Press, Calgary, Alberta, 1998.

Arieh Tartakower and Kurt R. Grossmann, *The Jewish Refugee*, Institute of Jewish Affairs, New York, 1944.

Nechama Tec, *When Light Pierced the Darkness: Christian Rescue of Jews in Nazi-Occupied Poland*, Oxford University Press, New York, 1986.

Nechama Tec, *Defiance: Jewish Partisans in Belorussia During World War II*, Oxford University Press, New York, 1993.

Golda Tencer (editor), *And I Still See Their Faces: Images of Polish Jews*, American-Polish-Israeli Shalom Foundation, Warsaw, 1998.

Rita Thalman and Emmanuel Feinermann, *Crystal Night, 9–10 November 1938*, Thames and Hudson, London, 1974.

Gordon Thomas and Max Morgan-Witts, *Voyage of the Damned: The Voyage of the St Louis*, Hodder and Stoughton, London, 1974.

George Topas, *The Iron Furnace: A Holocaust Survivor's Story*, University of Kentucky Press, Lexington, Kentucky, 1990.

Avraham Tory, *Surviving the Holocaust: The Kovno Ghetto Diary*, Harvard University Press, Cambridge, Massachusetts, 1990.

Dezider Tóth (editor), *The Tragedy of Slovak Jews*, Datei, Banska Bystrica, 1992.

Barry Turner, *...And the Policeman Smiled: 10,000 Children Escape from Nazi Europe*, Bloomsbury, London, 1990.

Rudolf Vrba (with Alan Bestic), *I Cannot Forgive*, Sidgwick and Jackson, London, 1963.

Zorach Warhaftig, *Refugee and Survivor: Rescue Efforts during the Holocaust*, Yad Vashem, Jerusalem, 1988.

Leon Weliczker Wells, *Shattered Faith: A Holocaust Legacy*, University Press of Kentucky, Lexington, Kentucky, 1995.

Leon Weliczker Wells, *The Janowska Road*, Macmillan, New York, 1963.

Harold Werner, *Fighting Back: A Memoir of Jewish Resistance in World War II*, Columbia University Press, New York, 1992.

Elie Wiesel, *Night*, MacGibbon and Kee, London, 1960.

Elie Wiesel, *And the Sea is Never Full, Memoirs, 1969–*, Alfred A. Knopf, New York, 1999.

Samuel Willenberg, *Surviving Treblinka*, Basil Blackwell, Oxford, 1989.

The Yellow Spot: The Extermination of the Jews in Germany, Victor Gollancz, London, 1936.

Susan Zuccotti, *The Italians and the Holocaust: Persecution, Rescue, Survival*, Basic Books, New York, 1987.

Yitzhak Zuckerman ('Antek'), *A Surplus of Memory: Chronicle of the Warsaw Ghetto Uprising*, University of California Press, Berkeley, California, 1993.

ARTICLES

David Borde, 'Wiesel, a Man of Peace, Cites Need to Act,' *New York Times*, 2 June 1999.

Victor Breitburg, 'The return to Lodz – biographical episodes', *Holocaust Survivors '45 Aid Society Journal*, issue number 23, London, autumn 1999.

Tricia Deering, 'Czechs claim Holocaust gold,' *Jewish Chronicle*, 19 November 1999.

Joseph Finkelstone, 'Fifty-year victory for waifs of war: how we gave life and love to death camp orphans', *Evening Standard*, 14 August 1995.

Abraham H. Foxman, 'A Broken Silence', *Dimensions: A Journal of Holocaust Studies*, Volume 6, Number 3, New York, 1992.

Ya'akov Friedler, 'Nazi spirit not dead in Germany, rescuer of Polish Jews says,' *Jerusalem Post*, 21 October 1969.

John and Carol Garrard, 'Barbarossa's First Victims: The Jews of Brest', *East European Jewish Affairs*, volume 28, number 2, 1999.

Ben Giladi, 'The Unforgotten', *The Voice of Piotrkow Survivors, Special Edition, 'Clandestine Education in a Ghetto under the Swastika'*, Kew Gardens, New York, Fall 1999.

Ruth E. Gruber, 'New foundations at Auschwitz,' *Jewish Chronicle*, 19 November 1999.

Hugo Gryn, 'Hugo's address to the boys, May 1947, *Holocaust Survivors '45 Aid Society Journal*, issue number 23, London, autumn 1999.

Abraham Gutt, 'Past and Present', *Holocaust Survivors '45 Aid Society Journal*, issue number 23, London, autumn 1999.

Lorraine Justman-Wisnicki, 'The Children of Gorzkowice: My Personal Memories,' *The Voice of Piotrkow Survivors, Special Edition, 'Clandestine Education in a Ghetto under the Swastika'*, Kew Gardens, New York, Fall 1999.

Howard Kaplan, 'Escape!' (the story of an Auschwitz escapee, Czeslaw Mordowicz), *Moment*, Washington DC, 1981.

Lorraine Kirk, 'Euro-Parliament chiefs endorse Ann Frank rights declaration,' *Jewish Chronicle*, 19 November 1999.

Bronka Klibanska, 'In the Ghetto and in the Resistance: A Personal Narrative', Dalia Ofer and Lenore J. Weitzman, *Women in the Holocaust*, Yale University Press, New Haven, 1998.

Brian Laghi, 'Ottawa moves on war-crimes prosecutions,' *Globe and Mail*, Toronto, 12 October 1999.

Dov Levin, 'Ruins and Remembrance', in Dennis B. Klein (general editor), *Hidden History of the Kovno Ghetto*, Little, Brown and Company, Boston, 1997.

Edward Lynne, 'Brave Lady from Holland: Israel Honours Saviour of 10,000 children,' *Jewish Observer*, London, 21 April 1967.

Ernie Meyer, 'The second Wallenberg: Giorgio Perlasca saved thousands of Hungarian Jews....', *Jerusalem Post*, 29 September 1989.

Mordecai Paldiel, 'Jan Zabinski', in Israel Gutman (Editor in Chief), *Encyclopedia of the Holocaust*, four volumes, Macmillan, New York, 1990.

Herbert Rosenkranz, 'Austria', Israel Gutman (Editor in Chief), *Encyclopedia of the Holocaust*, 4 volumes, Macmillan, New York, 1990.

Ruth Rothenberg, 'Holocaust day debate at United Synagogue council meeting,' *Jewish Chronicle*, 19 November 1999.

Marek Rudnicki, 'My Recollections of the Deportation of Janusz Korczak', *Polin: A Journal of Polish-Jewish Studies*, volume 7, Blackwell, Oxford, 1992.

Dennis Sharp, 'Walter Bor,' obituary, *Independent*, London, 11 October 1999.

Rafael F. Scharf, 'Fragments of Truth', *Holocaust Survivors '45 Aid Society Journal*, issue number 23, London, autumn 1999.

Shmuel Spector, 'Einsatzgruppen' (with map), Israel Gutman (Editor in Chief), *Encyclopedia of the Holocaust*, four volumes, Macmillan, New York, 1990.

Elie Wiesel, 'The Question of Genocide,' *Newsweek*, 12 April 1999.

Hans-Heinrich Wilhelm, 'Julius Streicher', Israel Gutman (Editor in Chief), *Encyclopedia of the Holocaust*, four volumes, Macmillan, New York, 1990.

Regine Wosnitza, 'Survivor says she is ready to lead German Jewry,' *Jewish Chronicle*, 19 November 1999.

Michel Zlotowski, 'France will compensate Holocaust-era orphans,' *Jewish Chronicle*, 19 November 1999.

Alexander Zvielli, 'A Haunted Land,' *Jerusalem Post*, 27 January 1978.

TRIAL TRANSCRIPTS

Yehuda Bakon, testimony of 7 June 1961, and Benno Cohn, testimony of 25 April 1961, in State of Israel, Ministry of Justice, *The Trial of Adolf Eichmann: Record of Proceedings in the District Court of Jerusalem*, six volumes, Jerusalem, 1992.

UNPUBLISHED MANUSCRIPTS

Jack Brauns, *'Recollections and Reflections'* (pre-war Kovno, the Kovno ghetto, Dachau), Covina, California.

Gisele Naichouler Feldman, *'Hiding in the Famous Castle of General Lafayette: Conversations with my students'* (a hidden child's recollections), Farmington Hills, Michigan.

Lord Kagan, *'Knight of the Ghetto'* (recollections of the Kovno ghetto), London.

Mania Tenenbaum-Salinger, *'Memoirs'*, (recollections of liberation at Belsen), West Bloomfield, Michigan. .

Stella Tzur, *'Suppose it happened to your child: memoirs of the "Shoa"'* (a hidden child in Poland), Haifa, Israel.

Rella Wizenberg, *'It is not easy to forget....'* (recollections of Radom, Poland), Farmington Hills, Michigan.

I have also taken eye-witness testimonies from my own books: *Sir Horace Rumbold: Portrait of a Diplomat*, Heinemann, London, 1973; *Final Journey: The Fate of the Jews in Nazi Europe*, George Allen and Unwin, London, 1979; *Auschwitz and the Allies*, Michael Joseph and George Rainbird, London, and Holt, New York, 1981; *The Holocaust: The Jewish Tragedy*, HarperCollins, London, and Holt, New York, 1986; *The Boys, Triumph over Adversity*, Weidenfeld and Nicolson, London, and Holt, New York, 1996; *Atlas of the Holocaust*: revised edition, Routledge, London, and William Morrow, New York, 1993; *The Day the War Ended: VE-Day 1945 In Europe and Around the World*, HarperCollins, London, and Holt, New York,1995; and *Holocaust Journey: Travelling in Search of the Past*, Weidenfeld and Nicolson, London, and Columbia University Press, New York, 1997.

On the day in November 1999 when I completed this manuscript, there were eleven items of news relating to the Holocaust in the London *Jewish Chronicle*. Each week's newspapers, each new volume of memoirs and new historical study – and no week passes without some new publication – adds to our knowledge of the mass murder of six million human beings, killed solely because they were Jewish.

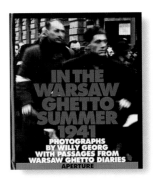

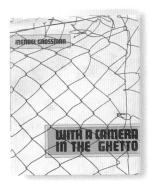

Index of Places

First published in

the United States of America in 2000

by UNIVERSE PUBLISHING

A Division of

Rizzoli International Publications, Inc.

300 Park Avenue South

New York, NY 10010

EDITOR Michelle Pickering

LAYOUT DESIGNER Mark Stevens

PHOTOGRAPHER (book jackets) Richard Palmer

ISBN 0-7893-0409-0

Printed and bound in Great Britain
by Bath Press Colourbooks

Author's note

Every effort has been made to trace ownership of copyright in the
illustrations printed in this book. I am grateful to those copyright
holders, institutions and individuals who have given me permission to
reproduce material; they are AKG Photo, London (on pages 28–9,
31, 180), Akropolis Publishers, Prague (11, 20), Archive Photos,
New York (135), Archives of the State of Israel, Jerusalem (161),
Associated Press (49), Auschwitz State Museum, Oswiecim, Poland
(76, 77, 120, 122, 123, 180), Bibliothèque Historique de la Ville de
Paris (85), Bildarchiv Preussischer Kulturbesitz, Berlin (35, 39, 43),
Central Zionist Archives, Jerusalem (159), *Evening Standard* (56),
The '45 Aid Society, London (154, 155, 156, 157, 171), Victor Gollancz,
Publishers, London (32, 33), Estate of Rabbi Hugo Gryn (170), Art
Collection, Beit Lohamei Hagettaot, Ghetto Fighters' House, Israel
(86–7, 131), Henschel Verlag, Berlin (109), Her Majesty's Stationery
Office, London (110), Hulton-Getty Picture Library, London (37, 45,
47), Huntington Library, California (37), Imperial War Museum,
London (36, 150), Interpress Publishers, Warsaw (18), Jewish
Historical Institute, Warsaw (73, 175), Kapon Editions, Athens (10),
Keter Publishing House, Jerusalem (12, 13, 94, 95), Beate Klarsfeld
Foundation, Paris (1, 138, 139), Main Commission for the Research
of Crimes Against the Polish Nation – The Institute for National
Memory, Warsaw (52, 74, 90, 91, 93), News International
Syndication (178, 179), Martinus Nijhoff, Publishers, Dordrecht, The
Netherlands (143), Osterreichisches Staatsarchiv Austrian State
Archives, Vienna (40, 41), R. Paknys Publishing House, Vilnius (163),
Panstwowe Wydawnictwo Naukowe, Warsaw (130), Polish Institute
and Sikorski Museum, London (131), Red Cross, Netherlands (134),
Shalom Foundation, Warsaw (12, 16, 17, 25, 111), March Tenth
Inc., Haworth, New Jersey (136, 137), United States Signal Corps
(153), United States Holocaust Memorial Museum, Washington DC
(96, 97, 99, 142), Wiener Library, London (33, 42, 45), Yad Vashem
Film and Photo Department Archives, Jerusalem (5, 43, 49, 50–1, 52,
53, 54, 56, 57, 59, 60, 61, 65, 67, 72, 73, 83, 88–9, 98, 100, 108,
113, 114–5, 118, 132, 137, 144, 146, 148–9, 152, 153, 159, 160,
161, 175, 180), and the Zionist Organization Youth Department,
Jerusalem (110, 111). Freddie Knoller and Eric D. Sugerman provided
the postage stamps reproduced here (13, 42, 48, 83, 87, 91, 105,
119, 135, 142, 151, 165). The following individuals have given me
permission to reproduce their material: Tom Bermann (44), Eve Line
Blum (125), Ian Clifford (173), Gisela Feldman (47), Mark Gerson,
(170), Paul Halter (87), Ben Helfgott (166), Rabbi Harry M. Jacobi
(48), Jack Kagan (6, 15, 26, 27, 101, 158, 166), Felicja Karay (79),
Robert Krell (103), Dov Levin (171), Judy Mandel (172, 173), Robin
O'Neil (2), Rafael F. Scharf (133), Malcolm Smith (38), Eric D. Sugerman
(20, 64), Stella Kochawa Tzur (102), Mara Vishniac-Kohn (15, 22–3),
Rudolf Vrba (140), Jacek Weislo (169), Helga Weisová-Hosková (4,
82-3) and Leon Weliczker Wells (164). I have also used my own
photographs (11, 14, 69, 70, 74, 85, 126, 128–9, 147, 162, 163, 165,
167, 168, 169 and 177), illustration (21) and postage stamps (28, 64).